Taiwan and Chinese nationalism

For China, Taiwan is next in line to be unified with the People's Republic, after Hong Kong in 1997. China's claim on Taiwan is of great importance to the politics of Chinese nationalism. However, the democratic challenge from Taiwan is very potent and its status and identity within the international community is crucial to its survival.

Taiwan and Chinese Nationalism explores how Taiwan's status has come to be seen as a symbol for the legitimacy of the Chinese regime in the evolution of Chinese nationalism. It also demonstrates how this view has been challenged by demands for democratisation in Taiwan. The KMT regime is shown to have allowed sovereignty to be practised by the population of the island while maintaining the claim that it is a part of China. The result is a 'post-nationalist' identity for the island in an intermediate state between independence and unification with the PRC.

Taiwan and Chinese Nationalism places these developments in the context of the discourse on Chinese nationalism at the end of the twentieth century. It is crucial reading for those wishing to gain a much deeper understanding of one of the world's most volatile regions.

Christopher Hughes lectures in Chinese Politics and History at Middlesex University and in the International Politics of the Asia-Pacific at the London School of Economics.

Politics in Asia series
Edited by Michael Leifer
London School of Economics

Taiwan and Chinese nationalism

National identity and status in
international society

Christopher Hughes

Routledge
Taylor & Francis Group

LONDON AND NEW YORK

First published 1997
by Routledge
2 Park Square, Milton Park, Abingdon, Oxfordshire OX14 4RN

Simultaneously published in the USA and Canada
by Routledge
711 Third Avenue, New York, NY 10017

First issued in paperback 2014

Routledge is an imprint of the Taylor & Francis Group, an informa business

© 1997 Christopher Hughes

Typeset in Times by LaserScript, Mitcham, Surrey

British Library Cataloguing in Publication Data
A catalogue record for this book is available from the British Library

Library of Congress Cataloging in Publication Data
A catalogue record for this book has been requested

ISBN 13 : 978-1-138-86302-6 (pbk)
ISBN 13 : 978-0-415-15768-1 (hbk)

To Jiafong

Contents

Figures

Foreword

The abiding tension between nation and state within international society has been pointed up in singular form by the circumstances and tribulations of the off-shore island of Taiwan which has been ruled separately from the mainland of China by a Chinese government for nearly half a century. This political-territorial legacy of civil war within China and also of the Cold War has remained a source of irredentist and international contention which was demonstrated most recently by the renewed crisis in the Taiwan Strait during the run-up to the first direct popular election for the island's president which was held in March 1996. In this timely and illuminating exploration of the complexities of the relationship between nation and state in Taiwan's case, Christopher Hughes has succeeded admirably in locating the study of nationalism within the discipline of International Relations.

Dr Hughes points out that Taiwan possesses all the attributes of a separate state and additionally plays an important role in the world economy. The government in Taipei maintains, however, that the island and its inhabitants are part of the Chinese nation and by implication an expression of Chinese identity. Correspondingly, the government in Beijing acknowledges that identity as part of its claim that the island is a renegade province whose political destiny is restoration to the motherland. At issue, in this rigorous scholarly analysis, are the nature, role and relevance of national identity for the competing governments in Taipei and Beijing as well as the international implications of its adverse interpretations.

Chinese national identity was critical for the credentials and legitimacy of the retreating Kuomintang administration which imposed itself on an alienated island population in claiming an entitlement to rule the mainland. Dr Hughes traces the nature of political change within Taiwan attendant on a remarkable economic development in order to explain how the bases of legitimacy changed for government within the island. He demonstrates with great skill how the initial link between Chinese identity and the legitimacy of the government in Taipei was broken by the dynamics of democratisation leading to the deconstruction of Chinese nationalism, albeit without its total rejection. This decoupling of the exercise of sovereignty from the question of the island's identity has had an important international significance, especially as the government in Beijing has been obliged to enthrone Chinese nationalism as the legitimising alternative to a defunct Marxist dogma. Taiwan's international status has always been problematic but has been acutely so ever since the government in Taipei was obliged to vacate China's seat in the United Nations in 1971 and then, at the end of the decade, lost the international recognition of the United States. Taiwan has not only had to confront the persisting threat from an irredentist government in Beijing but also the orthodoxy of international society whereby sovereignty is treated as an absolute quality in which it is deficient.

Beyond the dynamics of Taiwanese politics, Dr Hughes addresses the international dimension of the island's predicament as its government has sought an international position which will serve the cause of upholding its separate political existence without precipitating armed conflict with China which, at the very least, would be disruptive to an economic activity which has underpinned that separateness. Dr Hughes explains with dispassion the difficulties experienced by Taiwan in seeking, without success, to break out of its 'intermediate state' and the attendant problems of coping with a diplomatic purgatory. As Taiwan continues to register a separate international identity and as an irredentist China reasserts a traditional one, drawing confidence from the restoration of its sovereignty over Hong Kong, the status of the island will be a matter of growing international interest and concern. This volume makes an outstanding contribution to understanding the complexities of a problem capable of disturbing the peace of Asia in the twenty-first century.

Michael Leifer

Preface

This work began as a doctoral research project at the London School of Economics in 1990. At that time the research agenda for Taiwan tended to reflect what had been a decade of economic growth for the island and several years of improving relations across the Taiwan Strait. By the middle of the 1990s, though, this situation had changed dramatically. A process of rapid constitutional reform in Taiwan had enabled the development of electoral politics that culminated in the island's first election of its president, on 23 March 1996. At the same time, the improvement in relations between Taiwan and mainland China appeared to have peaked only to plummet back to a situation of military tension not seen in the Taiwan Strait since the crises of the 1950s. One of the things this work set out to do was to keep track of these helter-skelter developments and to understand how they are interrelated.

In such a rapidly changing situation, however, the researcher's task is like that of Sisyphus on a very slippery slope. The best way to get a grip is to focus on one of the most salient problems to emerge from the train of events and then locate it within a much broader historical and theoretical perspective. That this research was begun in 1990 had much to do with the problem and perspective that were chosen. This was the time of the fall of the Berlin wall and the dissolution of the Soviet Union. It was the beginning of a decade that ended the Cold War and started with the Gulf War. It has seen the world map transformed as a host of communities make the claim to statehood, some with little trouble and others with tragic consequences. In short, it was the beginning of a period in which understanding the re-emergence of nationalism was to become a dominant theme on the research agenda. To attest to this, one only had to squeeze into the large classroom at the London School of Economics in which James Mayall and Anthony Smith held their weekly seminar on the subject.

It was in such an atmosphere that the focus of this work became an attempt to understand what the Taiwan problem can tell us about the relationship between the national unit and the political unit in Chinese thinking (as Ernest Gellner might have put it). For the outsider the problem seems baffling at first. Taiwan is an island of twenty-one million people that lies some 100 miles off the Chinese coast and has only been ruled by a mainland Chinese government for four years this century (1945–9). It possesses all the characteristics of a state and plays an important role in the world economy. Despite this, the government in Beijing claims that Taiwan is a part of China and is prepared to go to war if any major international actor recognises the island as a state. Moreover, to make matters even more confusing, although the government in Taipei claims that the island is a part of the Chinese 'nation', it is not clear whether it claims that the island is a separate state or not. From the perspective of nationalist theory, then, Taiwan offers an interesting case of failure to agree over the relationship between Chinese identity and the political units that have come to exist within it. For International Relations, Taiwan's position between the two possible statehoods of unification with the PRC and independence, combined with its attachments to a trans-state Chinese community, presents a case study that can further our knowledge of the kinds of problems that arise with the expansion of international society.

Understanding the Taiwan problem as a problem of Chinese nationalism, then, is useful for understanding the political dynamics of cross-Strait relations, for gaining an insight into the politics of national identity and for understanding something about the role of nationalism in international society. Above all, though, the Taiwan problem is useful on all these counts due to the fact that it has generated numerous debates in Chinese on all these subjects. Of course, much of what is said gets obscured by state propaganda. However, as political transformation in Taiwan fits increasingly uneasily with Chinese nationalism, arguments over the relationship between being Chinese and being part of the Chinese state steadily transform the way that concepts of state and nation are articulated. If some sense of the depth of emotion, creativity and innovation that this gives rise to has been conveyed below, this work will have achieved much of what it set out to do.

Acknowledgements

It hardly needs to be said that this book would not have been possible without the insight, stimulation and guidance provided by the supervision of Michael Yahuda. A studentship from the Economic and Social Research Council of the United Kingdom enabled the writing-up of the results of the original research. Naturally, the author is responsible for any mistakes.

Note on romanisation

The political division between Taiwan and the Chinese mainland extends to the systems of romanisation used by each side. This presents problems for a work that deals with both sides of the Taiwan Strait when it comes to presenting Chinese proper names in English.

The principle that has been adopted here is to use the Pinyin system for names of individuals and places in the Chinese mainland. For individuals and places in Taiwan, however, preference has been given to how those names are presented in English-language materials published in the island. This makes it easier to match names in the text with primary English-language sources. It also seems right because this is how such people have decided to name themselves.

To minimise confusion, Pinyin only has been used for all references of Chinese-language works. The Pinyin versions of names from Taiwan have been given in parentheses when they first appear in the text. A glossary of such names and their Pinyin equivalents has been provided for quick reference.

Abbreviations

Note The abbreviations used for newspapers are listed separately in the Bibliography on p. 169.

ADB	Asian Development Bank
AIT	American Institute in Taiwan
APEC	Asia Pacific Economic Co-operation
ARATS	Association for Relations Across the Taiwan Strait
ASEAN	Association of South-east Asian Nations
CCNAA	Co-ordination Council for North American Affairs
CCP	Chinese Communist Party
CCPD	Council for Cultural Planning and Development
CEC	Central Election Commission
CEPD	Council for Economic Planning and Development
CNP	China New Party
CSC	Central Standing Committee
CYACL	Chinese Youth Anti-Communist League
DPP	Democratic Progressive Party
FDI	foreign direct investment
GATT	General Agreement on Tariffs and Trade
JCRR	US–ROC Joint Commission on Rural Reconstruction
KMT	Kuomintang (Guomindang)
LDP	Liberal Democratic Party
MAC	Mainland Affairs Council
MFN	most favoured nation
MOFA	Ministry of Foreign Affairs
NAC	National Affairs Conference
NAFTA	North American Free Trade Agreement
NPC	National People's Congress
NUC	National Unification Council
OCAC	Overseas Chinese Affairs Commission

PBEC	Pacific Basin Economic Council
PECC	Pacific Economic Co-operation Council
PLA	People's Liberation Army
PRC	People's Republic of China
ROC	Republic of China
SAR	special administrative region
SEF	Straits Exchange Foundation
UN	United Nations
WTO	World Trade Organisation

1 Taiwan in Chinese nationalism

On 30 January 1995, Jiang Zemin, would-be successor to Deng Xiaoping as paramount leader of the People's Republic of China (PRC), put his stamp on Beijing's Taiwan policy. In a speech to welcome in the lunar new year, he quoted the words of the 'National Father' of China, Dr Sun Yat-sen (1866–1925): 'Unification is the wish of the whole body of Chinese citizens. If there is unification then the whole people will be fortunate; if there is no unification then there will be suffering' (Jiang 1995).

Fifteen months later, on 23 March 1996, after a series of missile tests and military manoeuvres by the People's Liberation Army (PLA) in and around the Taiwan Strait, leading to a stand-off with the biggest US naval force in East Asia since the Vietnam War, the twenty-one million people of Taiwan elected their president for the first time. When Lee Teng-hui gave his inauguration speech, however, he stated that his government was also committed to unification with the Chinese mainland (Lee 1996a). When one attempts to unravel the relationship between Taiwan and China that lies behind such events, it is perhaps tempting to accept the conclusion reached by *The Economist* some years ago, that if Taiwan were a person it would be in the hands of a psychiatrist (Hartland-Thurnberg 1990: 121).

Perhaps the nearest it is possible to get to submitting a state to psychoanalysis is to look at its history. To understand the nature of the various claims to sovereignty over Taiwan, however, engaging in the historical debate as to how cultural, trade and administrative links developed over the centuries can be a rather sterile exercise. This is because such enquiries tend to presuppose the truth of the claim that these kinds of links somehow become political and binding down the generations. Although pursuing such a position has been the motivation behind much state-sponsored historical research on the Taiwan problem (Taiwan Affairs Office 1993: 1–5), its validity as a political principle is rejected by those who advocate the independence of Taiwan from China. As the Taiwanese writer Li Ao puts it, why should claims to Taiwan based on the historical record hold any more than the claim of, say, modern Turkey to the lands which once formed the Ottoman empire (Li 1987: 6)? If history is to tell us anything about the Chinese claim to Taiwan, what needs to be understood is when that claim was made and why it should have become so important for Chinese politics.

MAKING THE CHINESE CLAIM TO TAIWAN

The official version of the claim to Taiwan as made by the PRC asserts that Taiwan has belonged to China 'since ancient times'. This is then used as the basis to insist that the island should be part of the Chinese state (Taiwan Affairs Office 1993). Some preliminary observations about the nature of such a claim, however, are needed to understand its true significance for Chinese politics. The first of these is that such a claim is essentially a nationalist claim. That is to say, it is made according to what Ernest Gellner has called the 'nationalist principle', namely that 'the political and the national unit should be congruent' (Gellner 1990: 1).

If it is accepted that the Chinese claim to Taiwan is made according to this nationalist principle, the problem of anachronism is raised. This is because most recent works on the history of nationalism conclude that it is a doctrine that emerged in Europe in relatively recent times (Anderson 1991; Gellner 1990; Hobsbawm 1991; Kamenka 1976; Mayall 1993; Smith 1986). If the nationalist principle is to mean anything at all, it presupposes what Mayall calls the 'national idea'. This is the argument that the world is (or should be) divided into nations, and that the nation is the only proper basis for a sovereign state and the ultimate source of governmental authority (Mayall 1993: 2). This in turn requires the conception of politics as an activity conducted between states without the recognition of any authority above themselves, such as emerged in Europe between the *realpolitik* of the Italian city states and the 1648 Peace of Westphalia. The 'anarchical society' of states that was the result could only exist so long as there was a rejection of the supra-state authority of church or empire. Various institutions, such as the balance of power, international rules of conduct and diplomacy, were developed to ensure that no one state would be able to achieve preponderance over the rest (Armstrong 1993; Bull 1993).

The emergence of this society of states also made possible the later doctrine that the sovereignty of those states ought to be located within the populations who live under them. This was the principle that had come to fruition in the challenge to the idea of dynastic rule represented by the era of the American and French revolutions (Mayall 1993: 26–7). As well as implying that humanity is naturally divided according to nationality, this vision also proposes that rule by foreigners constitutes a denial of natural rights, and that each nation therefore has a right to constitute a separate state (Mayall 1993: 40). This was ultimately to be enshrined as the principle of national self-determination at Versailles in 1918. It was also seen as a valuable weapon by the international Communist movement, from its endorsement by Marx and Engels in 1865 to its incorporation in the world revolutionary strategy of the Third International during its existence from 1919 to 1943 (Connor 1984: 5–61).

The argument that nationalism is a relatively modern, European doctrine sits well with the evidence concerning its emergence in China. The very term *minzu*, used by Jiang Zemin as the equivalent of the English 'nation' in his new year speech, was only introduced into the Chinese vocabulary in 1899 by the constitutional reformer Liang Qichao (1873–1929) (*Minzu cidian* 1987). The Chinese term for 'nationalism' (*minzu zhuyi*) was probably also used first by Liang, in 1901. Sun Yat-sen himself did not begin using it until 1904 (Jiang 1985: 177–8). The realisation that nationalism is a modern Chinese doctrine imported from outside makes it possible to arrive at a correct interpretation of historical claims to Taiwan made according to the nationalist principle.

For example, those claiming Chinese sovereignty over Taiwan often point out that it was incorporated by the Qing dynasty in 1684 (Taiwan Affairs Office 1993: 2). In a purely legal sense this may be true. However, that the Qing court showed little interest in occupying Taiwan or even bringing it under complete military control indicates that to understand this relationship in terms of the creation of a nation-state may be anachronistic. The same charge could also be made if the Qing response to an attempt by Japan to colonise the eastern part of the island in 1874 were interpreted in terms of building a modern nation-state. Whereas in 1874 Japan was clearly making claims to Taiwan according to the principle that it is legitimate in international law to settle unadministered territory, the Qing's response of trying to establish visible measures of control over the island are better understood as an attempt to preserve a very different vision of world order (Kim 1980: 68–76; Yen 1965). This was the vision of a hierarchical, or Sinocentric, world order, which in turn was rooted in the particular form of legitimisation cultivated by the Qing. Central to this was the belief that all legitimate power originated from the Qing emperor, or Son of Heaven. This power was believed to have been bestowed by the Mandate of Heaven, and was legitimate so long as the emperor performed certain rituals prescribed by neo-Confucian culture. As there could only be one superior culture, it followed that there could only be one Son of Heaven, whose legitimate rule ought to extend to 'all under heaven' (Fairbank 1968).

To see how Taiwan's position in the Qing world order had to be radically opposed to that as it is imagined in Chinese nationalism, it is necessary to realise that the Qing rulers were actually perceived by many of the people over whom they ruled to be an ethnically foreign group. Originating from Manchuria, conquering the previous Ming dynasty by force of arms, the Qing ruling class was in fact outnumbered one hundred to one by its new subjects (Laitinen 1990: 15). To enlist the loyalty of the Ming bureaucracy and gentry, the Manchurian rulers propagated neo-Confucian ideology so as to legitimate their own dynastic rule as an alien group. As the Manchurians could themselves be legitimate rulers over the empire, it followed that any people could eventually be acculturated into the Qing empire. Peoples such as the aboriginal inhabitants of eastern Taiwan could thus be deemed barbarians who would eventually willingly join the empire when they had come round to accepting its cultural-political norms. A *laissez-faire* policy was thus adopted towards them, in the hope that they would eventually mend their ways and enter 'civilised society' (Yen 1965).

As international society spread out from Europe and clashed with the Qing empire in the nineteenth century, the 'culturalism' of the latter had to give way. It was in the resulting process of erosion that Taiwan began to play a significant role for the later development of Chinese nationalism. The Qing only had some twenty years after the Japanese attack of 1874 in which to attempt to fulfil the task of asserting military and political control over Taiwan. When the dynasty was defeated in the Sino-Japanese War (1894–5), Taiwan was ceded to Japan by the Treaty of Shimonoseki. On one level the war had been a conflict over influence in the Korean peninsula. On a far deeper level, however, it represented the first successful blow to the Qing international order by an East Asian power (Kim 1980: 68–76). Although the gentry and merchants of Taiwan expressed their desire to deny Japanese claims and remain loyal to the Qing court by establishing a Taiwan Republic on 25 May 1895, the court refused even to acknowledge the republic's existence or communicate with its leaders during its ten-day existence (Lamley 1964: 143–72).

If the Qing court was thinking in terms of sacrificing Taiwan in the cause of preserving the Sinocentric order, however, Shimonoseki was to have a profound impact on those who were discontented with the dynasty. It was in fact in the same year as Shimonoseki that Sun Yat-sen established the first revolutionary nationalist association, the China Revival Society (Xing zhong hui), in Hawaii and Hong Kong. After Shimonoseki, Sun was able to convince reformers and revolutionaries that achieving a status of equality in international society was fundamentally incompatible with the universalistic principles upon which the political culture of the Qing state rested. It was after Shimonoseki, then, that the search for a nationalist foundation for state power and sovereignty began. It was in this context that Taiwan began to feature in a list of territories claimed to have been lost by the 'Chinese nation'.

If the defeat of the Qing by Japan in 1895 and the cession of Taiwan might be said to have been one of the sparks that started off the prairie fire of Chinese nationalism (Spence 1982: 7–26), it would still be premature to conclude that Taiwan became a revanchist issue for Chinese nationalism at this time. When it comes to explicit claims to sovereignty over Taiwan, there is a deafening silence between 1911 and the next great transformation of East Asian international relations, the Second World War. It is noteworthy, for example, that although Taiwan had been made a province of the Qing empire in 1885, it did not appear as a province in the draft constitutions written for the new republic in 1925, 1934 and 1936. Moreover, that the other lost territories listed alongside Taiwan in the Three Principles of the People (see p. 7) include Korea, Vietnam, Burma, the Ili basin, unspecified territory north of the Heilong River, the Ryukyu Islands, Bhutan and Nepal (Sun 1969: 13–14) indicates that although Taiwan initially played a symbolic role as a 'lost territory' of the Qing order, this did not necessarily imply that the sovereignty of the Chinese nation should be asserted over it.

Evidence concerning attitudes towards anti-Japanese activists from Taiwan who had based themselves in China after 1895 also reveals a distinct ambivalence about whether or not such people should be considered to be part of a Chinese or a Taiwanese nationalist movement. Individuals from Taiwan in mainland China were generally treated as foreigners in the same way as Koreans. In general there was a range of opinions over the future status of Taiwan, ranging from retrocession to independence and international trusteeship. In February 1941, the League of Taiwan Revolutionary Organisations (Taiwan geming tuanti lianhe hui), a broad umbrella grouping of various Taiwanese organisations operating in the mainland, renamed itself the Taiwan Revolutionary Alliance (Taiwan tongmeng hui) as a satellite organisation of the KMT. When it was recommended by members that the group should become a KMT party organisation, a Section for the Preparation of the Taiwan Party Under the KMT Central Organisation Department was established by the KMT, but the character for 'province' (*sheng*) was omitted from this title due to the unresolved status of Taiwan. This issue was not settled until the establishment of the Taiwan Province Executive Committee (Taiwan sheng zhixing weiyuan hui) in September 1945 (Hong 1995).

It appears, in fact, that it is only with the turning of the tide against Japan in the Second World War that Taiwan begins to take on a more significant meaning in China (Copper 1980; Hsiao and Sullivan 1979).

The earliest known official claim of China's right to recover Taiwan came on 6 October 1942, when Chiang Kai-shek met US Presidential Representative Wendell Wilkie (Hsiao and Sullivan 1979: 464). In Chiang Kai-shek's *China's Destiny*, the writing of which began in November 1942, it is clearly asserted that Taiwan is crucial for China's national security. Along with the Penghu archipelago, the four North-eastern Provinces (Manchuria), Inner and Outer Mongolia, Xinjiang and Tibet, Taiwan is described as an integral part of 'a fortress essential for the nation's defence and security' (Chiang 1947: 36). This position that Taiwan is a part of China finally received international recognition when the ROC was represented at the Cairo Conference with Great Britain and the United States in November–December 1943. The relevant section of the Cairo Declaration announced that 'all the territories Japan has stolen from the Chinese, such as Manchuria, Formosa [Taiwan], and the Pescadores [Penghu Islands], shall be restored to the Republic of China'. This commitment was later restated in the Potsdam Declaration (*Important Documents* 1955: 7–9).

The available evidence, then, indicates that the application of the nationalist principle to Taiwan only occurred after the American entry into the Second World War. The most obvious factor that can be put forward for this timing is that the alliance of the ROC with the Allies in the Second World War provided Chiang Kai-shek with a degree of influence in international affairs never before enjoyed by a leader of the post-1911 Chinese state. When Roosevelt and Churchill had made restoration of self-government to occupied territories one of the principles of the Atlantic Charter in August 1941, Chiang's advisers urged him to use his new influence to insist that this should be applied not only to territories occupied since 1937 or 1939, as Churchill had intended, but also to territories taken by Japan since the 1894–5 Sino-Japanese War (ZMZS 1981: 796–7). With the Allies determined to keep China in the war against Japan, the ROC was in a good position to make such demands (Tuchman 1970: 396–414). By the time of Cairo, these included insisting that the declaration of the Conference would include a clause stating that Taiwan and the Penghu Islands should be ceded to China on the defeat of Japan. Despite objections from the British delegation that the declaration should insist only on Japan giving up Taiwan and Penghu, rather than their being ceded to China, Roosevelt's sympathy and his keenness to ensure Chinese participation in the war enabled the ROC version to enter the final document (ZMZS 1981: 527–34).

Such an explanation, however, still needs to account for the motive behind the Chinese claim to Taiwan, which is crucial to grasp if the later development of the Taiwan problem is to be understood. For such an explanation it is necessary to locate that claim firmly within the politics of Chinese nationalism, and in particular in the relationship between the problems of nation-building and the legitimacy of the system of party dictatorship.

NATIONALISM, NATION-BUILDING AND DICTATORSHIP

When Sun Yat-sen gave a series of lectures on Chinese nationalism in 1924, he defined the new ideology as 'the doctrine of the clan of the state' (Sun 1969: 2), which bears a striking parallel to Gellner's nationalist principle.[1] Collected together and published under the title *San min zhuyi* (Three Principles of the People), these lectures were to become the foundation of the nationalist tradition of thinking about the relationship between state and community without which Taiwan could not have its later significance for Chinese politics. Without this tradition there would be little sense in Jiang Zemin extending an invitation for unification to the 'twenty-one million Taiwan compatriots' who, 'no matter whether from Taiwan province or other provinces, are all Chinese people, are all flesh and blood compatriots, brothers as in hands and feet' (Jiang 1995a).

The problem with such a doctrine for China at the beginning of the twentieth century, however, was that it presupposed the existence of a Chinese national identity. That Sun Yat-sen was aware that such an identity hardly existed is made clear when he goes on to describe the members of the Chinese nation as being like a 'heap of loose sand', fragmented by the parochial bonds of clan ties (Sun 1969: 1). Indeed, according to the seminal work on Chinese nationalism by Chalmers Johnson, concepts such as 'China' and 'Chinese nationality' only really begin to penetrate rural areas of the Chinese mainland as late as the 1930s, during the war against Japan (Johnson 1962: 5). What Sun and his successors realised, though, was that if a strong Chinese state was to be built on this 'heap of loose sand', it would mean shifting loyalties away from peripheral and parochial identities and towards the central organs of a new state. In other words, the successful harnessing of state power would depend on completing a programme of nation-building.

For nation-building to be successful, however, certain conditions must be present. These include a relatively well-developed system of communications and mass regimentation of the population. Such phenomena only appear, however, when a society has taken some steps down the road of industrialisation (Gellner 1990). But for the early Chinese nationalists, industrialisation had barely begun. Moreover, the territories of the former empire, already segmented as a mosaic of provinces, colonies and protectorates under the Qing, had been further fragmented by foreign encroachment, internal rebellion and lack of central control over local military units. When a military coup overthrew the dynasty in 1911 and established the Republic of China on 1 January 1912, the result was the dictatorship of the Bonapartist general, Yuan Shikai. Rather than build a republic as envisioned by Sun and his followers, Yuan proceeded to institute a constitutional monarchy with himself as emperor, and to disband the KMT. His death in 1916 left a power vacuum in which military leaders who drew their support from provincial ties vied for succession. The former empire descended into the 'Warlord' period and became acutely vulnerable to partition and colonisation by foreign powers.

In his earlier years, Sun Yat-sen had looked to the liberal democracies, especially the United States, as the ideal model for converting public sentiments into political power. The situation he now faced led him to turn to the theory of party dictatorship. Starting from the premise that the Chinese people had no significant understanding of the workings of constitutional democracy or the modern state, Sun went on to elaborate a blueprint for a revolution in three phases. A military stage would come first, during which martial law would be imposed while remnants of the Qing dynasty were eradicated. This would be followed by a 'tutelary' period during which the party would exercise a dictatorship over the population until it had become sufficiently familiar with the new ideology to engage directly in democratic politics. The revolutionary government would then hand over power to the president, and government by constitution would begin (Sun 1927: 120–3). This programme of the three-stage revolution was officially promulgated as the Nation-building Programme of the National Government (Guomin zhengfu jian guo dagang) by Sun Yat-sen in April 1924 (Pan 1945: 210–13).

Although this legitimisation of party dictatorship in terms of the mission of national salvation was supposed to have a democratic outcome, the vision of the KMT as the vanguard revolutionary party was also largely inspired by an alliance Sun Yat-sen made with Moscow in 1924. At the First Congress of the KMT, in January of that year, the task was set of instilling ideological unity, organisation and discipline into the party. Sun's lectures on the Three Principles of the People were made the party canon and the organisation was restructured along Leninist lines of democratic centralism. When Sun died on 25 March 1925, he left his successors a theory of party dictatorship legitimised by the nationalist revolution in China.

Sun's theory began to be put into practice by his successor as leader of the KMT, Generalissimo Chiang Kai-shek. He led a National Revolutionary Army north from the KMT's base in Canton, which took control of Beijing in 1928. The nationalist theory of legitimacy was then codified by the Central Committee of the KMT in the form of an organic law. This located sovereignty in the party, which claimed to be governing on behalf of the people (*China Year Book* 1929–30: 1185, 1931–2: 513). With the KMT divided between various factions, however, Chiang was able to manipulate executive power through the party machinery and as the Japanese advanced on Manchuria in March 1934, the context was provided for an ever increasing concentration into his own hands. When Chiang was kidnapped in the city of Xian, on 12 December 1936, by troops whose commanders demanded an end to the campaign against the Communists and the formation of a Second United Front, this time directed against Japanese aggression, his release provided an immense boost to his charisma as leader of the nation (Coble 1991: 344; Eastman 1986: 163). If the political party might have been too nebulous a concept towards which to express one's patriotism, the figure of the charismatic leader in the shape of Chiang, the man who had 'united China', offered a more concrete symbol. The foundations of a dictatorship presided over by a paramount leader arbitrating between factions in a one-party state had been legitimised by the cause of national salvation.

After the defeat of Japan, moves were made to shift the KMT towards a more democratic form of legitimacy, a significant motivation being threats from the United States that aid for the civil war against the CCP could otherwise be withdrawn. A constitution was adopted on 25 December 1947, and elections were held in 1947 and 1948 for the three representative chambers of government (National Assembly, Legislative Yuan and Control Yuan). However, the renewed civil war with the CCP also provided the context for strengthening the relationship between party dictatorship and nationalism, ultimately consolidating Taiwan's significance in Chinese politics. First of all, the elections were marred by the occupation of large areas of the country by Communist forces, protests from other states over the participation of their Chinese residents, and the lack of a genuine census and the unavailability of electoral registers in many areas. In the chaotic circumstances of the civil war, the government claimed that twenty million people voted, out of a population of around 540 million, and that KMT candidates won nearly all the seats (Liu 1992: 150; Long 1991: 57).

The constitution itself was written in a way that legalised the argument that the KMT was the only party fit to govern China, the Three Principles of the People being made the state ideology by Article 1. The system of checks and balances of Sun Yat-sen's five-power system of government was also overshadowed by the development of the excessively powerful presidency. Although the president's office was originally envisioned as akin to that of the limited presidency of the German Weimar Republic (Liu

1992: 151), the power that Chiang Kai-shek enjoyed as charismatic leader, embodiment of the nation and chairman of the KMT was not something that could be contained by any constitution. The civil war also continued the sense of national crisis that allowed constitutional restrictions on the power of the leader to be circumvented. This was achieved by one of the first acts of the First National Assembly after it was convened in 1948, when it appended to the constitution a number of additional clauses, called the Temporary Provisions Effective During the Period of Communist Rebellion. In effect, these overrode the constitution itself and enabled *ad hoc* measures to be put in place to legalise party dictatorship over the coming decades. The constitutional devices for linking dictatorship with the unification of China had thus already been put in place by the time the KMT was forced to retreat from the mainland to Taiwan by the Communists in December 1949.

NATIONALISM AND CHINESE COMMUNISM

If Sun's exclamation that 'China is a heap of loose sand' marks the crisis of Chinese national identity in the 1920s, Mao Zedong's proclamation on the establishment of the PRC that 'the Chinese people have stood up' has come to be something akin to a sutra chanted by the CCP in times of crisis. Ever since the CCP met in Shanghai for its First National Congress in July 1921, its members had felt the need to reconcile their internationalism with the Chinese nationalist movement. In resolving this problem they could look first of all to the Marxist tradition. Even Marx and Engels had accepted that Communists should align themselves with any movement against imperialism, with the important proviso that the Communists themselves remain ideologically untainted (Connor 1984: 11; Hoston 1994). Faced with the triumph of nationalism over proletarian internationalism in the First World War, Lenin had developed his theory of imperialism as the highest stage of capitalism, under which mercantilist nations come to take the place of classes as the chief actors in world conflict (Gilpin 1987: 38–40). By the time the CCP met for its Second National Congress in July 1922, it was ready to adopt the strategy of the United Front with the KMT as party policy.

This importance of nationalism to the CCP must be understood as developing within the broader context of the deepening relationship between Sun Yat-sen and the Soviet Union. This partnership between Sun's nationalism and Communist internationalism was awkward from the beginning. Sun appears to have understood the Russian revolution more as a movement by the Slav nation against imperialism than as any kind of internationalist supersession of the national idea (Sun 1969: 36). In the joint communiqué he signed with Soviet representative Adolf Joffe on 26 January 1923, the application of Communism to Chinese society was explicitly rejected. Yet Sun still decided to welcome Communists into the KMT. As Chiang Kai-shek rose to the position of leader of the KMT following Sun's death on 12 March 1925, his suspicions of CCP influence over the party coupled with fear of Stalin's designs on China finally led him to break with Moscow and the CCP through the purging of leftists and the massacre of labour activists in Shanghai in April 1927.

In the atmosphere of intense rivalry between the KMT and CCP that resulted, the latter's links with international Communism left it open to charges of being the puppet of a foreign power. Mao Zedong, who shared Sun's and Chiang's suspicions of Soviet intentions towards China, was particularly sensitive to this accusation. If Communists are supposed to remain untainted by the nationalism they co-opt in their revolutionary strategies, this golden rule of Marxism-Leninism had never been high on Mao's list of priorities. From his earliest days, Mao's thinking had been heavily coloured by the anti-imperialist sentiments that arose during the First World War and came to a climax when students and intellectuals, enraged by the handing over of German concessions in China to Japan at Versailles, took to the streets in the patriotic May Fourth Movement of 1919. These were the events that were to spill over and provide much of the potential support for the embryonic CCP and KMT. In such a climate, it was natural for Mao to go a step further than the Leninist strategy of alliance with national liberation movements in the cause of world revolution, by developing a Marxist tradition which saw the dignity of the Chinese nation and the greatness of its contribution to the world as values in themselves (Meisner 1967; Schram 1989: 49–50).

Rather than the withering away of the state, one of the greatest attractions for Chinese Communists under Mao's leadership was the vision of a world revolution aimed at establishing equal states free from imperialist oppression (Liu (undated): 50). If Sun's links with Moscow had been tenuous, Mao was equally unwilling to submit to foreign leadership. While links with the Soviet Union were strained during the war against Japan, he seized the opportunity to purge Moscow-trained cadres and consolidate his own leadership, sowing the seeds of a fractious relationship that would eventually blow up into the Sino-Soviet split of the 1960s. Even after the Second World War, when Mao had to 'lean to one side' to ensure Soviet recognition and economic and military support in the run-up to the establishment of the PRC, this was intended above all to serve the goal of national revival, rather than to align Beijing's foreign policy with proletarian internationalism (Goncharov *et al.* 1993: 32–3).

Within the domestic politics of the emerging Chinese state, if the KMT had legitimised its dictatorship in terms of the narrative of national salvation, the Communists felt that their role in the Second United Front against Japan and their defeat of the KMT in the civil war had allowed them to claim that cause for themselves. According to the CCP version of the revolution, the Communists had become the true heirs to Sun's revolution. When Sun Yat-sen had agreed to form the First United Front with the Communists, he had realised that the world situation had changed from one of bourgeois national revolutions to that of division into socialist and imperialist camps. In this situation, only alignment with the socialist camp could be an anti-imperialist doctrine, and therefore truly patriotic. By extension, anybody who opposed the CCP was not just opposing Communism but in doing so was betraying China in the struggle against imperialism, as Mao made clear during the war against Japan (Mao 1939: 365).

It is in this context of the argument over nationalist credentials that the CCP's identification of Taiwan as part of China should be understood. A shift on this issue paralleling that undertaken by the KMT after 1941 is apparent from a survey of the evidence concerning the CCP attitude to Taiwan before the Cairo Conference. The most frequently quoted piece of evidence here is the remark made by Mao to the American journalist Edgar Snow in 1936. In response to a question posed by Snow concerning what China should do about the territories it had lost to Japan, Mao replied:

> Manchuria must be regained. We do not, however, include Korea, formerly a Chinese colony, but when we have re-established the independence of the lost territories of China, and if the Koreans wish to break away from the chains of Japanese imperialism, we will extend help in their struggle for independence. The same thing applies for Taiwan [Formosa]. As for Inner Mongolia, which is populated by both Chinese and Mongolians, we will struggle to drive Japan from there and help Inner Mongolia to establish an autonomous state.
>
> (Snow 1978: 128–9)

What comes out clearly from this statement is that Mao divided the territories formerly linked with the Qing empire into at least two categories. On the one hand were those like Inner Mongolia, where the large number of ethnic Chinese meant they should have 'autonomous' status. On the other hand were those such as Korea and Taiwan which were not peopled by Chinese, and whose opposition to Japanese imperialism thus constituted independence movements.

This interpretation of Mao's statement to Snow has been given weight by an analysis of CCP documents from the period 1928–43 by Hsiao and Sullivan, who claim that before 1943 the CCP did in fact recognise that anti-Japanese resistance on Taiwan constituted a national liberation movement by a distinct Taiwanese nation (*minzu*) (Hsiao and Sullivan 1979). A survey of Taiwanese revolutionary organisations in the mainland in the 1920s and 1930s (Lan 1994) indicates that the objective of Taiwan's independence from Japan, rather than one of unification with China, was in fact the clarion call of both Taiwanese and Chinese leftists in the mainland. The relationship of the CCP to Taiwanese anti-Japanese organisations operating in the mainland thus mirrors the KMT's ambivalence and suggests that the link was conceived as one between fraternal parties opposing imperialism, rather than as one implying membership of the same nation.

The evidence available, then, indicates that it was only at the time of the Cairo Conference that the CCP began to identify Taiwan as part of the Chinese nation. Many good reasons can be put forward for this change of position. First of all, rejection of the claim that Taiwan is a part of China would have meant rejection of a major international agreement, which in turn could have complicated future international recognition of a CCP regime (Hsiao and Sullivan 1979: 464–5). In the context of the development of Chinese nationalism, though, there were additional reasons of a far more pressing nature. These arose from the fact that the CCP had made the preservation of territorial integrity an issue of political legitimation ever since it had contrasted its own declaration of war on Japan following the September 1931 invasion of Manchuria with Chiang Kai-shek's 'selling the whole of China' (Mao 1934: 249–55; Provisional Central Government 1934). By 1943, to deny an international agreement presenting China with territories deemed to have been stolen by Japan would hardly have been consistent with the CCP's claim to be the true party of national salvation as the post-war contest with the KMT approached.

Aside from the competition with the KMT, however, the claim to Taiwan must also be understood in terms of the consolidation of Mao Zedong's leadership of the CCP. For Mao, as for Sun and Chiang, the goal of the revolution was not to dismantle the remnants of the Qing empire but to transform them into a modern Chinese state. Whereas before 1949, advocating national self-determination was useful to mobilise minority ethnic groups against the Japanese and the KMT, after liberation it was viewed according to what Mayall calls the 'conventional interpretation' held to by anti-colonial liberation movements throughout the world (Mayall 1993: 55–7). That is, once the colonialists had been expelled, state borders were not to be tampered with. Thus, whereas Mao had explicitly stated in his report to the Second Congress of the Chinese Soviet Republic in January 1934 that the presence of comrades from Taiwan, Korea and Annam (Vietnam) proved the party's commitment to allowing minorities to form independent states (Mao 1934: 277), by the time of the 1954 constitution of the PRC, areas populated by national minorities had become 'inalienable parts of the PRC' (NPC 1954: Art. 3). The suppression of a movement such as the 1959 revolt in Tibet could then be described in patriotic terms as a victory over a 'clique of traitors and foreign imperialism' (Leng and Palmer 1961: 137).

This changed role of the national minorities in the post-1949 PRC constitution must be understood in its relationship to the consolidation of the institution of CCP dictatorship. With the existence of large numbers of minorities, particularly in sensitive border areas, the CCP adopted theories and policies similar to those used by the Russian Communists when faced with the potential threat to the state by ethnic diversity. Stalin's formula of 'national in form, socialist in content' and the Sunist notion of a superior Han culture were synthesised in the shape of a superior Chinese socialist civilisation. This is the thinking behind the words of the vice-chairman of the Nationalities Affairs Commission who stated that:

> Only by uniting themselves in the big united family of the motherland, can the various nationalities of China construct socialism and resist imperialism. Any nationality, if it attempts to secede from the big family of the motherland, is bound to leave the socialist road and follow the imperialist and colonial road.
>
> (Wang 1958: 138)

Under the Communists, then, as much of the former Qing empire as possible was to be held together by a system of CCP rule. When Mao finally announced that the Chinese people had stood up, he was not only announcing the foundation of the PRC state, he was also addressing the first meeting of an organisation which would lay down the foundations for the legitimacy of CCP dictatorship. This was the First Plenary Session of the Chinese People's Political Consultative Conference, a United Front organisation led by the CCP. The resulting document, the Common Programme, adopted on 30 September 1949, established the system of People's Democratic Dictatorship. No less than four formal constitutions were to follow in 1954, 1975, 1978 and 1983. Despite the turbulence of the decades of the Great Leap Forward and the Great Proletarian Cultural Revolution, one theme that remains constant in the preambles to all these documents is that of the CCP as the party of national salvation presiding over a system of People's Democratic Dictatorship.

If CCP dictatorship was to be established on a strange hybrid of nationalism and proletarian revolutionism, what is particularly relevant for the longer-term significance of Taiwan in PRC politics is how the former element comes to take on an increasing prominence as belief in the revolution and CCP governance declines. In fact, Taiwan is not even mentioned specifically in the 1954 version, promulgated before the disaster of the Great Leap Forward, or in the 1975 version, promulgated during the final spluttering of the Cultural Revolution. The 'liberation' of Taiwan is only cited in the constitution for the first time in the preamble to the March 1978 version (NPC 1978: 130). This was the period when Mao's then apparent successor, the uninspiring Hua Guofeng, was struggling to assert himself by striking a compromise between Maoism and economic reform in the face of mass discontent with CCP governance.

It was only after Deng Xiaoping consolidated his power in December 1978 that the party was finally to depart from 'the mistakes' made by comrade Mao in his later years (Central Committee 1981: 73). And when Deng set out his programme for the 1980s he made the return of Taiwan one of the three major tasks of the decade, along with opposing international hegemonism and stepping up economic construction (Deng 1980: 224–5). In the preamble to the 1983 version of the constitution that followed, the 'reunification' of Taiwan with the motherland kept its place in the CCP's history of national salvation. In emphasising the call for national unification at the time of his succession, Deng thus located himself in an unbroken tradition of leaders and would-be leaders of the Chinese nation, stretching back to Sun Yat-sen and forward to Jiang Zemin, who link the issue of the integrity of the Chinese nation with the legitimacy of party dictatorship. As Deng reminded his audience in a speech of 16 January 1980, 'China always used to be described as "a heap of loose sand". But when our party came to power and rallied the whole country around it, the disunity resulting from the partitioning of the country by various forces was brought to an end' (Deng 1980: 252).

Looking back at the Communist revolution in China, then, the Taiwan issue can be seen to have become increasingly significant in the PRC's domestic politics whenever the CCP has fallen back on nationalist appeals as its revolutionism has fallen out of favour. First of all, during the civil war with the KMT the issue of Taiwan became one over which neither side could afford to compromise without damaging its credentials as the true saviour of the nation. Taiwan again takes on more prominence in domestic politics following the death of Mao, when the party has to face up to the catastrophic failures of the first four decades of its rule. Under Deng, the true essence of Mao Zedong Thought was now to be found not in the doctrine of class struggle, but in a combination of CCP dictatorship legitimised by economic development and national salvation. Deng was playing for high stakes in making unification with Taiwan one of the main tasks for the CCP in the 1980s, and he made no secret of his view that the island's status was linked with the integrity of the PRC's own international status and the stability of CCP rule. It was thus that, when outlining his new Taiwan policy, Deng emphasised that, 'Under no circumstances will we allow any foreign country to interfere. Foreign interference would simply mean China is still not independent, which would lead to no end of trouble' (Deng 1983: 19).

Yet this increasing prominence of the Taiwan issue in PRC politics may not have been either possible or desirable without the changes that took place in the international scene of the 1970s. There would have been little point in replacing Mao's doctrine of the class struggle by the cause of unifying the motherland, had not resolving the Taiwan problem appeared to be an increasingly attainable prospect. It was changes in the wider international scene, especially the PRC–US rapprochement of the 1970s, that had made it one.

INTERNATIONALISATION OF THE TAIWAN PROBLEM

From an international perspective, the revival of the civil war in China after 1945 had made it unclear which government legitimately represented the Chinese state. At first it seemed that the course of the civil war would resolve this issue. By 1948 it was assumed by most foreign governments that the fall of Taiwan was imminent. Most significantly, this was the view of the Truman administration (Chang 1990: 13; Lasater 1989: 12; MacFarquhar 1972: 70–1). When the PRC was established on 21 September 1949, the CCP had already made it clear that the new government would adopt a one-China policy under which there could be no acceptance of recognition by any state which still recognised the ROC. In April 1949, Mao had rejected overtures from both the USA and Britain to develop relations with the new government, unless they first of all cut relations with the KMT regime.

This chain of events, however, was interrupted by the position Taiwan came to take in the complex balance of power that evolved between the PRC, the Soviet Union and the United States during the Cold War. In the end, it was not Mao's planned attack on Taiwan by the PRC that pushed the Truman administration into taking military action to defend the Chiang regime, but the outbreak of the Korean War on 25 June 1950. Already under intense criticism for having 'lost China', two days after the outbreak of hostilities Truman reversed his previous position on Taiwan's status and took the view that the island was now essential to the security of the Pacific and US forces in that area (Truman 1950: 83). The US Seventh Fleet thus began regular patrols in the Taiwan Strait to prevent any attack on Taiwan from the Chinese mainland, and the USA continued to supply the ROC with economic and military aid.

Recent works on this period have shed light on why preservation of the KMT regime in Taiwan could have served the interests of both Washington and Moscow. For Stalin, the existence of the KMT regime on Taiwan was useful in so far as it ruled out improved relations between the PRC and the United States (Goncharov *et al.* 1993: 99–109). For the Truman administration, on the other hand, supporting the KMT regime became part of a strategy of maintaining pressure on the PRC that would force the new state to make increasingly high demands on its Soviet ally, thereby straining the Sino-Soviet alliance (Chang 1990). With the addition of intense pressure from the 'China lobby' on all US administrations since Truman had 'lost' China, the ROC came to be viewed as a US ally, important both militarily and symbolically for the US strategy of containment. The alliance between Washington and Taipei was consolidated by the US–ROC Mutual Defence Treaty of December 1954.

The development of the Cold War thus froze the unsettled status of Taiwan. Meanwhile the ROC regime was still saddled with the nationalist form of legitimacy it had developed in the Chinese mainland and the claim that it was the government of all China. Faced by this complex situation, most international actors had preferred to suspend their judgement over the final status of Taiwan, especially since the Truman administration had kept open a window of flexibility on the issue by insisting that the future status of the island was undecided. Originally the USA had insisted that this matter should await the restoration of security in the Pacific, a peace settlement with Japan, or consideration by the United Nations (Truman 1950: 83). However, when a peace treaty was finally signed on 8 July 1951 between Japan and forty-eight Allied powers (excluding the USSR and the PRC), it was not stated to whom Taiwan was being ceded. Similarly, in a separate peace treaty with the ROC, signed in April 1952, Japan recognised its renunciation of title to Taiwan without specifying to whom it was being given. From Washington's perspective, what these treaties achieved was nothing more than formally to take the Japanese element out of the Taiwan problem, while leaving the situation otherwise unchanged (Crawford 1979: 145).

The framework was thus in place for the broader dynamics of the Taiwan problem to develop. Two rival governments existed, both claiming exclusive sovereignty over one nation, 'China', and both claiming that Taiwan had been returned to the motherland in 1945. So long as the United States recognised the ROC government as the legitimate government of the Chinese nation and continued to support it as such in international organisations, especially the UN, the regime's claim was given a degree of credibility. Conversely, as only one Chinese government could be recognised, this implied the illegitimacy of the PRC.

This situation began to be reversed with the realignment of power in East Asia signalled by the PRC–US rapprochement of the 1970s. In 1971, the same year that National Security Adviser Henry Kissinger made his secret visit to Beijing, the ROC withdrew from the United Nations and the majority of states began to recognise the PRC government as the representative of China. Yet the status of Taiwan still remained unresolved. Pushed into a fudged compromise on the status of the island by the wider necessities of opposing a resurgent Soviet Union, President Nixon mobilised the vagaries of the English language to 'acknowledge' and 'not challenge' Beijing's claim to Taiwan when he agreed on the PRC–US Joint Communiqué of 28 February 1972 (the 'Shanghai Communiqué'). This avoidance of explicit *recognition* that Taiwan is a part of China was maintained in the joint communiqué establishing diplomatic relations between the Carter administration and Beijing on 1 January 1979, and the joint communiqué under the Reagan administration of August 1982, which tried to establish limits on US arms sales to Taiwan (Han 1990: 514–18, 525–9; Harding 1972).

It was in this uncertain situation that the ROC began to develop formulas by which it could assert Taiwan's status as an independent state while not being recognised as such and while not betraying the KMT's own position that the island is a part of China. This meant finding formulas by which Taiwan could join various international conventions and international organisations. Although courts could treat the island as having a well-established *de facto* government capable of committing the state to certain classes of transaction, in strictly legal terms Taiwan, as distinct from the ROC, could not be recognised as a state because its government did not make such a claim. Its status thus came to pose something of a problem for legal experts, the more dispassionate of whom concluded it to be that of a consolidated *de facto* government in a civil war situation (Crawford 1979: 151).

The costs of this international confusion over Taiwan's status have been high for all sides. The issue brought the USA and the PRC to the brink of war during the Taiwan Strait crises of 1954 and 1958. When relations between Washington and Beijing finally began to thaw in the 1970s, the status of Taiwan was again the main obstacle to overcome in reaching agreement on the wording of the joint communiqués which were to establish some kind of *modus vivendi*. Although normalisation of Beijing–Washington relations on 1 January 1979 reduced the prominence of the Taiwan problem in PRC–US relations somewhat, the issue of the continuing supply of arms to Taiwan by the USA could still cause significant tensions in the early 1980s. The threat of the use of military force against Taiwan if the island was to declare independence or become unstable is also a threat to the regional stability of East Asia. More recently, the PRC's linkage of US arms sales to Taiwan with its own sale of arms to third states shows how the problem continues to have global implications. The potential ramifications of these points of friction are magnified by the PRC's position as a permanent member of the UN Security Council.

Yet the costs for the ROC on Taiwan were high. Apart from living under the constant military threat from the PRC and the massive defence burden which that entails, the greatest sacrifice made by the regime on Taiwan in clinging to the one-China policy has been its international isolation. At the time of writing, the ROC is recognised by only thirty-one states, among which only South Africa approaches the status of a regional power. The ROC is also excluded from international organisations. Yet Taiwan plays an extremely active role in the world economy. By 1993 Taiwan could boast the world's fifteenth largest volume of merchandise trade (*ROC Yearbook* 1993: 203) and its foreign exchange reserves could compete with those of Japan for the position of the world's highest. The biggest sacrifice that the regime in Taipei has had to pay for adhering to the one-China principle, though, was the breaking of relations with its main ally, the United States. According to one well-placed source, there would have been much pressure in the USA to grant recognition to Taiwan as a separate state at the time of US–PRC rapprochement, if Taipei had made such a claim. The reason that it did not make such a claim can be found in the implications that this would have had on the constitutional situation of the regime in Taipei (Feldman 1989: 30). It is to this problem that we turn in Chapter 2.

TAIWAN IN CHINESE NATIONALISM

Theories of state legitimacy, from Rousseau to Bendix, point out the necessity of an element of *belief* in the fitness of rulers to rule if a stable political situation is to be achieved (Bendix 1978: 16–17; Rousseau 1979: 212–13; Weber 1978: 212–13). In the process of the transformation of the Qing dynasty empire into the Chinese state, this belief came to be articulated and expressed in terms of Chinese nationalism. The founding figures of this ideology propagated the belief that the system of party dictatorship was legitimate so long as its purpose was to achieve the integrity of the Chinese nation-state. Conversely, representative government and calls for self-determination by those who did not consider themselves to be part of the Chinese nation had to be postponed or forbidden. It was according to the imperatives of this ideology that Taiwan came to play a highly symbolic role in the legitimisation of the Chinese system of party dictatorship. This role began to develop in the closing years of the nineteenth century when the cession of Taiwan to Japan represented the weakness of the *ancien régime* and the injustice inflicted on the Chinese nation by imperialism. When the Second World War provided the conditions within which the ROC could gain international recognition for a claim to the island after the defeat of Japan, this symbolic role was dramatically enhanced.

Yet Taiwan only became one of the central problems of Chinese politics when the KMT-led regime was expelled from the Chinese mainland and established itself on Taiwan. This was when the situation was created of two rival governments in Beijing and Taipei, both claiming to be the legitimate government of the whole Chinese nation. When this situation was frozen by the Cold War balance of power in East Asia, other international actors could only recognise one of them as a *de jure* government. The Chinese nation had been imagined, achieved, then quickly divided.

When Jiang Zemin made his lunar new year speech in 1995, then, he was locating himself within the narrative of Chinese nationalism that had become central to the discourse on state legitimisation throughout the long Chinese revolution. By presenting his appeal to compatriots in Taiwan in terms of a story stretching back to the decline of the Qing dynasty (Jiang 1995), he was reminding his audience throughout the Chinese reading world that the Taiwan problem is not only an argument about the international status of Taiwan, it is also an argument about the legitimacy of the Chinese nation-state itself. To understand how such an overture was received on the other side of the Taiwan Strait, it is necessary to look at the very different historical experiences that have shaped the relationship between national identity and status in the politics of Taiwan itself.

2 The crisis of Chinese nationalism in Taiwan

Having looked at how Taiwan came to be of importance to Chinese nationalism, it is possible to understand why any challenge to the claim that Taiwan is a part of China should be of great significance in Chinese politics. A combination of factors internal and external to the island in the decades after its occupation by the ROC in 1945, however, did ultimately lead to such a challenge. That the island had passed through a very different history from that of the Chinese mainland makes this perhaps unsurprising. It is Taiwan's alternative history, therefore, that should be the starting point for explaining how another vision of the relationship between Chinese state and Chinese nation ultimately developed.

If the defeat of the Qing dynasty and the cession of Taiwan to Japan at Shimonoseki stands at the beginning of the search for the Chinese nation, in Taiwan it marks the beginning of half a century of Japanese colonial rule. This started with a brief but traumatic attempt to resist the Japanese by establishing a Taiwan Republic, the first such political body in East Asia. Rather than an experiment in popular government, however, the republic's ten-day existence and the four months of resistance that followed its disbandment by the Japanese should be seen more as a last-ditch attempt to remain within Qing suzerainty. That the Qing failed even to acknowledge the republic's existence or communicate with its leaders resulted in resentment towards the court's betrayal amongst the gentry and merchant classes, and apathy on the part of common people and soldiers (Lamley 1964: 143–65).

Having crushed the Qing loyalists of the Taiwan Republic, the early Japanese administration then attempted to govern the island by initiating self-rule within the Japanese empire. Within the Treaty of Shimonoseki, a clause had been included which allowed any resident of Taiwan to leave the island within two years. After that time, all would take up Japanese nationality. To prevent the development of secessionist tendencies, this measure was accompanied by a policy of cultural assimilation. Yet if the people of the island had become Japanese subjects, they did not enjoy equal rights with Japanese citizens. The island was ruled by an appointed governor while local people were discriminated against in employment and educational opportunities. Under these conditions, a Home Rule Movement was formed which pressed for increased representation for the people of Taiwan in the governance of the island. Although the Home Rule Movement's demand for an island-wide assembly was not met, limited representation was eventually achieved in district assemblies where half the members were elected and half appointed by the Japanese administration.

When militarists gained control of the Japanese government in the 1930s, however, the colonial power's approach changed to one of complete 'Nipponisation'. A decree by the governor demanded that people should change their names to Japanese, adopt Japanese customs, and use the Japanese language as their everyday vernacular. All Chinese-language publications were banned from 1 April 1937. Although throughout most of the Japanese period the distinction between coloniser and colonised had been preserved by the Japanese authorities, the increasing economic and military incorporation of the island into the Japanese system ultimately led to intense efforts being made to persuade the Taiwanese that they were Japanese citizens obliged to die for the emperor in combat. No less than 207,183 were conscripted during the Second World War, 30,304 of whom became casualties.

Yet the result of Nipponisation was not simply the inculcation of a Japanese identity in the population. It has also been maintained that under Japanese colonisation there was created an island-wide definition of political incorporation as 'Taiwanese' (Winckler 1988a: 54). According to this view, the unequal status between Japanese and Taiwanese during the period of occupation had made the success of cultural assimilation unlikely. Rather, as is usually the case with state-imposed attempts at cultural homogenisation (Bloom 1990: 143–6), a feeling of resentment against the colonialists had been a significant by-product of the Japanese policy and a possible binding force for the islanders (Lin 1987, 1993; Lin 1994a, 1994b; Ye 1990). But can such a binding force be called a form of 'national' consciousness?

From the perspective on nationalism adopted in this work, a 'national' consciousness is one in which group identification is the premise for a claim to statehood. At least in 1945, it seems unlikely that any emergent Taiwanese identity among the island population was a 'national' identity in this sense of the term. The sentiments of the younger residents of Taiwan were very different from the nationalist emotions of Koreans and the residents of European colonies in Asia. Rather than making any great clamour for independence, Taiwanese leaders argued for a special place within the Japanese empire through participation in an elective island administration and representation of Taiwan's interests in the National Diet at Tokyo (Kerr 1974: xiv).

It would actually have been very difficult for the islanders to have developed a form of homogeneous Taiwanese identity before 1945, because they were neither linguistically nor culturally bound into a single ethnic group. Not only was there the distinction between colonial elite and the colonised, but the colonised themselves were divided into a mosaic of ethnic groupings. These often stretched back to clan origins in the Chinese mainland. The majority of the population consisted of islanders whose ancestors had migrated from Fujian province over the centuries and who retained much of the parochial dialect and customs of that area of mainland China (Lin 1994a: 1–8). Yet there were also the remnants of aboriginal tribes, now a small minority, and a large minority of Hakka who originated from the province of Guangdong. All these groups possessed their own dialects and customs. Even among the majority who originated from Fujian, there were conflicts between groupings who took their identities from specific places of origin in that mainland province. Rather than being identified as 'Taiwanese', this fragmented population was labelled by the Japanese as 'islanders' (*bendao ren*). If they were referred to as 'Chinese' at all, it was only in a derogatory sense (Dai and Ye 1992: 17).

Those historians who wish to stress that the residents of Taiwan maintained loyalty to the Chinese 'motherland', on the other hand, need to explain such phenomena as the enthusiasm shown by the Taiwan gentry class towards the short-lived pan-Asiatic 'Taiwan Acculturation Society' (Taiwan tonghua hui). Established by forty-four Japanese liberal reformers in Taiwan in 1914 with the aim of making Taiwan a bridge between the Japanese and Chinese nations, this had the support of no less than 3,178 members of the Taiwan gentry. One of these Taiwanese members was so enthused by the organisation's rhetoric that he publicly pierced his flesh to write in blood, 'The Acculturation Society is our loving mother' (Wu and Cai 1990: 17–24). Indeed, if we can assess the strength of an identity in terms of the bonds of loyalty it entails, then it is noteworthy that many influential members of the pre-1945 population did not seem to find it difficult to identify with the Japanese authorities under the occupation and then switch their allegiances to the ROC authorities after the change in administration. Other occurrences that throw doubt on nationalist interpretations of Taiwan under the Japanese are the fact that many of the individuals who chose to leave Taiwan for the mainland after Shimonoseki quickly returned to the island to take up Japanese nationality, while many of Taiwan's business community spent the period of the War of Resistance Against Japan in the mainland providing supplies to the Japanese army (Lin 1996: 36–40). Then there are the cases of the young men who, having been schooled in Japanese militarism, were only too proud to volunteer to fight for Japan in the Second World War (Chen 1995: 158–69; Chen 1996: 78–87).

Following the arrival of the ROC forces from the mainland after the defeat of Japan, and the accompanying influx of immigrants, there began to arise an identity crisis concerning the relationship between being Chinese and being Taiwanese. What Chinese consciousness did exist in Taiwan had come to take a distinctly Taiwanese form as one element in a complex relationship between being Chinese, being Taiwanese and being Japanese. Formative experiences under the colonial administration consisted of speaking, acting and moving as a Japanese while at school, but returning to the traditional culture of the family, speaking in a provincial local dialect, worshipping local deities, and occasionally listening to stories about China from the older generation on returning home (Ye 1990: 2). What Chinese patriotism had taken shape in these circumstances was largely a form of personal self-strengthening by Taiwanese intellectuals in their rejection of Japanese colonialism. The image of China such people clung to was handed down in lore but often not based on any first-hand knowledge of the other side of the Strait (Ye 1990: 14–15). On the other hand, the residents of Taiwan had also achieved limited representation in government under the Japanese occupation, and there were high expectations that liberation from colonial rule would mean that this would be extended to full representation. To pursue this aim a Taiwan People's Association was established on 2 February 1946, which was later reorganised as the Taiwan Political Reconstruction Association.

From the other side of the Strait, however, Taiwan was seen in something of a negative light, as a backwater suffering from the collaborationist stigma left by fifty years of Japanese rule. Unlike the liberated mainland Chinese provinces, Taiwan was singled out as not ready for its own provincial government. The system of rule by appointed governor used by the Japanese was thus continued under the new rulers. A variety of views exist concerning the character of the first governor, General Chen Yi. Some see him as having already established a record for brutal rule from his previous governance of Fujian province (Kerr 1966: 47–57). Others say he was something of an idealist whose hopes for making Taiwan a model Chinese province were frustrated by a lack of first-hand knowledge and the post-war economic crisis (Chen *et al.* 1994: 4). All agree, though, that Chen Yi's policies failed in several important respects.[2]

First of all, it was Chen who insisted on treating Taiwan as a special administrative case. The harsh executive system he imposed on the island, with its restrictions on freedom of expression, created the feeling that the Taiwanese were to be seen again as second-class citizens, quelling any initial patriotism felt towards the new regime. Such sentiments were fed further when Chen undertook measures that reflected a lack of understanding of the predicament that the islanders had been left facing when abandoned by the Qing dynasty. These included the arrest of leading figures he considered to have been collaborators, his unwillingness to employ islanders in important posts (even preferring to continue using the previous Japanese occupants), and his hindering the return of Taiwanese stranded in the mainland. This special treatment meted out to the Taiwanese, accompanied by a certain supercilious arrogance shown towards the islanders by the new arrivals, was hardly likely to consolidate feelings of loyalty towards the new regime. When complemented by measures taken in the mainland against supposed collaborators, which were applied across the board to Koreans as well as Taiwanese, it is not surprising that the outcry went up that the islanders were being treated like foreigners.

The general style of Chen's administration was that of the victor over the vanquished, rather than that of the liberator. With a corrupt bureaucracy and failure to take economic measures to stem chronic inflation, it is hardly surprising that the first years of ROC administration in Taiwan resulted in a growing resentment towards the newcomers from the mainland. When the ROC government in Nanjing promulgated its constitution on 1 January 1947, disillusionment intensified with Chen Yi's announcement that it would not apply to Taiwan because the population required several more years of political tutelage. Questions began to be asked about the future of Taiwan's relationship with the mainland. Critics started to point to Taiwan's separate history, while radical youths questioned the validity of the wartime declarations of the Allies (Kerr 1966: 281–93).

The growing frustration finally erupted into island-wide violence on 28 February 1947. The immediate cause of the disturbances was the beating of a woman tobacco pedlar in Taipei by officials enforcing a monopoly that Chen had kept in place after the departure of the Japanese. As the violence spread, the islanders tried to arm themselves and form a defence corps. The overwhelming power of ROC military reinforcements from the mainland ensured consolidation of the new state, however. In the purges which followed, the potential leadership among the residents of Taiwan was either annihilated, or co-opted into collaboration, or fled overseas. These events, mythologised as the '228 Incident', were to become perhaps the most significant formative experiences in preventing the consolidation of a Chinese national identity for the island over the following decades.

LEGITIMISING CHINESE NATIONALISM IN TAIWAN

If belief in political legitimacy is like the faith depositors place in a bank (Bendix 1978: 16–17), by the time the ROC regime moved its capital to Taipei on 7 December 1949, it had precious little credit left in the eyes of the native population of Taiwan. The popular slogan 'Dogs go and pigs come!' which came to be scrawled on Taipei walls soon after the ROC occupation (Kerr 1966: 97), indicates that there was no huge difference between the Japanese and the mainland Chinese rulers in the eyes of some of the indigenous population. Also worrying for Chiang Kai-shek, battling the Communists in the mainland civil war, must have been reports that the Truman administration was considering withdrawing support for his regime and exploring the possibilities of an autonomous Taiwan by backing indigenous forces there (Chang 1990: 18–19). As defeat of the ROC on the mainland became a certain prospect, the KMT had to begin to develop a more effective administration for Taiwan if the party was to survive there, let alone make the island a base for the nationalist mission of return.

The type of administration that was developed had to be limited by the KMT's constitutional claim to legitimacy. This meant that the legality of the KMT regime in Taiwan would depend on an ROC constitution devised for the whole of China, with the addition of a number of emergency measures justified in terms of the Chinese nationalist revolution. These were the legal devices for maintaining party dictatorship that had been put in place in the mainland in April 1948 by the first meeting of the ROC National Assembly. Entitled the Temporary Provisions Effective During the Period of Communist Rebellion, these suspended most of the constitutional constraints on the president. The president's powers were enhanced even further by the Legislative Yuan in December 1949, when it issued an administrative order declaring Taiwan a combat zone. This allowed Chiang Kai-shek to activate martial law on the island by emergency decree (Tien 1989: 110). Over the following decades a police state was established under two powerful institutions, the Taiwan Garrison Command and the National Security Council, both under the office of the president. The military penetrated civilian life at all levels, and military tribunals were authorised to try civilians and impose restrictions on civil rights.

In short, then, when the ROC moved to Taiwan, the KMT continued to legitimise its dictatorship in terms of constitutional measures that made sense in terms of the Chinese nationalist project. There were strong reasons for maintaining this argument. First of all, flawed though the elections of 1947 and 1948 might have been, they did enable the KMT to claim that the source of its legitimacy to rule lay in the sovereign will of the Chinese nation, as stated in Article 2 of the constitution. As only elections in mainland constituencies could express the will of the Chinese nation, the representatives elected on the other side of the Taiwan Strait in 1947 and 1948 could be frozen in office until unification could occur.

Another factor shaping the KMT's theory of legitimisation on Taiwan was the attitude of the individuals who had followed the party there and formed its base of popular support. When the KMT had retreated to Taiwan, it had brought with it some 2.5 million people, swelling the island's population of just under six million to just over eight million.[3] These migrants looked to the KMT party-state to provide them with protection, work and housing. The difficulties faced by individuals from the Chinese mainland who could not identify themselves in terms other than those they had brought from the mainland is conveyed by literature about their nostalgic attempts to recreate the clubs and dance halls of Shanghai in downtown Taipei (Bai 1978). Only the narrative of return embodied in the KMT's nationalism could provide what Breuilly would describe as the intellectual map that describes and prescribes the state of affairs for such people (Breuilly 1993: 381). In providing an answer as to why they found themselves in their present predicament and promising future victory over all adversaries, Chinese nationalism was to become their political mythology (Tudor 1972: 139).

The KMT's mythology was also given a degree of plausibility as the Cold War developed and the United States developed its doctrine of the 'roll back' of Communism, redrawing its defensive perimeter in East Asia to include Taiwan. US support for the ROC as the representative of China in international organisations, especially the UN, perpetuated hopes that the KMT might return to the mainland. Perhaps more significantly, this also enhanced the party's legitimacy as a government which could provide security from Communist attack in the eyes of the population of Taiwan. With the USA providing military protection and the economic aid that would lead to the 'Taiwan miracle', it appeared that the foundations could be laid for building a workable relationship between the regime and diverse social groupings. In any case, Chiang Kai-shek, as one of the strongest believers in the nationalist mission, saw no contradiction in developing Taiwan as a model Chinese society from which a political offensive against Communism could be launched (Tsang 1993b: 48–72).

If the KMT was to continue to root its legitimacy to rule Taiwan in terms of Chinese nationalism, however, something had to be done to bring the pre-1945 population of the island into the Chinese nation. It would be an over-simplification to envision the resulting process as one of a homogeneous 'mainlander' minority imposing its rule on a native 'Taiwanese' majority, because both groups were fragmented. The 'mainlanders' were sub-divided by their own provincial origins, by belonging to different shades of the political spectrum and by the political factionalism going back to the intra-party struggles of the mainland. As for the natives of Taiwan, apart from the ethnic divisions mentioned above, they saw themselves as belonging to at least three categories. There were those who had stayed in Taiwan under the Japanese and who had not had connections with the KMT before the end of the Second World War. Then there was a small minority, mostly of small businessmen and independent professionals, who had remained in Taiwan but supported Chinese nationalism. Finally there were the returnee Taiwanese who had gone to the mainland during the Japanese occupation, worked for the KMT government and who came back to Taiwan in 1945 as part of the new establishment (Winckler 1988b: 164). All of these political attitudes overlay the much longer-standing provincial, clan and ethnic divisions among the population. Perhaps the complex system of identification that resulted is best encapsulated by a recollection of the Hakka writer Tai Kuo-hui (Dai Guohui), who, unable to prove his identity through speaking in the Fujian dialect when faced with a Taiwanese mob during the 228 Incident, had to resort to singing the Japanese national anthem to show he was not from the Chinese mainland (Dai and Ye 1992: 3).

The KMT adopted a number of measures to consolidate power over this mosaic. First of all, the autonomy of the state enabled a radical policy of land reform to be carried out between 1949 and 1953. This increased the amount of land worked by owner-cultivators from 50.5 per cent to 75.4 per cent (Gold 1986: 66). The political effect, however, was to destroy the large landlord class which had formed the political leadership in the countryside, and to create a large owner-cultivator class, grateful to the KMT for their new status and higher income. Political influence in the countryside was also developed by the formation of KMT-controlled Farmers' Associations, which controlled credit and access to new technology and markets. Organisational control and elite selection were also developed through a radical restructuring of the party and state organisations in the early 1950s, after which large numbers of the native Taiwanese elite were encouraged to enter organisations at the lower levels. Candidates for co-option could be cultivated through military conscription, the representation of the military on campuses, and the establishment of a Chinese Youth Anti-Communist League (CYACL), with Chiang Kai-shek's son, Chiang Ching-kuo (Jiang Jingguo), as its first leader (Tien 1989: 87–8).

Yet if such a system was to have the 'faith of its investors' it still had to cultivate the loyalty of the population by devising symbols and institutions through which individuals could identify their own interests with the interests of the larger, 'imagined' Chinese nation upon which the KMT's whole constitutional theory of legitimacy was premised. Before this could be done, the administration had to expunge all traces of Japanese colonial culture and redirect the identification of individuals towards the KMT's version of a Chinese tradition. When the ROC forces arrived in Taiwan, however, there was even a shortage of newsmen on the island who could handle Chinese (Jang 1967: 78). Moreover, apart from using Japanese, the islanders also communicated in a wide diversity of Chinese dialects. While in power in mainland China, the KMT had already attempted to impose on the linguistic mosaic there a standard 'National Language' (*guoyu* – often referred to as Mandarin in English). In Taiwan this policy was to be continued. Control was taken of what had been the leading Japanese-language newspapers, and in 1948 a *National Language Daily* (*Guoyu ribao*) was set up by a Mandarin Promotion Committee. The National Language was also made the language of instruction and identified with love for the country, while the use of other dialects within school grounds was punishable by on-the-spot fines (Wilson 1983: 95–9).

The inculcation of a Chinese national identity went much further than language policy. Time was also 'nationalised' by counting from 1912 as year one: this is held to be a continuation of the system of basing year designations on periods of dynastic rule (*ROC Yearbook* 1993: x). Space was nationalised with maps showing the national territory as including the whole of the Chinese mainland and Outer Mongolia. Streets were renamed after mainland places, while educational and cultural institutions (such as the National Palace Museum, where much of China's cultural heritage from the mainland was preserved) were held to be the true successors to their mainland counterparts. Following the death of Chiang Kai-shek in April 1975, icing was added to this nationalist cake in the form of the Chiang Kai-shek Memorial, a massive square in the centre of Taipei which bears more than a passing resemblance to Tiananmen Square in Beijing.

The educational environment was also geared to an intense process of familiarising children and students with respect for national symbols, in particular the national flag, national anthem (also the KMT party song), national designation of the ROC and the national leader. Mind-numbing exercises were inflicted on children, such as remembering the names of mainland railway stations as they had existed before 1949. The cult of the charismatic leader was propagated, with portraits of Sun Yat-sen and Chiang Kai-shek hung in every classroom and government office. Sunism became a compulsory part of the school curriculum and passing an examination on the Three Principles of the People was made a prerequisite for university entrance, after which discipline was instilled by the presence of the military on campus.

Despite the rigour with which the KMT attempted to exercise hegemony over Taiwan's society, the fact that the whole edifice rested on Chinese nationalism meant that this foundation would ultimately prove insufficient for state legitimisation. Violence and cultural homogenisation may be more likely to be successful when applied in societies without any strong pre-existing sense of national identity or statehood. However, the symbols of the state should also be able to present an appropriate attitude in the face of perceived threats and behave beneficently towards the individual (Bloom 1990: 61). The KMT's initial attempts at building a Chinese national identity in Taiwan failed in both respects due to a number of domestic and international factors.

THE INTERNATIONAL CHALLENGE TO LEGITIMACY

One fundamental flaw in KMT legitimacy was that although the party could present itself as the guardian of Taiwan against attack from the mainland, the credibility of this claim was contingent upon increasingly uncertain American support. Although the Truman administration had hardened and consolidated its support for the ROC at the time of the Korean War, in practice it had always kept Chiang Kai-shek 'on a leash'. The international turmoil caused by the outbreak of hostilities in 1954 and 1958 between the two sides of the Taiwan Strait over the islands just off the coast of Fujian, still occupied by ROC forces, pushed the Eisenhower administration further towards considering the adoption of a two-China policy (Chang 1990: 144–9). Pressure was also put on the ROC to renounce the use of force against the mainland. By the time of the Kennedy administration, high-ranking officials had begun to suggest publicly that 'two Chinas' already existed and to urge a policy that would encourage the evolution of a 'Sino-Taiwanese' state on Taiwan. US press reports, meanwhile, floated a 'successor states' theory as a possible solution to the problem of PRC representation at the UN (MacFarquhar 1972: 183–4).

The real external crisis for the KMT regime, however, came with the Beijing–Washington rapprochement of the 1970s. The 1971 visit of the US table tennis team to the PRC and the Kissinger and Nixon visits to Beijing not only damaged the credibility of the ROC claim to be the government of China but raised questions over the issue of future US support. The PRC–US Joint Communiqué of 27 February 1972 was careful in its wording to 'acknowledge' and 'not challenge' the position that 'all Chinese on either side of the Taiwan Strait maintain that there is but one China and that

Taiwan is a part of China', rather than to recognise Beijing's claim to sovereignty (Harding 1992: 43). But the improved relations between Beijing and Washington contributed to the forced withdrawal of the ROC from the UN on 25 October 1971 and to recognition of the PRC by Japan in September 1972. In the context of US troop withdrawals from East Asia under Nixon's Guam Doctrine, the scaling down of US arms sales to the region, and Communist victories in Indochina, fear of isolation and Communist expansion could only grow in Taiwan. Dissidents overseas readily took advantage of the increasing evidence of the KMT's impotency, pointing out that the aim of retaking the Chinese mainland was militarily impossible, the ROC's forces being defensive and relying entirely on US military support for their survival. The rationale behind the myth was perceived to lie elsewhere, namely in the maintenance of what was claimed to be the illegal rule of Chiang Kai-shek over Taiwan through the imposition of martial law (Peng 1972: 121–31).

When the United States finally established diplomatic relations with the PRC on 1 January 1979, it was increasingly obvious to the KMT's critics that the ROC government would probably never be the government of all China, that the state was losing what little control it had over the destiny of even Taiwan itself, and that the future was to be one of increasing isolation in which security relied ultimately on the good will of the US Congress. Such critics began to feel bold enough to declare that the party was faced by a crisis of domestic legitimacy in the face of the international obstacles of the 1970s because it had overlooked the principle that 'diplomacy is an extension of domestic politics' (*Formosa* 1979a: 6–7).

Yet if US recognition of the PRC destroyed the myth of KMT nationalism for many in Taiwan, it did not do so in a way that decisively resolved Taiwan's status through unification with the mainland or independence. Instead, when the US Congress passed the Taiwan Relations Act, provisions were made which effectively froze Taiwan's status in an intermediate state between these two possible statehoods. This was done not by extending recognition to Taiwan, but by treating the island as a legal personality in US law. This international status was fixed by the overall provision in Section 4 (b) that whenever the laws of the USA refer to foreign countries, nations, states or governments or similar entities, they would also apply to Taiwan.

As the Taiwan legal expert Hungdah Chiu has put it, such measures amounted to a denial of the legal effect of the non-recognition of a foreign state carried out for political reasons (Chiu, H. 1992: 6). The Taiwan Relations Act was thus drawn up as a unique piece of legislation to deal with a unique situation in which the presidency had its hands tied in pursuing its version of the national interest by a Congress reflecting a deep sense of moral indignation over the betrayal of a long-standing ally. The result was to create and perpetuate a unique international status for the island between two possible statehoods. It was in this intermediate state that the domestic challenge to legitimacy was to come to a head.

THE DOMESTIC CHALLENGE TO LEGITIMACY

The international question mark hanging over the legitimacy of the KMT's claim to be the rightful government of China was underlined by developments in Taiwan itself. By the 1970s, the conditions for a burgeoning of political consciousness were coming into place. An increasingly wealthy and urbanised society was developing on the back of strong economic growth. Nine years of compulsory schooling and the expansion of higher education had led to a rise in the general level of knowledge, while many students were exposed to foreign, especially American, values while studying overseas. By the beginning of the decade student magazines had begun to campaign openly for democratic participation in politics, the upholding of basic human rights and the funding of social welfare.

The resolution of various anomalies arising from the imposition on Taiwan of a constitution designed for the Chinese mainland was also leading to a process of creeping democratisation. First of all, there was the relationship between Taiwan's provincial authorities and the rump national government of the ROC. In accordance with the wishes of Sun Yat-sen, the ROC constitution had paid much attention to local autonomy, so as to encourage political participation and tutelage. The Legislative Yuan had also drawn up a legal basis for self-government for what had been the thirty-six provinces of the ROC, in a document entitled *Principles for Local Self-Government*. Yet with the withdrawal of the ROC government to Taiwan in 1949, the island had been left with a central and a local government sharing the same jurisdiction.

If these problems were to be resolved through a reform of the ROC constitution, difficult questions concerning the ideology upon which KMT dictatorship was premised would be raised. Rather than face up to this, a tentative solution to the local–national government relationship had been found by replacing the *Principles for Local Self-Government* with a one-page document entitled *Main Points for Implementation of Local Self-Government by the Cities and Counties of Taiwan Province*. This allowed for a nominal provincial government for Taiwan which was to be clearly subordinate to the central government. The office of provincial governor was to be appointed by the president, while matters of personnel and legislation also had to be approved by the central authorities. The capital,

Taipei, and later the second main city, Kaohsiung, were placed under direct rule by the national government (Li 1993: 76–85).

Although local government had been neutered, its very existence did allow a semblance of democracy to be practised at the lowest levels. From 1951 elections were held for county magistrates and city mayors, and from 1954 for the Taiwan Provincial Assembly. The threat of dissent was largely countered at this level by the development of a complex system of local factions (Bosco 1992: 157–83). With the KMT acting as 'king maker' between groups competing for control over the allocation of resources and for prestige, effective leverage could be exercised over elections (Bosco 1994: 28–62). Despite this, local politics did provide a forum in which Taiwanese-born politicians could develop a political career.

In 1958, a group of such local activists established an Association for the Study of China's Local Self-Government. As any linkage of the issue of democracy with that of national identity was severely dealt with by the state, the group limited its aims to calling for the reform of corrupt electoral politics. In 1960, these local politicians joined forces with a number of critics of the Chiang regime who had migrated from the Chinese mainland and organised themselves around the magazine *Free China Semi-Monthly* (*Ziyou Zhongguo ban yue kan*) to try to establish a China Democratic Party (Zhongguo minzhu dang). The limits of KMT tolerance were revealed when the leading member of the group, the mainlander Lei Chen (Lei Zhen), was imprisoned. But the project did mark the first stage in an uneasy alliance between activists from two different constituencies who shared the common desire to bring about democratic politics.

Creeping democratisation was also encouraged when a solution had to be found to the process of natural attrition among the ageing representatives in the three chambers of central government who had been elected on the mainland A partial answer to this was found by introducing a system of supplementary elections from 1969 onwards for seats that had become vacant in the National Assembly and the Legislative Yuan. A small number of new seats were also created in the parliamentary chambers to represent the increased population of Taiwan. Yet the possibility of politicisation of the population that might arise from regular elections for the supplementary seats was avoided by allowing members to hold those seats in perpetuity. When, in 1972, the regime initiated regular elections for a small number of seats to represent Taiwan, this signalled a more significant move towards representative government. However, the party guarded against the dangers of interpreting this as the first step towards a parliamentary system to represent Taiwan by insisting that this small number of seats was supposed to represent Taiwan only as the 'free area of China'.

The conditions were gradually being created, however, for the cause of dissent to be taken up by a younger generation of activists. Such activists organised themselves around the magazine *The Intellectual* (*Daxue zazhi*) and called for greater representation for the native population. Although one of their highest concerns was to consolidate Taiwan against outside aggression (Halbeisen 1993: 79–80) and even though this was expressed in terms of Chinese patriotism, such autonomous activity was viewed with suspicion by the state. This was particularly clear when the government condemned as part of a CCP-inspired united front the patriotic demonstrations staged by students across the Chinese-reading world following the US-handover to Japan in 1971 of the Senkaku (Diaoyutai) Islands, an archipelago to the north of Taiwan which the Americans had occupied in the Second World War (Taida 1971: 28–31). The inconsistency of such attitudes held by the KMT, let alone this demonstration of the inability of the regime to safeguard the territory it claimed as Chinese, only contributed to the long-term erosion of the KMT's nationalist mythology and to a call for bold and independent initiatives in foreign policy (Wang 1971: 4).

When Chiang Kai-shek died on 6 April 1975, a powerful symbol was denied the KMT and fears arose over a succession crisis. He had already placed his son, Chiang Ching-kuo, in line for succession and Ching-kuo had actually been in charge of the administration since the early 1970s. The Moscow-trained Chiang Ching-kuo was not a widely trusted figure, however, having overseen the construction and implementation of much of the state's policing and control operations. But Chiang Ching-kuo set out on a course radically different from that expected of him. First as chairman of the KMT and premier, and from March 1978 as president, he presented a comparatively moderate and flexible approach to society and politics. One of his first acts was to offer amnesty to a number of prisoners, including some 130 political detainees. He also worked hard through the mass media to cultivate his leadership charisma and shed his previous hard-man image.

If Chiang Ching-kuo was to reduce the alienation that had developed under his father, however, he was hampered in this task by a number of things. First of all, despite his new image, Chiang continued to crack down on dissent and the organisation of new political parties, while talk of secession remained illegal. Moreover, if Chiang was to ensure the allegiance of the population of the island to the state, he was hampered by the cultural policy he had inherited. This had become particularly inept since a movement to 'revive Chinese culture' had been launched in 1967 to counter the Cultural Revolution in the mainland. Harking back to the New Life Movement initiated by Chiang Kai-shek in 1934 in the mainland, this presented a formalistic interpretation of Chinese tradition which focused on the moral legitimacy of the ROC regime and its leader (Chan 1985: 136–7). This kind of policy could hardly act as a panacea for the erosion of the symbols of international recognition that was taking place in the 1970s. Incidents such as the withdrawal of the ROC team from the 1976 Montreal Olympics when the Canadian government, at Beijing's request, refused to allow it to participate as the ROC, indicated that the claims of Chinese nationalism could impose a heavy cost on Taiwan.

The observation that nation-building through this kind of direct manipulation of culture tends to evoke alienation rather than identification (Bloom 1990: 143) is borne out by the ultimate appearance of dissatisfaction with the straitjacket imposed under Chiang Kai-shek. Until the mid-1970s the main alternative to the state-imposed version of Chinese tradition appeared to be literary theories from abroad, which, according to critics, were imported wholesale by the cultural 'compradores' of the Department of Foreign Languages and Literature at National Taiwan University. By the middle of the decade, however, a more appealing alternative finally began to appear in the shape of a literary trend called *xiang tu* ('native literature'). This harked back to a tradition of social realist writing about Taiwan which had been first mentioned in a 1930 essay by the writer Huang Shih-hui (Huang Shihui). Although the Taiwanese consciousness that was emerging here did not yet go so far as to call for a Taiwanese state, it encouraged the perception that Taiwan had suffered a loss of its own identity in the face of Japanese and American 'imperialism' and it stimulated a sense of loyalty to the island (Gold 1993: 183–92, 1994: 61–4; Lau 1983: 138–47). As *xiang tu* came to merge with the rising tide of political dissatisfaction, questioning the links between national identity, regime legitimisation and international status became unavoidable.

DECONSTRUCTING CHINESE NATIONALISM

Underlying the voices of protest and dissent emerging from Taiwan's creeping democratisation and growing sense of its own identity was the development of a refutation of the principles and imperatives of Chinese nationalism. Probably the earliest comprehensive critique of KMT ideology came in the form of the 1964 *Declaration of Taiwanese Self-Salvation* (*Taiwan zi jiu yundong xuanyan*) (Peng Mingmin Educational Foundation 1994: 187–98), drawn up by a professor of law at National Taiwan University, Peng Ming-min (Peng Mingmin), and two students. All three were promptly arrested and imprisoned, and their publication destroyed. Peng later fled to the United States, where he propagated his views amongst students studying overseas. There he developed his argument in the 1972 autobiographical work, *A Taste of Freedom* (Peng 1972).

Peng tells the familiar story of the talented Taiwanese growing up under Japanese colonial rule, the consequent confusion of identity, and the trauma of the ROC occupation of Taiwan. A student of international aviation law, under the patronage of reform-minded mainlanders, in 1961 he was made head of the department of politics at National Taiwan University. As a young academic amongst an elite dominated by immigrants from mainland China, Peng soon found himself torn between attempts by the regime to co-opt his services on one side, and jealous hostility from his mainlander colleagues and superiors on the other. His eventual politicisation as a critic of the KMT regime arose, however, from the international exposure and knowledge of international relations demanded by his work. The turning point came after he was sent to the UN to advise the ROC delegation on its attempts to veto membership for Mongolia, which the ROC still claimed as Chinese territory, against pressure for recognition of Mongolia from the Soviet Union and African states.

When Peng returned, disillusioned, to Taiwan he began to hold discussion meetings at his home and to develop an argument against the proposition that because Taiwan had always been part of China, it ought always to be a part of China in the future. In part, he challenged this principle by reinterpreting the historical relationship of Taiwan with the Chinese mainland, portraying it in terms of a people struggling to escape the yoke of the mainland through a process of frequent rebellions (Peng 1972: 239). He also opposed sentimentality over the links between the two sides of the Taiwan Strait with a reminder that attitudes towards the island by the mainland have been characterised by ambiguity, with Taiwan seen for long periods as a haunt of pirates and opium fiends whom the Qing court was glad to be rid of. Actions such as allowing the heads of aboriginal tribes to sign a treaty with the United States in 1869 and the decision to cede Taiwan to Japan are taken as further evidence of the tenuous nature of Qing sovereignty.

Since Shimonoseki, Peng reminds us, there have been only the four years between 1945 and 1949 of direct contacts across the Taiwan Strait. Yet those four years were a time of turbulence and suffering in which the 228 Incident occurred and the island's elite was wiped out by 'the Chinese' (Peng 1972: 240). With the history of Taiwan thus portrayed, Peng is able to make the analogy with other pioneering peoples who have fled to new lands and created new states, regardless of the principle that the ethnic nation and the state should be congruent. In this light, it is as wrong to lump the residents of Taiwan together with 'the Chinese' as it is to maintain that the Americans, Australians and British are all the same (Peng 1972: 241).

Peng's attack on Chinese nationalism also attempts to reject the linking of the problem of Taiwan's status with the issue of China's crisis at the hands of imperialism. Although China may well have suffered as a semi-colony under the powers, Peng points out that its status as victim was terminated with its recovery of sovereignty and self-respect at the time of the establishment of the 'New China' in 1949. Peng is quite clear that Taiwan only became an issue for China later on, when the KMT made the island its base for attacking the PRC with US support (Peng 1972: 242). Meanwhile, he claimed, the Chiang Kai-shek administration was using nationalist mythology to maintain a regime so undemocratic that it could not claim to represent Taiwan, China or even the KMT itself. It could in fact speak for no more than a small faction within the party.

What is particularly interesting about Peng Ming-min, however, is that in questioning the links between nation, state and party, he also creates space for the development of an alternative conception of political community which reveals a concern for bridging the divisions in Taiwan society created by KMT rule. When, for example, the *Declaration of Taiwanese Self-Salvation* points out that the KMT's economic policies are intended to divide the islanders according to their origins, what is meant by 'islanders' is all the individuals who live in Taiwan, 'regardless of place of origin'. This is significant as indicating a willingness to work towards a conception of political community which would not be defined by criteria that exclude those who arrived in Taiwan after 1945. The concept of political community in Taiwan, it is argued, must include all the diverse groups living in the island while maintaining their political separation from the Chinese nation.

This conception of political community is developed further in *A Taste of Freedom*, where more is revealed about the sources that inspire Peng's views on the subject. Being fluent in French, he was influenced at an early stage by the works of Ernest Renan, in particular *What Is a Nation?* What strikes Peng about Renan's views is that they raise the idea that neither race, nor language, nor culture forms a nation but rather a deeply felt sense of community and shared destiny (Peng 1972: 26). This idea of the nation as a community of shared destiny is clearly attractive to Peng Ming-min in the situation of an ethnically divided Taiwan. Yet it also enables him to reject the 'feudal prejudice' that anyone of Han descent, no matter how divided they have been from China in history and geography, should be under Chinese rule. For Peng, the Chinese must learn to distinguish between ethnic origin, culture and language on the one hand, and politics and law on the other. They must give up the idea that those who are ethnically, culturally and linguistically Chinese must be politically and legally Chinese as well (Peng 1972: 244). Individuals should be able to be proud of their Chinese culture and ancestry, but at the same time divorce their status from China politically and legally. Eisenhower, after all, was proud of his German ancestry but did not shirk at leading the Allies against the Germans in the Second World War (Peng 1972: 245).

Although it is difficult to say what kind of impact Peng's works had inside Taiwan in the early 1970s, they do at least indicate the kind of thinking that was developing at that time amongst those dissatisfied with the KMT regime. Many of those themes could only come into the open inside Taiwan in the late 1970s and the 1980s when conditions had allowed for the coming together of opponents of the KMT in a loose grouping identified as the Dang Wai (literally 'outside the party'). As democratisation crept forwards, the signal went up that such opposition was growing from being a marginal activity to one which could rally mass support when members of the Dang Wai won 34 per cent of the vote in the 1977 elections for the Taiwan Provincial Assembly. The tense mood among sections of the ruling party and the public was also revealed when the election witnessed the first outbreak of mass violence.

When in 1979 a number of leading Dang Wai figures formed an organisation around the journal *Formosa* (*Meili dao*), with an eye to developing a political party, they continued to explore the links between democracy and national identity. Acknowledging the modernity of nationalism in China (Yao 1979: 93–7), they pointed out that the KMT's argument for legitimisation was fundamentally flawed through its separation of the state from the Chinese nation upon which its legitimacy was said to rest. This had left the KMT on the horns of a dilemma, premising its rule on an ideology incompatible with democracy in Taiwan. On the one side, the regime's weak link with the Chinese nation was maintained by the idea of 'legitimate succession' (*fa tong*), according to which the regime was legal so long as representatives who had been elected in the mainland continued in office. On the other hand, any expansion of democracy in Taiwan must imply an acknowledgement that the *demos* is limited to the island, and that the idea of 'legitimate succession' is invalid. If those in power insisted on maintaining their positions through the idea of 'legitimate succession' instead of establishing their legitimacy on democratic grounds, warned the magazine, then the KMT would be 'adding wings to the tiger' of revolution, and would witness a replay of the demise of the Qing dynasty (*Formosa* 1979b: 7).

Having stated that parliament clearly does not represent 'the compatriots who live in the Taiwan area' (Huang 1979: 15), *Formosa* writers began to develop an alternative conception of the relationship between people and state which comes close to the community of shared destiny adopted by Peng Ming-min. The government and the people of the ROC on Taiwan, they maintain, have become like two people with one body who actually share the same destiny. If the government is to survive in this situation, it will have to understand the common demands and aspirations of the compatriots living in the Taiwan area (Huang 1979: 18).

In defence of such aspirations against charges of treason, the idea that patriotism involves the individual sacrificing his or her interests for the sake of a sacred mission of national salvation is rejected. Instead, patriotism is described as depending on the quality of the relationship between the individual and the community: if the place where the individual lives provides a good living, then the individual will identify with that place and will be a good patriot (Liu 1979: 76). Even the Chinese classics are invoked to provide examples of patriotic statesmen who had willingly betrayed a bad state in favour of an alien state which offered policies more beneficial to the people. Further afield, did not George Washington, an English patriot, throw in his lot with the Thirteen States after seeing the results of bad British government (Huang 1979: 18)?

In conformity with this idea of patriotism, and in opposition to the principle of loyalty to Chinese nationalism, the *Formosa* writers develop a contractarian vision of society. In this view a state arises when individuals identify with each other due to shared interests, forming a community to protect their territory and to take control of their destiny through democratic government. As in Peng Ming-min, it is stated again that it is particularly important in a society such as Taiwan's to accept that, although the population can be divided into numerous ethnic groups, all of these are only distinguished by their time of arrival, and that all the settlers who have come to Taiwan over the centuries have ended up developing a primary attachment to Taiwan's soil. The 'mainlanders', it is held, will be no exception to this trend (Liu 1979: 76). The alternative, to demand 'patriotism' in terms of loyalty towards an ethnic community, can only be disastrous. What, for example, is to become of the unfortunate Manchurian who is labelled a 'Han traitor' in mainland China because he has worked for the Japanese, moves to Japan where he is called by a derogatory epithet for 'Chinese', escapes to Shanghai to be labelled a 'Manchurian', then eventually settles in Taiwan only to be identified as a 'mainlander'?

What the Dang Wai activists were working towards by the late 1970s, then, was an ideology linking the individual with the political community that reverses the subservience of the individual to the nation-state in Chinese nationalism. In evaluating the legitimacy of a regime, the true patriot should not consider its ethnic identity but the quality of life it provides. The only real criterion to decide whether or not a person's actions are patriotic is whether or not those actions are good for the life of the people. But 'the people' in this formula is now talked of in terms of the Chinese term *renmin*, denoting a political community, rather than the term *minzu*, implying an ethnic nation.

DEMOCRACY AND SECESSIONISM IN THE DEMOCRATIC PROGRESSIVE PARTY

Despite their oblique theoretical strategies, the leading figures in the *Formosa* group were actually imprisoned following an outbreak of rioting at a rally they had organised on International Human Rights Day, 10 December 1979, in the southern city of Kaohsiung. This initially left the Dang Wai movement under the guidance of reformers who concentrated on working for democratic reforms within the parliamentary system. When supplementary elections to the Legislative Yuan that had been postponed during the international and domestic crises of December 1978 were finally held in December 1980, the Dang Wai made some significant gains, increasing their number of seats from five to eleven, out of a total of fifty-two contested seats, with 26 per cent of the vote. However, a widening split in the movement was also evident as discontent grew with the slow pace of reform. By 1982 calls were being made by some Dang Wai members to defy the law and establish a formal opposition party. When moderates and radicals ran in the same districts in the 1983 Legislative Yuan supplementary elections, their vote was split and the Dang Wai only won nine seats, out of fifty-three contested, despite gaining 29 per cent at the polls.

The fact that all the moderate Dang Wai candidates were defeated did not bode well for any compromises with the KMT either. By 1984 an 'activist' faction had organised itself around a new journal, *The Movement* (*Xin Chaoliu*). Its members rejected the validity of working towards elections for a legislature which could only have very limited influence over the executive in a KMT-dominated party-state. It also claimed that it was not realistic to expect to bring about real change in a system where the opposition won only a tiny fraction of the legislative seats when gaining around a quarter of the votes cast (Lu 1992: 126–7). Its members thus advocated mass extra-parliamentary activity and launched a campaign to criticise moderates within the Dang Wai who hoped to work for reform within the system. Meanwhile, they took up the discussion of the links between national identity and democracy that had been initiated in *Formosa*. Thinly veiled secessionist ideas were developed in the form of academic discussions and through translation of foreign texts on the issues of self-determination and national identity (*Xin Chaoliu* 1984a, 1984b).

A further degree of radicalisation was provided by support from Taiwanese living overseas. In particular this came from the United States, where secessionist groups had mushroomed during the 1970s and were increasingly co-ordinating their activities. By 1986, this overseas opposition had become impatient with its counterpart in Taiwan. Some successes had been achieved in the United States through agitating American public opinion and lobbying Congress, resulting in visits by Senators to Taiwan in August 1986, and the passing of a resolution on 1 August by the House of Representatives Foreign Relations Committee, urging the KMT to lift its ban on new political parties. In mid-1986 a committee was set up by activists in the United States to prepare to establish an opposition party to launch in Taiwan by the end of the year.

The setbacks suffered by the Dang Wai in the 1983 elections had in fact already convinced leading members of the movement in Taiwan of the need to form an organisation that did not just operate for election campaigns and would be able to avoid the chaos which tended to arise when elections approached. A Taiwan Public Policy Association was thus formed with staff in Taipei and branch offices throughout the island (Lu 1992: 128). Under pressure from overseas, and encouraged by the successes of the 'People's Power' movement in the Philippines and the popular opposition movement in South Korea, the Dang Wai movement defied the law and finally announced the establishment of the Democratic Progressive Party (DPP) on 28 September 1986.

The problem that confronted the DPP on its founding was how to weld the disparate opposition groups which had formerly operated as a loose political alliance into a force which could unite around a common platform (Sun 1992; Xie 1990). The lowest common denominator uniting the old Dang Wai movement had in fact been no more than a shared commitment to democratic reform. That there was a genuine demand and necessity for such reform had become increasingly obvious by the late 1980s as growing tensions over a series of domestic issues led to a series of mass movements and demonstrations. A year after the lifting of martial law, protests were running at a rate of two per day (CP, 7 November 1988). Violent incidents began to break out, the worst of which occurred on 20 May 1988, when a farmers' demonstration in Taipei erupted into a full-scale riot causing widespread damage to property and people.

Public opinion surveys found that the atmosphere of reform combined with the strains of rapid economic growth and measures taken to integrate Taiwan into the world economy was also causing widespread cynicism (CP, 14 November 1988). This was coupled with a new confidence to take a dissenting stand on long-standing issues of contention. Industrial relations, for example, were high on the agenda as employers and the government adopted high-handed tactics in dealing with labour disputes, such as the mass dismissal of bus drivers and the indiscriminate clubbing of reporters observing strike-breaking by the police. Another particularly emotive theme that gathered island-wide support was that of environmentalism. Between 1983 and 1987 there were 382 environmental protests (CP, 7 November 1988) as the public began to question the costs of economic growth. These too began to turn violent, with more than thirty riot police and twenty environmental activists injured in a clash outside the Linyuan plant of the Chinese Petroleum Corporation on 31 May 1988.

Such developments took on a particularly poignant significance in the context of the democracy movements that were sweeping the Philippines, South Korea, Burma and, by 1989, the Chinese mainland. Indeed, as the mainland student movement began to take the road to Tiananmen Square, its counterpart in Taiwan was emboldened to make dramatic gestures to discredit the KMT. National Taiwan University felt the need to give two reprimands to a student leader who directed the play *Totem and Taboo*, in which actors crowned the statue of Chiang Kai-shek with a dunce's cap and draped it with a white banner reading 'ROC's first, second, third, fourth and fifth President'. Students also shouted slogans criticising personality cults and the presence of the KMT and military officials on campuses.

A significant sign that this was something more than high spirits but was tapping a well of popular feeling was that the campus authorities stopped short of expulsion when a writer and a social worker staged a hunger strike in support of the students. Underlying such activities was a widespread move towards more campus democracy in the shape of demands for a change to the university laws, according to which the Ministry of Education could appoint student union officials, enabling the KMT to exert control. It was increasingly difficult for the authorities to deal with such challenges at the same time as voicing support for the growing student movement on the other side of the Taiwan Strait. As DPP legislator Wu Che-liang (Wu Zheliang) put it on 24 May, how could the KMT support the mainland students but accuse supporters of the farmers' movement of being dissidents? Why should leading KMT members donate funds to the mainland movement while ignoring the plight of their own students? And how could the KMT demand the lifting of martial law in Beijing when many were suggesting imposing it in Taipei?

The DPP could certainly align itself with such mass discontent with KMT rule by taking an active part in demonstrations and through symbolic gestures, such as choosing a green silhouette of Taiwan for its party banner. What the opposition's agreement on the principle of democratisation and reform concealed, however, was a rift on the relationship of reform to the issue of national identity. On this latter issue, there existed a range of opinion which embraced those who advocated self-determination, those who insisted that self-determination must mean independence, and those who were in favour of eventual unification with mainland China. Before the Dang Wai became an organised political party, the movement had been a sufficiently broad church to accommodate all these individuals. But if the new party was to fight elections on a united platform, consensus would have to be reached on the issue of national identity. This was hence to become a matter of internal division when policy had to be presented in the form of a manifesto at its first national congress, on 10 November 1986.

The DPP responded to this challenge by trying to skirt round the national identity issue through approving a manifesto which advocated that the future of Taiwan should be decided 'by the whole body of the residents of Taiwan in a free, democratic, universal, just and equal fashion'. It also called for the party to oppose KMT and CCP violation of the principle of self-determination by negotiated solution (Jia 1993: 219). In other words, it advocated settling Taiwan's status according to the principle of self-determination, without going so far as to advocate independence. Yet the party could not ignore the fact that its own origins lay largely in a burgeoning sense of Taiwanese consciousness and the gauntlet the Dang Wai had thrown to the KMT to renew its mandate to rule through full democratic elections in Taiwan. It would have been impossible to mount a serious opposition to the ruling party if these links between democratisation and Taiwan's identity were now to be ignored. The DPP challenge to the KMT's nationalist ideology of legitimisation thus became increasingly clear as its legislators called for a 'New People, New Constitution, New Country, New Body Politic' (Chen 1989: 39–59).

Such sentiments appear to have been strong not only amongst some of the DPP's elected representatives and activists overseas, but also at the grass roots of the new party. A series of meetings held throughout Taiwan by the DPP between January and April 1988 found that 61.5 per cent of those attending agreed that the statement 'People should have the freedom of advocating Taiwanese independence' should be included in the DPP's Action Programme (Lu 1992: 137–45). As committed secessionists began to flood back to Taiwan from overseas after 1986, extra weight was added to this tendency. Relations between the radical advocates of independence and the advocates of unification deteriorated badly. Some radical activists adopted a kind of exclusive Taiwanese nationalism, refusing to speak the National Language or associate with Dang Wai members who had their origins in the mainland (Sun 1992: 12). Senior mainlander Dang Wai members, Lin Cheng-chieh (Lin Zhengjie) and Fei Hsi-ping (Fei Xiping) were singled out in particular for criticism as members of the unification faction and were subjected to what Lin called 'Taiwan-independence fascism' (CDN, 4 June 1991). Both eventually withdrew from the DPP.

However, voices of moderation were also forthcoming from party stalwarts, such as that of *Formosa* founder Huang Hsin-chieh (Huang Xinjie), who recommended that careful attention should be paid to the kind of language used by the opposition on the independence issue. Huang urged that if the DPP were to claim that 'the people have the freedom to advocate Taiwanese independence', the issue would best be put as one of freedom of speech and rephrased as 'the people have the freedom to advocate Taiwanese independence, or Chinese unification'. The possibility of making real progress on democratisation even encouraged some radical members of the DPP to put the independence issue on the back burner. Shih Ming-teh (Shi Mingde) and Hsu Hsin-liang, core members of *Formosa* and future chairmen of the party, urged caution when dealing with the independence issue. Shih, imprisoned since 1979 for his involvement in the Kaohsiung Incident, issued a statement urging people to recognise that Taiwan was already independent and should not risk the process of democratisation by giving the CCP any pretext to invade. Meanwhile, there should be much more flexibility adopted over the issue of what name Taiwan could use to get back into international society. On this count, so long as it did not imply that Taiwan was subordinate to the CCP, anything could be accepted (Sun 1992: 83–4).

Hsu Hsin-liang also urged weighing the ideal content of policies against their practical consequences. When considering whether or not to advocate independence in the DPP charter, a simple affirmation or denial would be to misunderstand the techniques of political struggle. One principle of politics, he pointed out, was never to help your enemy, and there was no necessity for the DPP to help the KMT solve the independence issue. Hsu held that there was still no widespread understanding of the independence issue in Taiwan, so education was more important for the moment. Moreover, with states such as the USA and Japan still attentive to the CCP's one-China policy, any secessionist challenge would risk losing international sympathy and support. If the DPP could win a majority in elections, then many problems could be solved. As for the CCP, both the DPP and the KMT should strive to maintain a good, peaceful and mutually beneficial relationship, akin to the situation in the European Community (Sun 1992: 84–5).

Yet such attempts to keep the issue of democratisation separate from that of national identity failed as radical members of the Dang Wai movement continued to return from abroad. In the December 1989 elections for local and central representative bodies, a secessionist organisation called the Alliance for the Formation of a New State (Xin guojia lianxian) was organised by Dang Wai member Lin Yih-shyong (Lin Yixiong), who had remained outside the DPP. Thirty-two DPP candidates joined the organisation. The DPP as a whole did well in the elections, but candidates affiliated with the Alliance for the Formation of a New State did especially well, winning seven out of the ten new seats won by the DPP in the Legislative Yuan and thirteen in the municipal councils of Taipei and Kaohsiung. With evidence that campaigning as an affiliate of a secessionist platform was no barrier to electoral success, the secessionist line was growing in strength in the DPP. This posed a potential challenge to the fundamental link between Chinese nation and Chinese state that the legitimacy of both the KMT and CCP was premised upon. And it was to this challenge that the ruling parties on both sides of the Taiwan Strait had to respond, albeit in different ways and under different constraints.

3   Stretching the one-China principle

Faced with the challenge to Chinese nationalism posed by the events of the 1970s, the KMT had to begin to develop a new form of legitimacy for the ROC regime in Taiwan. If the party was to go down the road of true democratisation, however, its initiatives would have to take account of the constraints imposed by Chinese nationalism, both in the Chinese mainland and Taiwan. For Beijing, under Deng Xiaoping's leadership, playing up the theme of unification had become increasingly attractive. Normalisation of relations with Washington and progress in negotiations with the United Kingdom over the transfer of Hong Kong to PRC sovereignty had made real progress on the Taiwan problem look more feasible than at any time since 1949. For Chinese nationalists in Taiwan, on the other hand, and most significantly at the highest levels of the KMT, unification with China remained the foundation of claims to political privilege and a powerful mythology by which sense could be made of the world.

Chiang Ching-kuo's administration, then, was faced with the task of developing policies that could strike some kind of balance between the growing demands for domestic reform, the demands of Chinese nationalism, and the reality of Taipei's international isolation. Rather than resolving these problems, however, new initiatives could only widen the gap between nationalist claims and political practice. Chiang Ching-kuo's successor, the Taiwanese-born and -raised Lee Teng-hui (Lee Denghui), was thus left facing a party and a society increasingly divided over the relationship between national identity and reform. Following a nationalist-inspired challenge to Lee's position, an outbreak of public protest led to his consolidation of power and to the conditions in which new departures in democratisation could be made.

THE BALANCE BETWEEN FOREIGN, MAINLAND AND DOMESTIC POLICIES

At the same time as Deng Xiaoping was raising the status of the Taiwan issue to make its resolution one of the three main tasks of the 1980s, there also occurred a shift in Beijing's Taiwan policy away from the call to 'liberate' the island and towards a policy of 'peaceful unification'. The first full expression of this came after the normalisation of Beijing's ties with Washington, in the form of a 'Message to Compatriots in Taiwan from the Standing Committee of the Fifth National People's Congress', delivered on New Year's Day 1979 (*Beijing Review*, 5 January 1979: 16–17). Although this document was still presented as an appeal to Chinese nationalism, it was also couched in more pragmatic calls for families to be united and for Taiwan's business community to be able to enjoy a reforming mainland economy. Fears among the people of Taiwan that unification would mean a drastic change in their way of life were placated by maintaining that Beijing would respect the status quo on the island and the opinions of a broad range of people, while the problem would be settled in a way that would not cause them any losses.

Over the next five years, the concessions the PRC was prepared to grant Taiwan under the policy of 'peaceful unification' were systematised into Deng Xiaoping's formula of 'one country, two systems', also applied to Hong Kong.[4] This is encapsulated in a talk given by Deng Xiaoping to visiting American-Chinese Professor Winston Yang on 26 June 1983. In this talk, Deng summed up Beijing's policy so far as meaning that after unification Taiwan will be given the status of a special administrative region (SAR), like Hong Kong, which will assume a character and social system different from that of the mainland. Beijing will not station its own personnel in Taiwan, and the party, governmental and military systems of the island will be governed by the Taiwan authorities themselves. Taiwan will also enjoy its own independent judiciary and a number of posts in the PRC's central government will be made available to members from Taiwan. In a concession that goes beyond 'one country, two systems' as it is applied to Hong Kong, Taiwan will even be allowed to maintain its own army, provided it does not threaten the mainland (Deng 1983).

These apparently benevolent shifts in Beijing's policy were rejected by Taipei as a tactic to undermine the solidarity of Taiwan's society. A policy of 'no contacts, no compromise and no negotiations', known as the 'three nos', was adopted to counter what Taipei saw as Beijing's 'united front' tactics (Jiang 1991: 430, 439, 443, 558). Mainland sources themselves, in fact, also locate inspiration for Beijing's new initiatives in this well-established CCP strategy. As mentioned above (p. 10), this had first been adopted as a policy by the CCP as long ago as its Second Congress, in July 1922. It is credited by the Communists as being the theoretical foundation for the alliances with the KMT that led to the unification of China in the 1920s and the defeat of Japan in the Second World War. It was first applied to Taiwan in July 1956 by Zhou Enlai, when he appealed for a third united front with the KMT (Li Qing 1987: 91–6; Ye Yang 1985: 97–101).

Rather than representing any kind of compromise over the status of Taiwan, 'peaceful unification' is thus more of a political end-game for Beijing. With the ROC isolated internationally, Beijing can put pressure on Taipei by mobilising 'patriots' in Taiwan who wield economic resources, scientific knowledge and political standing against secessionist forces and their 'foreign supporters'. The patriotism of such people is to be encouraged by the possibility of visits to relatives, the lure of a reforming mainland economy and the attraction of being able to join in cultural, sporting and educational events there. If these overtures should fail to win hearts and minds, however, there is never any intention of dropping the threat to use force to prevent formal secession.

If Taipei was to have any kind of effective response to such a strategy, it would first have to appeal for domestic solidarity in Taiwan. Although the break with Washington had been a blow to nationalist mythology, it could also be seen as providing an atmosphere of unity in the face of adversity (Gold 1986: 116). Moreover, the successes of the KMT in Taiwan could be contrasted with the failures of the CCP in the mainland. While Deng Xiaoping was consolidating his power by manipulating, then suppressing, the Beijing Spring movement of 1979, even Taiwan's limited elections could be held up as a model of democracy by comparison. At the same time, the emergency situation allowed the advocacy of Taiwanese independence in elections to be portrayed as playing into the hands of the CCP and therefore a threat to security (Jiang 1991: 534). As has been seen above, fear of antagonising the PRC meant that even some of the regime's severest critics, such as the *Formosa* writers, agreed that change through incremental reform was preferable to revolution as the way forward.

Meanwhile, convincing comparisons could be made between Taiwan's economic achievements and the situation of the mainland in the wake of the Mao period. Between 1960 and 1980 Taiwan's gross national product had increased at an annual rate of 9 per cent in real terms. Exports expanded at around 20 per cent a year, accompanied by low inflation and improvements in the distribution of income. It could be claimed that this growth had been fostered by successful government policies which had begun to show a new commitment to the development of Taiwan's infrastructure and economy. The launching of a number of large development projects in the 1970s had stimulated the economy enough to survive the world economic crises of the decade. By 1980 Taiwan was the world's sixteenth largest exporter and was well placed to enjoy the global recovery of the early 1980s under economic plans which gave priority to upgrading the export-oriented electronics sector.

Integration into the global economy was also encouraged by measures such as allowing the opening of foreign commercial banks, while local banks were encouraged to establish offices overseas. Attempts were being made to diversify trading partners so as to reduce dependence on the USA and Japan, while the overseas Chinese community was courted as an important economic and political resource. As well as satisfying many material demands, Taiwan's developing economic muscle also provided Taipei with the means to begin to counter the island's international isolation by substituting economic ties for diplomatic recognition, and trade and cultural offices for consulates and embassies.

If Taiwan's resources were to be used to counter the island's growing international isolation, however, this implied the necessity for an increasingly flexible interpretation of the one-China principle. This had already begun to become clear concerning membership of international non-governmental organisations, in which Taiwan could be represented as something other than a state. In 1984, the Taiwan business community was granted membership of the Pacific Basin Economic Council (PBEC) under the name 'Chinese Member Committee of PBEC in Taipei', a move enabled by the PBEC amending its covenant to include standard references to 'member' rather than 'nation'. A more symbolic concession was made when organisations from Taiwan began to participate in international events alongside those from the PRC. The breakthrough on this front came when a team from Taiwan participated in the 1984 Olympics alongside the PRC under the compromise name of 'Chinese, Taipei' (zhonghua Taibei). The PRC's acceptance of this formula allowed Taipei to subsequently use this name to gain entry to the Pacific Economic Co-operation Council (PECC) in 1986, joining at the same time as Beijing (MOFA 1992: 236–43; Woods 1993: 129–36).

The limits of Beijing's flexibility on this formula were shown, however, when the PRC joined the Asian Development Bank (ADB) in 1986. Although the ROC was a founding member of this organisation, the PRC objected to its participation even under the Olympic formula of 'Chinese, Taipei'. According to Beijing this could only be used for cultural and sporting events and non-governmental organisations. Instead, Beijing insisted on the use of 'Taipei, China'. This implies that Taiwan is a locality of China, something that is rather more obvious in the Chinese equivalents of these English appellations. Here the use of 'Chinese' (zhonghua) implies being part of a cultural entity, while 'China' (Zhongguo) clearly indicates belonging to a state. Again, after much posturing, the ROC was prepared to give way, and in 1987 sent a delegation of observers who took part under the name 'Taipei, China', albeit under protest.

If the changing situation meant that new flexibility had to be shown in foreign policy, there was also growing domestic and international pressure for new initiatives in mainland policy (Clough 1993; Nathan and Ho 1993). The first opportunity that arose for a more flexible interpretation of the 'three nos' came in May 1986, when a Taiwan pilot defected in a Boeing 747 cargo plane. When the PRC requested that talks be held between airline representatives to secure the plane's return, representatives from both sides finally negotiated for the first time since 1949 when they met in Hong Kong on 17 May. The following year heralded a breakthrough in relations with the Chinese mainland that promised to have a far more profound impact on the lives of individuals in Taiwan. This was the establishment, on 16 September, of a KMT task force to study the possibility of allowing Taiwan residents to visit relatives on the mainland. On 1 November the ROC Red Cross Society began to accept applications from individuals wishing to visit relatives on the mainland. By the end of 1988 some 430,766 trips had been made from Taiwan to the mainland. By 1994 this figure had risen to a total of no less than 6.3 million (EY 1994).

Chiang Ching-kuo's responses to the domestic and international crises of the 1970s, then, had led to the development of a three-stranded policy. In domestic politics a commitment to democracy and development in Taiwan was held up to contrast KMT government with that of the CCP dictatorship in the mainland. In foreign policy the one-China principle was applied with increasing flexibility to counter Taiwan's international isolation. Meanwhile, pressure for initiatives in mainland policy was to be satisfied by allowing indirect transactions with the mainland. The unavoidable implication of this difficult balancing act, however, was that the one-China principle was becoming increasingly devoid of meaning. By allowing various 'unofficial' contacts with the mainland, policy was coming close to recognising the existence of the mainland regime. At the same time, foreign policy was edging towards asserting Taiwan's independence in international society. Meanwhile, if real democracy was to be instituted in Taiwan, the practice of sovereignty by the population of the island could hardly be compatible with the claim that the government in Taipei represents the Chinese nation.

On all of these fronts, however, Chiang Ching-kuo insisted that the one-China principle remained the priority. In mainland policy it continued to rule out a political solution with Beijing. In foreign policy it ruled out recognition of Taiwan as an independent state. In domestic politics, Chiang continued to insist that the ROC government took its legitimacy from elections held in the Chinese mainland under a constitution designed for the whole of China. Thus, before Chiang took the first concrete step towards liberalisation by abolishing the legal foundation for martial law, the Emergency Decree, on 15 July 1987, he declared that new parties would only be legal if they respected the constitution and did not advocate independence (CDN, 9 October 1986; Moody 1992: 92). The Emergency Decree was then replaced by a National Security Law which stipulated that the exercise of the freedom of assembly or association should not violate the constitution or be used to advocate Communism or separatism (Tien 1989: 112). Perhaps somewhat ironically, such attempts to ignore the implications of policy initiatives for the one-China principle could only grow more difficult in proportion to the success of the policies themselves. Following Chiang's death, on 13 January 1988, this balancing act was to prove increasingly difficult for his successor.

NATIVE SON

An important element of Chiang Ching-kuo's attempts to reduce the sense of alienation from the state that resulted from his father's rule had been a new wave of Taiwanisation of the party-state. By the mid-1980s more than 70 per cent of the KMT's 2.2 million members were native Taiwanese. Native Taiwanese candidates also became more numerous in the various limited elections. By 1986, it could be claimed that the KMT had become largely native Taiwanese and that decision-making had moved to a generation that had come to political maturity on the island (Pye 1986: 618–19). Moreover, unlike the earlier wave of Taiwanisation, this one was not confined to the lower ranks, and in 1984 Chiang had nominated the young Taiwanese technocrat, Lee Teng-hui, to be his vice-president. This signalled the possibility of a native Taiwanese succession which became reality on Chiang's death. Lee was immediately sworn in to complete the remaining two years of his six-year presidential term, and on 8 July, the Thirteenth National Congress of the KMT also elected him chairman of the party.

For the first time, the regime in Taiwan was headed by a leader born on the island. Lee's formative experiences in many ways paralleled those of the secessionist Peng Ming-min. Born on 15 January 1923 into a rural community of a few hundred people near Taipei, Lee Teng-hui, like Peng Ming-min, was one of the few Taiwanese to attend university in Japan. Returning to Taiwan at the end of the Second World War, both had experienced the trauma of the first years of KMT administration. Widespread rumours that Lee Teng-hui became a member of the Taiwan Communist Party and was arrested and put on the government's blacklist have been rather half-heartedly denied by Lee himself (UDN, 8 January 1995). Despite the turmoil, Lee and Peng both attended National Taiwan University from which they graduated in 1948, Lee with a degree in agricultural economics. Both joined the faculty. Lee was an economics teacher from 1958 to 1978, the years when Peng was an assistant lecturer and eventually head of the department of politics. Both also spent long periods studying overseas, Peng as a postgraduate in Canada, while Lee received a master's degree from Iowa State University in 1953, and a PhD from Cornell in 1968.

Given these similar backgrounds, Peng and Lee reacted very differently to co-option into government service, joining different sides of the political divide. Peng's political development and eventual exile have been covered above (pp. 35–8). Lee, however, worked first as a research fellow at the Taiwan Provincial Co-operative Bank, then entered public service in 1957 with a post at the US–ROC Joint Commission on Rural Reconstruction (JCRR). He became a senior specialist and took charge of the Rural Economy Division in 1970. He is credited with having promoted the rural economy, establishing farmers' associations, irrigation systems, warehousing, health programmes and farm mechanisation. From 1972 to 1978, while remaining a consultant to the JCRR, he became a minister without portfolio in the central government. He then moved up through the posts of Mayor of Taipei City (1978–81) and Governor of Taiwan Province (1981–4), to become Chiang Ching-kuo's vice-president in 1984.

Having moved in the same circles, it is not surprising that Lee and Peng have many personal connections. By the time Lee became president, among his close colleagues were Peng Ming-min's cousin, Finance Minister Shirley Kuo (Guo Wanrong) and many of Peng's students. These included key personnel, such as Minister of Justice Shih Chi-yang (Shi Jiyang), representative at the Co-ordinating Council for North American Affairs in Washington Frederick Chien (Qian Fu), and Vice-Premier Lien Chan (Lian Zhan). These individuals, along with many others who had risen to the highest ranks of the KMT, had been selected in 1976 to receive the highest-level cadre training as part of Chiang Ching-kuo's programme of Taiwanisation of the KMT. They now worked with Lee in the Central Standing Committee and were to end up holding key government portfolios, with Frederick Chien eventually becoming foreign minister, and Lien Chan premier when Lee had consolidated his position after 1990.

Although Lee Teng-hui could look to this new intake for support, the process of Taiwanisation of which he was a part could not but contribute to a growing feeling of identity crisis for the KMT itself. That this was leading to pressure on Lee from the rank and file was immediately made evident when the Thirteenth National Congress rejected thirty-three of Lee's nominees to the Central Committee. Most of these were representatives of the old guard, while some of the successful candidates had campaigned on the grounds that they were 'Taiwanese' (Moody 1992: 114–15). Taiwanisation of the KMT may have become a factor for improving the party's appeal, but it was already threatening to cause a split between native Taiwanese members and those who had arrived from the mainland after 1945.

If Lee was to address the growing division between political practice and the one-China principle in this situation of division, it would be difficult for him to gain support for any radical departure from Chinese nationalism from the more conservative wing of the KMT, who were rather resentful towards the newcomer anyway. Yet with democratic mass movements breaking out all over East Asia and the DPP share of the vote growing since supplementary elections to the Legislative Yuan had been held in 1986, the necessity to harness the desire for change was pressing. If Lee was to turn that desire into support for the KMT, he could not ignore the need for more radical initiatives in mainland policy, foreign policy and domestic reform.

DEVELOPING CHIANG'S BALANCING ACT

On assuming power, Lee Teng-hui initially continued his predecessor's balancing of mainland and foreign policies while keeping democratisation separate from the question of national identity. Mainland policy was maintained in such a way that it could both placate Chinese nationalist suspicions and allow the island's population to enjoy the opportunities offered by the other side of the Strait On 18 April 1988, the ROC Red Cross Society began forwarding mail from Taiwan to residents of mainland China, and in July the Executive Yuan approved regulations governing the import of publications, films and radio and television programmes from the other side of the Taiwan Strait. In April the following year permission was given for news-gathering and film-making to take place on the mainland.

Contacts between unofficial organisations also began to develop, with a civilian delegation being allowed to attend the twenty-second meeting of the International Council of Scientific Unions in Beijing in the summer. Guidelines laid down by the Executive Yuan in December opened up participation in international academic conferences and cultural and athletic activities on the mainland. In April the following year, it was announced that ROC athletic teams and organisations could participate in international sports events held on the mainland, under the name 'Chinese

Taipei'. The flow of exchanges had also begun to be two-way in November 1988, when regulations were altered to allow mainland residents to visit sick relatives or attend their funerals in Taiwan. Guidelines put in place in December also opened the way for visits to Taiwan by mainland scholars and students who were residing in third countries.

As with Chiang Ching-kuo, the possible implications for Taiwan's political status of this development of links with the mainland were balanced by initiatives to raise the island's international status. When the administration christened anew what had come to be called 'practical diplomacy' under Chiang Ching-kuo with the name 'flexible diplomacy' (*tanxing waijiao*), attention was drawn to a new boldness in interpreting the implications of the one-China principle when it came to maintaining relations with other states (Yao and Liu 1989: 71–6). On 13 November 1988, the day after Saudi Arabia and the PRC announced the first steps towards normalisation, the Taiwan press even quoted unnamed sources as indicating that Taipei would no longer insist on being recognised as the sole legitimate government of China (UDN, 13 November 1988). Meanwhile, a Foreign Ministry spokesman announced on television that Taipei would no longer 'flatly reject' offers to establish relations with countries which recognise Beijing (CP, 14 November 1988).

Although these statements were quashed by Foreign Minister Lien Chan (CP, 14 November 1988), as the PRC began to face the turmoil of the demonstrations in the mainland in spring 1989, Lee Teng-hui was provided with an increasingly advantageous position from which to test the international isolation imposed on Taiwan by Beijing. On 6 March 1989, he made the first ROC presidential visit abroad since 1950 when he paid a four-day visit to Singapore. This did not strictly break the one-China principle because Singapore had followed a policy of not recognising either Taipei or Beijing. The visit was in fact offered as something of a consolation to Taipei by Singapore when the city-state announced it was about to recognise Beijing following Indonesia's decision to do so. Despite this, when Lee was received as 'the President from Taiwan', it was felt in Taiwan that the manner of his reception was appropriate for a head of state. Lee's position was 'I am not satisfied, but I can accept it' (Moody 1992: 144). At any rate, the experience galvanised Lee with new confidence when he announced at the airport on his return that if he was invited to visit states that recognised Beijing in future he would certainly do so. In the same month, Lien Chan tipped the balance further towards a two-Chinas policy when he agreed with legislators that the ROC's mainland policy could be described as 'one country, two equal governments' (*yi ge guojia, liang ge duideng zhengfu*).

This movement towards dual recognition was finally put into practice on

20 July 1989, when the ROC established formal diplomatic ties with Grenada, a state already enjoying formal ties with the PRC. Relations with Liberia, Lesotho and Guinea Bissau followed on the same model, with no demand being made that these states must break relations with Beijing. Asked what this meant for the one-China principle, Lee Teng-hui pointed out that the simultaneous recognition of West Germany and East Germany by 122 countries had not prevented the unification of those states. Neither had recognition of the two Koreas by eighty-three countries stopped talks between North and South (Lee 1991a: 78). If dual recognition had become acceptable to Lee Teng-hui, however, the PRC responded by breaking off relations with those states which established relations with the ROC, complaining that Lee Teng-hui was adopting a 'two-Chinas' policy.

This departure from the one-China principle by Taipei was also complemented by activities aimed at using Taiwan's economic prowess to court reforming Communist states. With Eastern Europe and the Soviet Union engaged in economic reforms and eager for foreign investment there were plenty of ripe targets. Closer to home, Taiwan quickly became the largest foreign investor in Vietnam. The industrialised states could not overlook the importance of Taiwan in world trade either. When an application was made for GATT membership on 1 January 1990, Taiwan boasted the world's thirteenth largest volume of merchandise trade, standing at US$118.5 billion (*Accession* 1990: 4). No less than 32.7 per cent of this was conducted with the United States, where the Bush administration was increasingly concerned with gaining access to the Taiwan market. In mid-1991 Bush threw his support behind Taipei's application and was soon followed by the European Community. A working group was set up to review the application under an article of the GATT charter that would allow for membership while saving the one-China principle by giving Taiwan and the archipelagos under its control the status of a 'customs territory'.[5] The 'Customs Territory of Taiwan, Penghu, Kinmen and Matsu' was eventually granted observer status on 29 September 1992. Meanwhile Taipei announced it would lobby Third World countries enjoying close ties with the PRC, such as India and Pakistan, while plans were drawn up for a network of semi-official trade offices in the subcontinent (FT, 24 May 1990).

By the early 1990s, then, the balancing of Taipei's mainland and foreign policies had provided a pragmatic mode of responding to changes in the mainland and in the international arena. However, while the one-China principle was taking a back seat in Taiwan's external relations, inside the island Chinese nationalism still remained the ideological and legal argument for the legitimacy of the KMT regime. On this front, too, Lee Teng-hui had tried to continue his predecessor's policy of keeping the issues of constitutional reform and national identity separate. So as not to be overtaken by the pressure for domestic reform, he insisted that constitutional democratic development would be actively carried forward (Lee 1988a: 1–2). Under his leadership the KMT proceeded to push the process of democratisation when, on 3 February 1988, the CSC passed and promulgated a programme to begin reform of the two elected parliamentary chambers, the Legislative Yuan and National Assembly. These were to be made more representative of the population of Taiwan by expanding the number of members elected through supplementary elections, and by establishing a voluntary retirement plan for veteran legislators.

Despite these liberalising initiatives, however, in his first press conference, Lee continued to draw a clear line between democracy and secession. He dismissed the DPP's calls for Taiwanese independence as sloganeering which could not succeed because the independence move- ment was illegal, it was not condoned by democracy or Chinese tradition, and it did not have enough popular support to survive (Lee 1988b: 26–7). Ultimately, however, as initiatives in foreign and mainland policy became more adventurous, more radical constitutional reforms would be needed, if only for the sake of consistency. From the perspective of Chinese nationalism a vicious circle was developing between reform and the one- China principle. From the mainland perspective, although reform was not expected to lead directly to a vote for secession, warnings began to be given that divergence between the political systems on the two sides of the Taiwan Strait might be used by Taipei to set increasingly difficult conditions for the mainland to meet before progress could be made on unification (Li Jiaquan 1988: 13–16; Li Shenzhi and Zi Zhongyun 1988: 3–11). Lee Teng-hui's more immediate problem, however, was how to overcome the constraints imposed on his movements by Chinese nationalists in his own party.

THE CONSTRAINTS OF KMT NATIONALISM

That the top position in party and state had come to be held by a 'Taiwan son' certainly signalled a shift in the balance of power between KMT members of different provincial backgrounds. However, 65.6 per cent of the KMT Central Committee was still of mainland origin (Lu 1992: 132), and 'representative' bodies such as the National Assembly and the Legislative Yuan were still largely staffed by members elected in the mainland or elected for life in supplementary elections. Many in these constituencies were sceptical about continuing the trend towards representative government in Taiwan. For veteran members of bodies such as the National Assembly and Legislative Yuan, real elections could only spell the end of a life of privilege. Moreover, if the democratic practices being pioneered by the DPP were to be emulated inside the KMT, this risked undoing the tight relationship between the centre and local factions (Moody 1992: 115–18). When the KMT adopted a system of primary elections in 1989, for example, the centre lost control as weaker local factions which did badly refused to mobilise support for the official candidate and ran their own independent KMT candidates, splitting the party's vote.

Finally, there were still those in the KMT who were genuinely committed to the nationalist mission that had so dominated their lives. Even as late as the outbreak of the demonstrations in the mainland in early 1989, some senior KMT figures began to herald the long-awaited day of return. As the demonstrations in the mainland came to a climax, veteran legislators who had held office since the 1948 mainland elections began to complain that if Chiang Kai-shek had been alive he would have sent forces to the mainland. One CSC member criticised the KMT's indifference, pointing out that the KMT had always said it would fight for freedom and democracy in China, but now, when the movement had started, no actions were being taken (CP, 25 May 1989). In contrast, the government's view was muted. Government Information Office spokesman Shaw Yu-ming (Shao Yuming) declared that Taipei would give only cautious support to the mainland demonstrators so as to avoid accusations that it had instigated the developments. When Lee Teng-hui finally told a plenary session of the Central Committee, on 3 June, that the CCP governed the mainland (CP, 4 June 1989), the mood amongst true believers was one of frustrated impotency. Not only was this the first ever such admission from the lips of a KMT chairman or ROC president, it was also significant in implying that the KMT's strategy was to accept the existence of two Chinese governments: the Communists governed the mainland, and the ROC was now the 'ROC on Taiwan'. When the massacre of 4 June finally occurred in Beijing, Lee Teng-hui's response to calls from nationalists to mobilise Chinese world-wide against the CCP and recover the mainland (CP, 7, 8 June 1989) was merely to say that the KMT should 'use calmness to control motion' (CDN, 8 June 1989). Shaw Yu-ming reaffirmed that visits across the Strait would continue, and declared that from 10 June direct telephone links were to be permitted.

With discontent over Lee's leadership mounting in sections of the KMT, his position became highly vulnerable when the remainder of Chiang Ching-kuo's term expired at the beginning of 1990. This was particularly serious because if Lee was to continue as president, he would have to be reappointed by members of the National Assembly. It was thus in March of that year that Lee faced the first real challenge to his leadership. His opponents in the party mobilised the National Assembly to back a rival candidate for the presidency, the charismatic native Taiwanese politician and long-time rival of Lee, Lin Yang-kang (Lin Yanggang). Possibilities of a resurrection of the Chiang dynasty were even raised in the figure of his proposed running mate, Chiang Wei-kuo (Jiang Weiguo), Chiang Kai-shek's son and Chiang Ching-kuo's half-brother.

With his position under threat, Lee Teng-hui had to search for an acceptable compromise with his opponents. Addressing the CSC on 7 March, he thus gave assurances that he would demand severe punishment for 'a small number of people falsely using the name of democracy to pursue their riotous activities of conspiring to split the national territory' (Lee 1990a). This point was not lost on Lin Yang-kang, who gave it special approval as a clarification of doubts that people were having over the KMT's attitude towards Taiwanese independence (CDN, 9 March 1990). A formula was also tentatively reached whereby, as constitutional reforms led to elections, a semblance that the newly elected bodies would represent all of China could be maintained. According to this formula, 'national' (meaning Chinese mainland) and 'overseas' (meaning overseas Chinese) constituencies would be represented in parliamentary bodies according to the proportion of votes won by parties actually contesting elections in Taiwan (CDN, 9 March 1990). With a number of other concessions being made to limit the powers of the president, it appears that Lee had made enough compromises for his rival candidates to withdraw from the election.

Yet it was at this juncture that there occurred a series of dramatic events which signalled that the gradual changes creeping over Taiwanese society had finally culminated in a qualitative change in mass political behaviour. With Lee apparently reined in by the CSC, a series of short-sighted actions by the National Assembly designed to consolidate and expand its own powers and privileges led to an unprecedented chain of public protests in support of real constitutional reform. These came to a climax in March with a Tiananmen-style student sit-in and hunger strike in the Chiang Kai-shek Memorial Plaza in central Taipei, with the demonstrators being supported by Taiwan-elected KMT representatives in the Legislative Yuan and local government. Lee Teng-hui quickly identified himself with the popular cause. On 17 March he made a television broadcast emphasising that democratisation was the path that had to be taken and that 'the future of the nation must rely on the common will decided by all the people' (CDN, 19 March 1990). Just who 'the people' were in this formula was left unclear. Yet it is significant that they were no longer referred to as 'the nation' (*minzu*), but by an ambiguous collective noun roughly translatable as 'all the common people' (*quan min*).

When the demonstrations finally came to a climax on 18 and 19 March with a mass occupation of the Chiang Kai-shek Memorial Plaza, the party centre finally took a strong line with its National Assembly members and ordered them to give way. Lee Teng-hui sent his minister of education to read a personal assurance that reforms would be speedily carried out and people power appeared to have won the day. When Lee Teng-hui was appointed eighth president of the ROC by the National Assembly on 21 March, he had established himself in the public eye on the side of democratisation and 'the people' against conservatives in the party.

Riding on this wave of popular support for reform, when Lee made his inauguration speech (Lee 1990b: 8) he indicated that not only would he pursue the balancing act between mainland and foreign policy with new vigour, but he would also have to risk breaking nationalist taboos in several important respects. In mainland policy, this was most clear in Lee's statement that Taipei would not withdraw its organisations from Hong Kong and Macao when they came under PRC jurisdiction in 1997 and 1999 respectively, entailing a clear departure from the 'three nos'. Lee also said that when objective conditions were ripe, it might be possible to hold negotiations with the mainland on unification. However, that Lee stressed that any unification was to be based on the common will of the Chinese people on both sides of the Taiwan Strait equally indicated a significant move towards acknowledging the right of the population of Taiwan to exercise self-determination over this issue. Moreover, when Lee argued that the mainland authorities would have to implement democracy and a free market economic system, renounce the use of force in the Taiwan Strait and not interfere with the ROC's development of foreign relations before unification could be discussed, he was setting conditions for postponing unification that would not only be impossible for the PRC to meet, but could also make Beijing appear to be the side maintaining the conditions perpetuating division.

Yet if Lee was to maintain stewardship of the reform process after his reappointment, he also had to restore a semblance of unity and organisation to the KMT by making some concessions to the powerful nationalist constituency. His first opportunity came with the appointment of a new premier. This was a highly sensitive issue because, so far, Lee had always worked with a mainland-born premier as both a symbol and embodiment of the balance of power between mainlanders and native Taiwanese in the KMT. To appoint a native Taiwanese to this post might have widened the rift in the party to unmanageable proportions. Moreover, the heated political atmosphere following the March demonstrations was accompanied by a serious decline in law and order. For the sake of restoring unity to the party, and some stability to an increasingly anarchical society, Lee appointed the mainland-born four-star General Hau Pei-tsun (Hao Bocun), who took office on 29 May 1990. Hau had been chief military aide to Chiang Kai-shek, and his biography (Wang 1994) reveals a religious devotion to the Chinese nationalist cause. It is not surprising, then, that his relationship with Lee was not an easy one. Concerning the issue of national identity, Hau immediately made it clear that he was not going to tolerate any move from the one-China policy. He could accept 'pragmatic diplomacy', but only because it was not a form of Taiwanese independence.

Lee Teng-hui hoped to confine his premier to overseeing Taiwan's domestic affairs, making it clear that he expected mainland policy to become the prerogative of the president, and not the Executive Yuan (cabinet) (CDN, 6 May 1990). But in Hau's first report to the Legislative Yuan, on 12 June 1990, a sharp difference with Lee over mainland policy was already appearing. Hau decried the possibility of a 'one country, two governments' formula for dealing with the PRC on a government-to-government basis as the result of Communist and US policy which was not recognised by the ROC. Most poignantly, in reply to a question from DPP firebrand Chen Shui-bian (Chen Shuibian) about where he would stand if the people of Taiwan and the president were to advocate independence, Hau stated that, according to the constitution, the army was the guardian of the ROC, not of Taiwan. As the president was the president of the ROC, without the ROC there would be no legal foundation for his position (CDN, 14 June 1990; Wang 1994: 266).

With uncertainty in Beijing over Lee's true intentions, mainland observers began to speculate that such events indicated that the long-term development of party politics in Taiwan would be along the lines of Japanese politics at the time. As with the Japanese LDP, the KMT would remain in power but its policies would be increasingly shaped by having to take account of various factions across the political spectrum (Yan and Yang 1990: 18–24). With the KMT divided into 'Mainstream' supporters of Lee and 'Non-Mainstream' supporters gathering around Hau, it was concluded that Lee's powers would be curtailed by the Executive Yuan. However, as the powers of the Legislative Yuan and National Assembly were also growing, the KMT leadership would have to negotiate with the growing number of DPP representatives. While the older generation did not dare to renounce the one-China principle openly, the entry of the third generation of politicians into the higher echelons of the political process and the increasing dependency of the political elite on public opinion pointed to the fact that future policy would have to strike some kind of balance between unification on the one hand and the interests of Taiwan and 'Taiwan consciousness' (*Taiwan yishi*) on the other (Zhu 1990: 1–4).

The mainland analysis turned out to be reasonably close to reality. During his three-year premiership, Hau was to become a rallying point for opponents of Lee Teng-hui in the KMT. Yet, although much of this opposition was presented in terms of sentimental attachment to the Chinese nation, Hau did also develop arguments against secession on more pragmatic grounds. In his view, the lesson of history is that Taiwan's destiny depends on events in the Chinese mainland (Wang 1994: 251–2). Yet he was also anxious not to over-exaggerate the dangers from the PRC at the expense of drawing attention away from what he saw as the more imminent threat to Taiwan, namely the possibility of conflict within the island between those with their origins in Taiwan and those from mainland China. In June 1990, with the PRC still in the international doghouse, Hau could thus argue that the ROC should concentrate on ensuring stability in Taiwan, avoiding military conflict and engaging in peaceful political, economic and cultural competition with the PRC (Wang 1994: 249). The main danger to Taiwan in this scenario was the threat to stability if the domestic 'provincial complex' (*shengji qingjie*) was stirred up by the secessionist enemy within. Domestic chaos in Taiwan could thus only be avoided by identification with the ROC (CDN, 21 June 1990). In these more pragmatic aspects of Hau's thinking, the premier was not that far removed from the president.

Yet agreement between Hau and Lee was ultimately prevented not only by public perceptions of their backgrounds, but more fundamentally by the degree to which each was prepared to concede the principles of Chinese nationalism in the process of bringing ideological theory into line with political practice. In Hau's view, any move to try to establish Taiwan's solidifying sense of its own identity in the process of constitutional reform would lay the KMT open to charges from both the PRC and the domestic opposition that the party was pursuing either a two-China policy or a policy of Taiwan independence. To go down this road would only add to an already acute sense of insecurity in Taiwan, threatening to destabilise the island's economy and divide the party and society in general. Such conservatism, however, did not sit easily with the radical tone set by Lee Teng-hui on his reappointment. If the democratic element of Lee's vision was to be put into practice, it would require constitutional reform in which the issue of Taiwan's national identity and international status would have to be directly addressed. It was in this situation of deadlock that Lee Teng-hui built on the wave of popular support for reform in Taiwan by beginning to cultivate a new consensus with the DPP. His master stroke in this respect was to call for a National Affairs Conference (NAC).

THE NATIONAL AFFAIRS CONFERENCE

When Lee's leadership position had been consolidated by alignment with the mass demonstrations of March 1990, he had announced that he would forge a new consensus between the KMT, the DPP and society in general (CDN, 21 March 1990). The preliminary step in this direction was to be the first meeting between Lee Teng-hui as president and the chairman of the DPP on 2 April. Of most significance, though, was Lee's call for the convening of the NAC to draw up proposals for constitutional reform and mainland policy. This would be attended by representatives of all parties and social groups and by academics. Invitations were even extended to overseas independence activists. Peng Ming-min, however, refused to return to Taiwan although Lee Teng-hui went to considerable lengths to persuade him to take part (CDN, 18 June 1990).

For Lee, the NAC was an attempt to reach a new consensus which would give him the mandate to carry out reform of the ROC constitution. That he was prepared to make radical changes was signalled when, on 8 May, he told eight opposition members of a preparatory committee for the NAC that he was prepared to contemplate abolishing the blacklist which prevented advocates of Taiwanese independence from returning to Taiwan from abroad. He also hoped for constitutional reforms which would address fundamental questions about the distribution of power, including making presidential elections more democratic and clarifying the balance between the presidency and the Executive Yuan (CDN, 10 May 1990).

If Lee was working towards co-opting the opposition, there still remained the task of instilling a clear sense of common direction among the disparate factions of the KMT before the NAC was held. Representatives who had been elected in Taiwan under the supplementary system of elections, though still a minority in the elected chambers, were broadly in support of a process which appeared to give democratic legitimacy to constitutional reform (CDN, 25 June 1990). As for the Central Committee, 53 per cent of representatives to the approaching plenum said that they could support abolishing the Temporary Provisions of the constitution, while 61 per cent could countenance some small revisions to the constitution itself. But they were overwhelmingly against enacting a new constitution, and 88 per cent were against participation in the NAC of individuals who did not identify with the ROC. Concerning the issue of unification, 91 per cent felt that the NAC should discuss it, but more than 80 per cent were opposed to looking into Taiwanese independence (CDN, 26 June 1990). When a working group was set up to develop the KMT position for the NAC, it came up with a compromise formula that could hopefully make real changes while still placating all sections of the party. According to this, the issue of national identity could be avoided if the main body of the ROC constitution was preserved and reforms were enacted through the *ad hoc* attachment of 'additional articles' (CDN, 20 June 1990). Radical changes could thus be enacted while legal continuity could be maintained with the ROC state.

When the NAC was held, from 28 June to 7 July, 150 representatives of the various political parties and social groups were registered to come and try to hammer out a wide consensus on the direction of constitutional reform. In the end, only 136 of these individuals actually took part. Aside from Peng Ming-min, those not attending also included prominent members of the DPP such as Chen Shui-bian and Peng's close associate, Frank Hsieh (Xie Changting). Perhaps even more of a blow to the credibility of the conference was the last-minute withdrawal of the respected National Taiwan University professor, Hu Fu, along with three other academics. These participants had all been seen as a neutral force, but they now complained that there would be no space for their opinions in a forum which had become an attempt to reach a compromise between two political parties while ignoring the opinions of the broader society (CDN, 29 June 1990). However, there did figure among the strong DPP representation veteran opposition figures such as Hsu Hsin-liang, newly returned from overseas exile and soon to be party chairman.

Wanting to appeal for constitutional reform within the bounds of Chinese nationalism, Lee Teng-hui's opening speech to the conference was framed in familiar terms. He portrayed the function of the conference as being to establish a consensus on constitutional reform that would facilitate the eventual reunification of a democratic and prosperous China (CDN, 29 June 1990). But DPP representatives such as Hsu Hsin-liang responded by arguing that if the KMT did not embark on a process of real reform then it was no better than the Communist reformers in Eastern Europe (CDN, 30 June 1990). The DPP's basic position on the broader issue of constitutional reform was that nothing short of a new constitution would do, and that this should be drawn up by a national conference.

To focus its fire on the link between democratisation and national identity, the DPP concentrated the debate on the weak point in the KMT's attempts at compromise by insisting on a resolution concerning the election of the president. In a special debate on this issue, the DPP insisted that the president must be directly elected by the whole people. As DPP Chairman Huang Hsin-chieh pointed out, only election of the president would mean that the people were the masters and that government had been returned to them (CDN, 4 July 1990). Faced with a lack of progress on this issue, on the afternoon of 2 July, DPP members formed an alliance with independent delegates to force the hand of the KMT by calling for a resolution that the president should be elected by the whole body of citizens. Huang threatened that if the resolution was not carried and a consensus was not reached, then the DPP would pull out and resort to alternative methods to achieve its ends.

What the DPP achieved by this tactic was to reveal how the KMT delegates were unable to reach a consensus among themselves on the key issue of presidential elections. In the ensuing heated discussion, some KMT members made it clear that their concern was over the link between representation and national identity. As second-generation mainlander legislator Jaw Shau-kong (Zhao Shaokang) pointed out, the issue was that of whether the president was to be president of 'Taiwan' or of 'the whole country'. Only if the president was selected by the National Assembly, with at least a token presence of 'national' (meaning Chinese) representatives, could an impression be preserved that he was the president of the 'whole country'. Yet there were others in the KMT who rallied to give more power to Lee Teng-hui by advocating the installation of a powerful American or French-style presidency and abolishing the National Assembly altogether. The DPP's tactic had worked and the split in the KMT was widening. Lee Teng-hui, meanwhile, stayed above the fray, explaining that as he was not going to run for another term, the decision did not really affect him (CDN, 4 July 1990).

Following more intense discussions between the two parties, on 3 July the NAC finally passed a resolution which effectively postponed a final settlement by stating: 'The president should be produced by election from the whole body of the citizens. The method and implementation of this will be discussed by all circles and fixed according to law.' Although this resolution fudged the fundamental issues of who actually constitutes the 'whole body of citizens', and how this body of people should actually elect its president, it did at least allow some kind of a consensus to be reached. While it put in place the principle of popular sovereignty, in the eyes of those opposed to the election of a 'president of Taiwan', the absence of clear guidelines on the method of election meant that it could still be interpreted to mean indirect election by the National Assembly acting as an electoral college. At any rate, the resolution had papered over the cracks in the KMT. That the covering remained flimsy was shown when the chairman of the NAC speedily passed the resolution and dissolved the meeting before allowing dissenting KMT delegates an opportunity to voice their opinions (CDN, 5 July 1990).

Although the NAC broke up with the KMT in disarray over the issue of presidential elections, it did issue a report concluding that consensus had been reached on several other items. The retirement of veteran representatives from the parliamentary chambers achieved a high degree of consensus. The majority of delegates also agreed that the status of the National Assembly had to be addressed, with suggestions for its future ranging from abolition to a drastic reduction of its powers. Concerning local government, there was agreement that direct election of the provincial governor was an important democratic factor and should thus be included in a law for local autonomy (CDN, 6 July 1990). What all this would actually mean in practice was not clear, however. The exact status of the NAC had remained unsettled from the beginning. When the DPP's Huang Hsin-chieh insisted that the president should be bound by the conference, he was informed by the Office of the President that Lee Teng-hui would select and implement what was of benefit to the country, the people and the nation (*minzu*) from the proceedings (CDN, 5 July 1990). Yet while the status of the NAC was thus downgraded, Lee Teng-hui could still use it to claim that he had a mandate for his vision of constitutional reform, and that he was acting according to the ROC constitution's stipulation that 'the sovereignty of the Republic of China shall reside in the whole body of citizens' (Lee 1990c).

Rather than directly implement the recommendations of the conference, which remained largely ambiguous anyway, Lee Teng-hui established a number of new organisations to look into the implications of its findings. In early July, a KMT working group, which included the heads of the Yuans, was set up to discuss the results of the NAC and to present a report to the CSC. A planning committee for constitutional reform was then made up of high-ranking KMT officials, to research further into the shape and implementation of reform. On 23 September, this committee agreed on the key formula by which the democratic and the nationalist arguments could be reconciled. This was in fact a restatement of the position arrived at by the KMT before the NAC, namely that rather than write a new constitution, additional articles would be added to the existing ROC constitution by the National Assembly. These would provide for elections to be held for a new National Assembly before 31 December 1991. Within three months of its election, this Second National Assembly would be convened by the president to make a second stage of amendments to the constitution. The Legislative Yuan would similarly be dissolved and a Second Legislative Yuan would be elected by 31 January 1993.

Central to this scheme of electoral reform was the development of the compromise on national identity that had first been raised during the intra-party struggles of the spring. A main element of this was the constitutional device that would enable the claim to be made that the bodies resulting from elections held in Taiwan would still be representative of the Chinese nation, not just of Taiwan. What this involved was the carving of the Chinese nation into four separate constituencies. Only in two of these would votes actually be cast: the 'free area', namely Taiwan and the various archipelagos under ROC jurisdiction, and an 'aboriginal constituency' consisting of a small quota of representatives elected by the remnants of Taiwan's aboriginal peoples. The other two constituencies were to be a 'nation-wide' and an 'overseas' constituency. These would be different from the first two constituencies in so far as their representatives would be appointed by proportional representation according to the number of votes cast for parties campaigning in Taiwan. As the number of seats allotted to the overseas and nation-wide constituencies would make up only a small proportion of the total, elections for a representative government could thus be held in Taiwan, while the appearance and myth that the resulting bodies represent 'China' would be maintained.

'RECOGNISING' BEIJING

With the adoption of the additional articles providing the formula for Taiwanese elections to be held without violation of the one-China principle, Lee Teng-hui could finally announce termination of the period of national mobilisation and the Temporary Provisions that had legalised the KMT dictatorship in Taiwan (see above, p. 26). The way to the first complete elections for national representative chambers ever to be held in Taiwan was now open. Yet if democratic reform meant ending the Period of National Mobilisation, this also had profound implications for relations with the Chinese mainland. Most importantly, it meant that the illegal status of the PRC regime as a 'rebellious organisation' had changed. The ground had already been prepared for this by Lee Teng-hui, when, on 15 May 1990, he had insisted that talks with the mainland authorities could be carried out on a government-to-government level. He now established a new organisation, the National Unification Council (NUC), under the Office of the President, to co-ordinate the emerging constitutional reforms with mainland policy. This new agency began operating on 1 October 1990 with the primary purpose of making suggestions to the president regarding overall unification policy. But its objective was also stated as being 'to integrate opinion at all levels of society and in all political parties concerning the issue of national unification' (*ROC Yearbook* 1991–2: 139).

In other words, the NUC was to play a key role in maintaining a broad consensus of opinion behind Lee's mainland policy. Its first task was thus to systematise and make into official policy the strategy of increasing activity between the two sides of the Taiwan Strait, while postponing the ultimate questions of sovereignty that this raised until an unspecified time in the future. This was achieved in the shape of a document entitled *Guidelines for National Unification*, adopted by the NUC at its third meeting on 23 February 1991 and by the Executive Yuan on 14 March (EY 1991). Consistent with Lee Teng-hui's previous announcements, this document preserved nationalist rhetoric but left it neutered by placing the goal of national unification in a distant future, separated from the present by numerous conditions that would have to be met by both sides before unification could take place.

From this perspective, what the *Guidelines* managed to achieve was a qualification of the overriding nationalist imperative that the political and the national units should be congruent, by clarifying various preconditions. Whereas under Chiang Ching-kuo, Taipei had insisted that China could only be united under the Three Principles of the People, this argument had now been clearly formulated as a process that would leave the onus of change on Beijing's side. More specifically, the kind of change that would have to take place was one that would promote Chinese culture, safeguard human dignity, guarantee fundamental human rights, and practise democracy and the rule of law (EY 1991: Sec. 3, Par. 3). Such conditions seem innocuous until interpreted by the ROC as meaning that 'China's unification is imperative not only for the sake of territorial unity alone, but for the political freedom and equitable distribution of wealth for all Chinese' (*ROC Yearbook* 1994: 147). It was becoming ever more clear that the unification of China was no longer the ultimate aim of the ROC, only the unification of a kind of China that might take generations to achieve. Meanwhile, the further apart the political and economic systems of the two sides of the Taiwan Strait might grow, the further away would be the actual act of unification.

What this means in terms of policy becomes clear when the conditions to be met before unification can begin to take place are spelled out. These conditions must be met in three stages: a short-term phase of 'exchanges and reciprocity', a medium-term phase of 'mutual trust and co-operation', then finally a long-term phase of 'consultation and unification'. Implicit in the conditions to be met in the short-term phase alone, however, is that there must be a qualitative change in the political and economic situation of the PRC which would be nothing short of a revolution. It is thus stated that, among other conditions, 'in the mainland area economic reform should be carried out forthrightly, the expression of public opinion there should be gradually allowed, and both democracy and the rule of law should be implemented' (EY 1991: Sec. 4, Par. 3). As such conditions as the above are open to a wide degree of interpretation, they may or may not be used as reasons for delaying moves to unification, depending on the judgement of the regime in Taipei.

Of more concrete significance in terms of the relationship between the one-China principle and ROC foreign policy objectives, though, is the *quid pro quo* expected by the ROC for moving beyond the short-term phase of the *Guidelines*. This is the demand that the two sides of the Taiwan Strait should end their state of hostility, resolve disputes through peaceful means, and respect each other in the international community (EY 1991: Sec. 4, Par. 4). In other words, the PRC must drop its right to use force to resolve the Taiwan problem and must allow the ROC to return to international society. Just as it was hoped that domestic reform need not impinge on the issue of national identity, it was now being proposed that Taiwan's status in international society could be improved without breaking the one-China principle. This would be achieved by allowing Taiwan to be active in international society as a state, but not insisting that the PRC recognise it as one. Instead, the regimes on both sides of the Taiwan Strait would recognise each other under a new concept. This is the 'political entity' (*zhengzhi shiti*), which is described by the ROC as an alternative to 'state' or 'government' which allows 'sufficient "creative ambiguity" for each side to live with' (*ROC Yearbook* 1994: 147).

Lee Teng-hui had already announced that the existence of the Chinese mainland as a 'political entity' was no longer to be denied. It had now become central to ROC policy that Beijing must accept that the ROC is a 'political entity' too, and one which must be allowed to join international organisations before progress can be made on unification. The concept of the 'political entity' thus promised to put aside the issue of sovereignty and allow a return to international society, while it could be held out to the PRC as a theoretical concept under which cross-Strait links could be developed.

A formula had now been reached that offered some kind of reconciliation of the democratic and the nationalist arguments over Taiwan. Legally, the additional articles to the constitution provided devices by which elections could be held in Taiwan while maintaining the appearance that they are elections for a government of the whole of China. In mainland policy, the *Guidelines for National Unification* provided a framework with sufficient Chinese nationalist content to allow figures such as Hau Pei-tsun to give it their support, while not over-antagonising the PRC. The *Guidelines for National Unification* also contained a teleological strategy that would enable the regime to postpone any actual moves towards unification while continuing to develop indirect private and commercial links with the mainland. As for dealing with the practical problems arising from contacts, the establishment of a 'private' organisation, the Straits Exchange Foundation (SEF), would allow what, in effect, are consular affairs to be dealt with, and contacts to be made with the PRC, while appearing to uphold the 'three nos'. The KMT was now faced with the prospect of testing out this compromise formula on the electorate. The DPP, however, riding high on its successes in setting the pace and direction of constitutional change, was preparing to force the KMT further on the issue of national identity by making it central to the elections for the Second National Assembly in December 1991.

4 National identity and democratisation

As far as the relationship between democratisation and national identity was concerned, the Second National Assembly elections were to show that popular support for the KMT and the Lee Teng-hui presidency could be maintained when the one-China principle was interpreted flexibly enough to allow constitutional reform to proceed. The longer-term cost of this, however, was to be growing antagonism from those within the KMT who still clung to Chinese nationalism and became dissatisfied as the rhetoric of 'one China' proved increasingly ambiguous. Underlying this ambiguity was the unavoidable fact that if sovereignty was to be practised by the residents of Taiwan, then it manifestly did not lie with the Chinese nation. As electoral politics led Lee Teng-hui to follow through the implications of the developing political dispensation, he faced increasing calls from all sides for a clarification of the relationship between the state on Taiwan, the population of the island, and the Chinese nation. The resulting interaction between reform, the constraints of the one-China principle and the need for new initiatives in mainland and foreign policies brought a search for a new definition of the relationship between Chinese identity and the state in Taiwan. As the reforms came to a conclusion with the 1996 presidential election, the limits of flexibility became increasingly salient.

THE SECOND NATIONAL ASSEMBLY ELECTIONS

The Second National Assembly elections were of critical importance to all sides not just as the first comprehensive elections to be held in Taiwan, but also because winning one-third of the seats would have allowed the DPP to block the KMT's constitutional reforms. This posed an acute threat in the context of an increasing shift in the DPP platform towards secessionism. This had become clear since the party had adopted a *Taiwan Constitution Draft* in August 1991. In September the DPP's CSC had approved including in the party platform a clause identifying the island as 'The

Republic of Taiwan which has independent sovereignty', which was also approved by an overwhelming majority at the Fifth National Congress in October. The DPP had also continued to focus political debate on the issue of constitutional reform that was most closely linked to the question of Taiwan's national identity, namely the holding of presidential elections. On 9 November, the institution of direct presidential elections had been made one of its main objectives and the slogan 'Be Taiwan's masters, elect your own president' had also been adopted for the coming National Assembly elections. Propaganda was distributed, including full-page and half-page advertisements in various national newspapers, which stated this to be one of the DPP's two main goals, along with the declaration of an independent Taiwan Republic.

As candidates began to advocate independence openly, DPP-controlled county governments defied the central government and the Central Election Commission (CEC) by not taking action against them. The CEC also banned the DPP from advocating Taiwanese independence on air, but this did not stop the party from broadcasting what were unmistakably the sentiments of Taiwanese nationalism in the television time it had been allotted. Its party political broadcast thus opened with the title 'Taiwan you are my mother', and included dialogue which looked forward to the day when 'people will have Republic of Taiwan passports and not Republic of China passports' (UDN, 13 December 1991). Meanwhile, the cost of unification was lambasted, the point being made that each individual in Taiwan would have to support sixty mainlanders, a common theme in Taiwan in light of the economic burdens placed on West Germans following German reunification.

Yet if the DPP was making Chinese nationalism the focus of its attack on the KMT, it ended up aiming at what had become something of a straw man. With Lee Teng-hui's policy having moved ahead, nationalism was conspicuously absent from the ruling party's campaign. Rather than using traditional slogans, such as 'Unite China under the Three Principles of the People', the KMT's campaign was conducted under the slogan of 'Reform, security, prosperity'.[6] Rather than unification with the mainland, the KMT portrayed itself as the party of reconciliation and rebirth in Taiwan. Looking to the past, the theme of reconciliation had been given substance by the release shortly before the campaign of a lengthy report on the 228 Incident, supposed to 'heal the historical wound', in the words of the chairman of the government's 228 Committee. Looking to the future, the idea of rebirth was symbolised by the image of a baby lying on the ROC flag, which closed the KMT's party political broadcasts and featured in its campaign literature. Moreover, the issue of unification was shunned by KMT candidates on the hustings. When pressed on the issue, they preferred to present their vision of the future in negative terms of opposing independence, striking fear into the hearts of their listeners with dire predictions, such as that given by a candidate in Tainan who warned voters that independence would mean that the dates on ancestral temples and graves would be changed and that the worship of Taiwan's cult deity, the Fujian goddess Mazu, would be banned (UDN, 6 December 1991).

This lack of a nationalist theme was also evident in the KMT's television campaign, in which Taiwan's achievements over the decades were stressed, in particular economic growth. In this respect the KMT could boast its commitment to Taiwan's economy and infrastructure following the launching of a Six-Year National Development Plan. A budget of no less than US$303.7 billion was to be spent on raising personal income, developing local industries, balancing regional development, and enhancing the quality of life. With increasing public concern over environmental problems, chaotic traffic, inadequate transportation systems and non-existent urban planning, grand projects were unveiled for high-speed railways, mass transit systems, environmental programmes and facilities for 'building culture'.

The theme of 'building our own culture' was used to steal the wind from the DPP, who had parodied the KMT's policies of instilling conformity in the population by comparing them to a production line for plastic dolls. The KMT countered by gathering Taiwan's star entertainers under a commentary reading: 'We have begun singing our own song, dancing our own dance, building our own bridge and laying down our own road.' The message the KMT now wanted to convey was that it was the party which had presided over a period of government in which the development of a vibrant native culture and identity had made possible the reconciliation of long-standing conflicts. This was the import of campaign material such as the KMT party political broadcast which showed images of a mainlander soldier visiting the home of a native Taiwanese in 1949, with resulting mutual incomprehension as the soldier talked in Mandarin while his host used a Fujian dialect. An image of the same two people in the 1990s was then shown, only this time criticising the DPP in Mandarin as they watched fisticuffs in the Legislative Yuan on television.

Much to the annoyance of the opposition, that the KMT was somehow a party of all the people was further underlined by showing Lee Teng-hui shaking hands with Huang Hsin-chieh, the former DPP chairman. Moreover, the KMT campaign was conducted at all levels in a variety of dialects, while 159 of its candidates for Taiwan and the aboriginal constituencies 'originated' from Taiwan province, and only thirty-three were 'outsiders'. Native Taiwanese thus made up the majority of candidates in all areas except the capital, with its high concentration of mainlanders, where twelve 'mainlander' candidates compared with eleven 'originating' from Taiwan.

That the KMT had found a formula on which it could fight and win was shown by its poll of 71.1 per cent in the election, an increase of 11 per cent on the 1989 supplementary elections to the Legislative Yuan. That the DPP had pushed the secessionist issue too far was the conclusion of most observers when it only polled 23.9 per cent, down from 28.2 per cent in 1989 and the first fall in its share of the vote since the party was founded. Crucially, this translated into less than the 25 per cent of seats required in the National Assembly to block the KMT's constitutional reforms.

Yet developments in the campaigning did also suggest that a consensus between the two parties on fundamental issues had begun to emerge. Some analysts, for example, saw that the DPP seemed to be making a late tactical move away from nationalistic appeals and towards a position where it could be seen as the party defending the status quo. If KMT candidates had shied away from the issue of unification, it was noted that DPP candidates on the hustings were equally reluctant to discuss independence. The DPP's Hsinchu (Xinzhu) County party manager, for example, said that if it was really necessary to discuss the independence problem, then DPP candidates should clarify their position by saying, firstly, that the objective of Taiwanese independence is to oppose the Chinese Communists ruling Taiwan and, secondly, that it means upholding the status quo. Whatever kind of unification might occur in the future, it will set Taiwan back, and the people of Taiwan cannot afford to pay such a price (UDN, 6 December 1991). On the national level, the adoption of slogans such as 'Be your own masters, not people subordinate to the Chinese Communists' (IMP, 10 November 1991), and a platform which emphasised self-determination and the fact that Taiwan was already *de facto* independent, was also said to reflect a shift away from the strident secessionist demands made at the DPP's National Congress.

DEMOCRATISATION AND STRAINS IN THE ONE-CHINA PRINCIPLE

If a consensus was emerging from electoral politics, then, it was the result of the KMT's decision not to join battle on the issue of national identity. This was done by ignoring the independence–unification debate altogether and concentrating on Taiwan's domestic transformation instead. What is most significant about the DPP's role in this is that the KMT had successfully been steered over the previous years into a position where the Lee Teng-hui leadership had realised that legitimacy could not be maintained in a democratising system by arguing from a Chinese nationalist platform. This would have to be ignored as much as possible in favour of focusing the debate on issues of gradual constitutional reform, economic growth and stability. Yet if such issues were to be addressed in a democratic fashion, there had to be at least a tacit understanding between the two main parties that the imperative of Chinese nationalism, although it might still have to exist in rhetoric, would not be transformed into concrete action. Yet it was precisely for this reason that victory also contained the seeds of division for the KMT, because there were still many in the party who were not prepared to agree to such a consensus.

Although a consensus had been built across much of the political spectrum through the holding of the NAC, this was fragile and could only hold so long as certain issues which linked democratisation most clearly with the question of national identity were left to one side. First and foremost amongst these remained the question of how the president was to be elected when Lee Teng-hui's term expired in 1996. This created a focus for opposition to Lee Teng-hui in the KMT from two sources. First of all, there were the bruised Chinese nationalists, such as Hau Pei-tsun and some senior members of his cabinet and the CSC. Such figures could look to war veterans and members of the Chinese communities overseas for support in their opposition to what they saw as a drift towards Taiwanese independence. Secondly, there were younger members of the KMT who in 1989 had formed a caucus called the New KMT Alliance to promote democratisation of the party and opposition to secession. These people now also feared that Lee Teng-hui was concentrating too much power in his own hands, a concern that was shared in much wider circles, especially academics, who favoured a collective, cabinet system of government. The unwillingness of Lee Teng-hui to dispose of the National Security Council and its subordinate organs during the reform process, for example, only fuelled suspicions that if he was to win a presidential election this could lead to a return to the type of strong-man government that had characterised the past. A complex coalition of positions was thus ranged against Lee, and when the newly elected National Assembly met on 27 May 1992, the strength of these forces was revealed by the fact that the eight 'additional articles' that were added to the constitution attempted to impose new limits on the powers of the president.[7]

Lee Teng-hui, on the other hand, had outlined his position on the issue of presidential elections by reminding a KMT working group set up to look into constitutional reform that the principle of direct presidential elections had been laid down by the NAC. Yet he also proposed that democracy in Taiwan need not break the island's links with the Chinese nation, because the results of the National Assembly elections showed that the majority of Taiwan's population identified with the ROC (UDN, 8 March 1992). He even made tantalising hints that the completion of constitutional reform would open up new vistas for the development of the Chinese nation beyond the narrow confines of the traditional conflict across the Taiwan Strait, waxing eloquent about new co-operation and mutual assistance between Taiwan, Hong Kong, the mainland and 'Chinese people the whole world over', so as to 'improve the lives of the whole body of the people of the Chinese race' (UDN, 14 March 1992).

Over the following years it was to become clearer that what Lee was beginning to develop here was in fact a delinking of the question of who exercises sovereignty in Taiwan from the question of the island's Chinese identity. Lee's opponents doubted whether such a breaking of the link between the state in Taiwan and Chinese national identity was either possible or desirable. Direct presidential elections, they believed, would herald both a move towards dictatorship and the creation of a president of Taiwan who could not feasibly be presented as the president of China. The working group thus split seven for direct elections against six in favour of the National Assembly electing the president. This division could have led to an open split in the CSC, had not another fudged resolution allowed the issue to be side-tracked again (UDN, 17 March 1992). This was eventually adopted by the National Assembly on 27 May 1992, in the shape of a twelfth additional article which read: 'Effective from the 1996 election for the ninth-term president and vice-president, the president and the vice-president shall be elected by the entire electorate in the free area of the Republic of China' (*ROC Yearbook* 1993: 729–30). The ability of such a resolution to appeal to a broad range of opinions was explained by one newspaper as being due to the fact that, although votes would only be cast by the voters of the 'free territory' of the ROC (that is Taiwan), there would still be a symbolic significance that the elections were for the whole of China (UDN, 17 March 1992). Moreover, it was still not stated whether the presidential election would be direct or by the National Assembly. The disputing sides had thus managed to create a breathing space, but at the expense of bringing divisions at the centre of the party back into the public eye.

If the conflict between presidential elections in Taiwan and the one-China principle could be papered over temporarily, however, the tensions between mainland policy and political practice continued to erode what little semantic content remained attached to the term 'one China'. As mentioned in the previous chapter, the first comprehensive statement of mainland policy following Lee Teng-hui's 1990 reappointment as president was made in the *Guidelines for National Unification*, drawn up by the NUC. Reflecting political developments inside Taiwan, this document put aside an ultimate resolution of the issue of unification until an unspecified time in the future. Such a postponement has the advantage of allowing sovereignty to be practised by the population of Taiwan, while preserving for Chinese nationalists the principle that there is only one China, albeit governed by two different regimes. Such a postponement of unification also has important ramifications for the future of Chinese nationalism, however. This is because, by advocating the possibility of a working relationship between two political entities that have come to exist within one China, it leaves a question mark hanging over the necessity of making the state congruent with 'China' at all. The unavoidable conclusion to this train of logic is, at the very least, that 'China' can be conceived of as an entity quite distinct from the two states that exist within it. As Huang Kun-huei (Huang Kunhui), chairman of the cabinet-level MAC, stated in a March 1991 commentary on the document:

> Our view is that Taiwan is of course a part of Chinese territory but the Chinese Communist regime is not 'China'. The current state of separation and mutual hostility is not a Taiwan problem but a Chinese problem. Thus we have the concept that 'Both the mainland and the Taiwan areas are parts of Chinese territory'. The Chinese mainland and Taiwan are 'one country, two areas'.
>
> (Huang 1991: 3)

Although this statement is clearly an attempt to present the *Guidelines* in terms acceptable to Chinese nationalists, the most that Huang conveys here is that there are evidently separate regimes on the two sides of the Taiwan Strait which can be said to coexist within some kind of a greater entity that has 'Chinese' characteristics. To maintain that this entity, called 'China', exists at all might give some comfort to Chinese nationalists. Yet if such a lack of clarity over the political obligations that are entailed by the existence of such an entity was supposed to allow space for Taipei to manoeuvre in foreign policy, it could also result in confusion. This was especially so when the actual implementation of policies generated tension between factions, parties and institutions holding different interpretations of the meaning of 'one China' for Taiwan.

An example of this can be seen in the problem of establishing a chain of command over the formulation and implementation of mainland policy. The official organisation set up by Lee Teng-hui in 1990 to oversee this process was the NUC, under the Office of the President. Yet a similar organisation had also been set up under the Executive Yuan (cabinet) by the KMT's Thirteenth Congress in 1988. This had begun life as the Mainland Affairs Task Force, but shortly after the establishment of the NUC it was renamed the Mainland Affairs Council (MAC). On 18 January 1991, the MAC's functions were institutionalised by an act stipulating that it should be responsible for research, overall planning and consideration of mainland policy as well as its partial implementation (*ROC Yearbook* 1991–2: 140).

As state organisations, however, neither the NUC nor the MAC could deal directly with official organisations in the mainland. A further 'non-official' organisation was thus established in February 1991 to make such contacts. This was the Straits Exchange Foundation (SEF), which had powers vested in it by the MAC and was contracted to handle all government-related contacts and communications between the two sides of the Taiwan Strait. Much of the funding for the SEF comes from the government, and that which comes from the private sector is appropriated by the MAC and subject to control by the Legislative Yuan. Moreover, most of the staff of the SEF are temporarily retired officials. Nevertheless, the organisation's status as a 'private' foundation could allow the policy of no official contacts to be circumvented, and members of the SEF to deal directly with mainland organisations.

One problem with this solution to having contacts under the policy of no official recognition or contacts was that the SEF was becoming increasingly autonomous in developing relations with the mainland within the guidelines laid down by the MAC and the NUC. Tensions between the MAC and the SEF became particularly salient. According to Hau Pei-tsun this was because the cabinet-level MAC had to take a more cautious approach to developing cross-Strait relations than the SEF, taking account of the much wider implications for policy of various initiatives than its 'unofficial' counterpart (Wang 1994: 28–9, 258–9). An example of this arose when the SEF invited fifteen mainland reporters to visit Taiwan in March 1992. This pre-empted the Executive Yuan's plans to draw up a law allowing CCP members to enter Taiwan, a highly delicate matter because it not only affected cross-Strait relations but also made it difficult for the KMT to maintain a ban on blacklisted advocates of secession from returning to Taiwan. Although a consensus was finally reached that Communists and Taiwanese independence activists should be treated equally (UDN, 30 March, 7 April 1992), the cabinet was left struggling to assert its control over the SEF (UDN, 29 April, 2 May 1992).

Yet if inconsistencies and friction arose from the bureaucratic organisations set up to oversee 'unofficial' contacts, there was also considerable pressure building up in the business community for a departure from the policy of no direct contacts. The rate of long-term investments by Taiwanese in the mainland was growing, and the nature of projects was moving from labour-intensive industry towards higher technology, marking a change from speculation to the putting down of roots. A new organisation of entrepreneurs, the Industrial Association for

Promoting Unification (Shang gong tongyi cujin hui), was established in March 1992 to promote closer links with the mainland. At one point the idea was floated that this new organisation might even become a political party and a third political force. At any rate, the government was being told it would have to prepare a more comprehensive response to deepening economic integration across the Strait (UDN, 20 April 1992). It is in the context of this kind of pressure that in the same month, representatives from the SEF went to Beijing for the first time to meet with a parallel 'unofficial' organisation set up by the mainland, the Association for Relations Across the Taiwan Strait (ARATS), to discuss issues relating to the verification of documents and implementation of indirect registered mail services.

The one-China principle was also coming under fire for the adverse effects it was having on foreign policy. Although flexible diplomacy had paid high dividends in terms of developing economic relations with other states, much of this achievement was overshadowed when the ROC's staunchest ally in the region, South Korea, announced it was switching allegiance from Taipei to Beijing. In keeping with the one-China principle, and largely to save face over the abrupt manner in which the Koreans made their move, on 23 August 1992 Taipei announced the breaking of diplomatic relations and air links with Seoul.

The issue of GATT membership also raised the impossibility of keeping foreign economic relations separate from the subject of statehood and national identity. Much jubilation was expressed when the Customs Territory of Taiwan, Penghu, Kinmen and Matsu gained representation on 29 September 1992. The government seems to have been hoist with its own petard, however, when a GATT spokesman announced that this representation would only be on the same level as the colonies of Hong Kong and Macao. That GATT membership was far more than a purely economic affair in Taiwan was shown by the words of Economics Minister Vincent Siew, who insisted that Taiwan would join GATT but not at the expense of national character, dignity or sovereignty. The Ministry of Foreign Affairs added that as a 'political entity', the ROC expected to be granted the same diplomatic privileges as all other members (FCJ, 2, 6 October 1992).

Although the position of GATT was later revised, press response to the humiliation had already added fuel to attacks being made on the one-China policy. Complaints were raised about the insufficiency of seeing Taiwan as a developed economy due to its rapid economic growth alone. It was insisted that a truly developed economy would let its people have 'self-esteem' and 'freedom', which the one-China principle was not doing. It was also pointed out that the GATT problem would not have arisen if

Taiwan was a member of the UN, another thing that the one-China principle ruled out (IMP, 5 October 1992).

As such issues developed, they could only continue to exacerbate divisions in the KMT itself over the relationship between Taiwan's political status and its identity as part of China. Independence-minded KMT legislators soon began to join the criticism, complaining that it was impractical and impossible to ask Beijing to belittle itself over issues such as Taiwan's entry to GATT. One solution proposed was to make the one-China policy sufficiently flexible to allow a referendum to determine whether or not Taiwan wants independence 'for now'. Reviving one of Lee Teng-hui's long-standing interpretations of the status of the divided nation, it was pointed out that the two Germanys had been separate sovereign states until the time was ripe for unification. In response, nationalists like Hau Pei-tsun could only shift the blame for the ROC's ostracism on to the PRC. If the Communists refused even to recognise Taiwan as a 'political entity', asked the premier, how could anyone expect the PRC to recognise the ROC as an equal, sovereign nation (FCJ, 6 October 1992)?

Such a position was far from satisfactory for many in the KMT. In the run-up to the Second Legislative Yuan elections scheduled for December, a caucus known as the Wisdom Coalition took a particularly high profile in criticising Hau's version of the one-China principle. Formed in 1988 by elected KMT legislators who were not satisfied with the direction and pace of reform, its members had become particularly dissatisfied with Taiwan's continuing estrangement from international society. Now they were calling for the 'Taiwanisation' of the KMT to be manifested in all KMT policy by giving Taiwan priority under the slogan of 'one China, one Taiwan' (*yi zhong, yi tai*). On the eve of the election, at least ten Wisdom Coalition legislators even went so far as to ask the Executive Yuan to consider adopting a two-Chinas policy. Echoing a traditional cry of the opposition, they expressed the view that conservatives within the party were using the threat of military action by Beijing to terrorise the people of Taiwan and to sell them out (IMP, 11 November 1992). One member of the Wisdom Coalition, Chen Che-nan (Chen Zhenan), a candidate for Taiwan's second city, Kaohsiung, went so far as to call Hau Pei-tsun and three other Central Committee members the 'four traitors selling out Taiwan' (IMP, 28 November 1992).

Chen Che-nan was expelled from the party and the 'one China, one Taiwan' platform was rejected by Hau Pei-tsun and KMT Secretary-General James Soong as being impractical and amounting to a call for independence. But the Wisdom Coalition's revelation of the depth of division within the KMT over the relationship between China and Taiwan goaded a wider debate to rage in the press. That other advocates of 'one

China, one Taiwan' remained inside the KMT and campaigned on that platform for the Legislative Yuan elections seemed to confirm suspicions that they had support at the highest levels of the party. Lee Teng-hui himself actually spoke out during a meeting of the CSC in defence of Chen Che-nan. He even repeated the accusation that some KMT members and media reporters had tried to distort the military threat from Beijing so as 'to suppress our comrades' (CT, 14 November 1992). An enraged Hau Pei-tsun stormed out of the meeting.

On the eve of the elections, Lee Teng-hui again attempted to reach a compromise on the national identity issue by calling for a KMT working group to clarify exactly what 'one China' implies. All that this group could do, however, was to clarify the vagaries that were emanating from the NUC by stating that 'one China' is the ROC and that the KMT does not accept the PRC's 'one country, two systems' formula or its position that the PRC represents China. Moreover, it was added that Taiwanese independence and advocacy of a 'one China, one Taiwan' policy would split the national territory and would thus be against the KMT's aim of unification. This resolution was passed by the CSC on 2 December 1992, at the same meeting at which Chen Che-nan's expulsion was finally agreed.

THE SECOND LEGISLATIVE YUAN ELECTIONS

Thus divided, the KMT suffered a serious setback in the Legislative Yuan elections. Its share of the vote fell to only 61.7 per cent, and if those who ran as KMT candidates without being officially nominated are excluded from the count, the figure was only 53 per cent. The DPP, on the other hand, boosted its vote to 36.1 per cent of the total. The nature of the DPP's achievement must be understood in context: most of its candidates were standing for election for the first time, and without the massive organisational, media and financial support available to the KMT. The scale of their overall success is revealed by the fact that out of a total of only fifty-nine candidates fielded, thirty-seven were successful. Moreover, DPP candidates scored the highest number of votes in fourteen districts out of a total of twenty-nine, while the KMT only came first in eight, although these results were not translated directly into seats due to the single non-transferable vote and multi-seat constituency system.

It was especially worrying, however, that candidates of the DPP's more extreme secessionist factions had done very well. The New Tide faction had seven candidates elected out of eight standing, with two non-constituency candidates added. The Taiwan Independence Alliance had two candidates out of four elected, with two non-constituency candidates added. One analysis of the views of the new legislators on the independence issue revealed that forty-three of them were advocates of and sympathisers with secession (UDN, 20 December 1992). Lin Cho-shui (Lin Zhuoshui), a leading member of the Movement faction who succeeded in being elected as legislator for Taipei City North, proclaimed confidently that, having passed through the 'darkest night' for Taiwan independence in the Second National Assembly elections, the 'flowers have now opened and Taiwanese independence is accepted by society' (UDN, 20 December 1992). Other commentators warned of a polarisation of the Legislative Yuan that might spill over to divide society along provincial lines.

Yet despite these enthusiastic early judgements, with hindsight it has become clear that rather than a swing in public opinion towards Taiwan's independence, the election results signalled the success of what amounted to a tactical withdrawal by the DPP from the openly secessionist platform adopted for the Second National Assembly elections of the previous year. The DPP had in fact softened its stance on independence since then, echoing instead themes already adopted by the KMT, such as the process of 'nativisation' and 'one China, one Taiwan', or putting Taiwan first. Rather than secession, the most prominent strand of the DPP's campaign themes had been the 'three antis, three demands'. These were anti-money politics, anti-military politics, anti-privilege politics; demand sovereignty, demand direct elections, demand lower taxes. Such a platform gained much sympathy from the public in the context of widespread dissatisfaction over a string of corruption cases concerning public works. Moreover, the KMT had lost a good deal of credibility and almost any sense of discipline since James Soong had looked for backing to candidates supported by business tycoons and large syndicates, known as 'Golden Bulls'. For the DPP, drawing attention to such problems proved to be far more effective than the bold declarations of independence which had characterised its platform for the Second National Assembly elections.

In contrast to the secessionist bravado of the Movement faction, an official post-election DPP statement preferred to interpret the results as the expression of a popular demand for speeding up political reform and re-establishing social order (IMP, 20 December 1992). The DPP campaign, in fact, had even gone so far as to recognise that voters did not yet have confidence in the party's ability to govern and assured sceptics that even if all their candidates were elected they would still not win half the total number of seats. For the present, it would be enough for the electorate to give them a chance to form a strong opposition party that could control and balance the KMT in the course of developing true party politics (CT, 20 December 1992). From this perspective, what the Legislative Yuan elections of December 1992 seem to mark is a confirmation by the DPP of Lee Teng-hui's strategy of trying to maintain a division between the issues of democratisation and national identity. As had been shown in the National Assembly elections, this had become the surest way to win votes from an electorate that wanted to see political reform without opening the Pandora's box of the national identity issue.

Yet another equally important outcome of the election had been a confirmation of the transformation of the role of the president himself. This resulted from the DPP's tactic of concentrating its fire on Hau Pei-tsun. Full-page advertisements appeared in the press to this effect, advocating support for Lee against the KMT's CSC through electing more DPP legislators. A vote for the opposition, argued the DPP, would ensure Lee's survival and, in consequence, continued balanced development of constitutional politics. The DPP thus lionised the president, giving him the role of a charismatic leader championing Taiwan's interests in a realm beyond party politics, and so fostering what was to become known as the 'Lee Teng-hui syndrome' in Taiwan's electoral politics.

Ironically, the success of the DPP's anti-Hau Pei-tsun campaign made the premier's position untenable in the new parliament. His departure on 2 February 1993, and his replacement by Lien Chan on 27 February, symbolised a radical shift of power in the KMT and removed one of the main obstacles to Lee Teng-hui's control over policy-making. Lien was firmly identified with Lee Teng-hui's policies, having faithfully implemented pragmatic diplomacy as foreign minister during Lee's first two years in office, only to be removed from the position and made governor of Taiwan province during the Hau cabinet. More significantly, Lien Chan was perceived to be 'Taiwanese'. Although he had been born in the mainland city of Xian, his father had migrated there from Taiwan. For the first time, both presidency and premiership were thus held by people perceived to be native Taiwanese.

THE FALL OF THE KMT NATIONALISTS

Having secured his own premier, Lee Teng-hui was in a better position to move against opposition to him on the KMT's CSC. The opportunity for this arose with the party's Fourteenth National Congress, scheduled for August 1993. A new Central Committee would be elected, which in turn would elect a CSC and approve the nomination of the party chairman. Riding on the wave of popular support delivered to him during the Legislative Yuan elections, Lee's first move to consolidate his power was to 'democratise' the Congress through initiating a secret ballot system for the election of the party chairman and vice-chairman. In addition, representation by party-nominated delegates would be weakened by allowing any KMT member who had been appointed to any post through election by the people of Taiwan to become an *ex-officio* delegate. This included the entire KMT membership of the Legislative Yuan, National Assembly, Taiwan Provincial Assembly, and Taipei and Kaohsiung city councils, KMT mayors and county magistrates, and heads of all KMT local chapters. For the 180 Central Committee members, this meant being swallowed up by a total of 700 *ex-officio* delegates, most of whom had been elected to their public positions by the population of Taiwan.

In response to Hau Pei-tsun's objection, now as a member of the CSC, that the increase in *ex-officio* candidates would give the impression that the KMT was the 'Taiwan KMT' (IWP, 28 May 1993), the preparatory committee for the Congress agreed to limit their proportion to one-third of the total. Yet the way in which this was to be achieved was not by reducing the number of *ex-officio* delegates, but by increasing the number of party-appointed delegates from a proposed 1,073 to 1,400. The conservatives on the CSC were too weak to squeeze any more concessions than this, and when the committee met on 19 May, no less than five veteran stalwarts of the Chinese nationalist cause announced that they would resign after the Congress.[8] All cited health concerns as their reasons for resigning. They did not, however, fail to give a swan song on the theme that the party should treat the Three Principles of the People 'like the Bible' and that the younger generation should carry the creed back to the mainland as Chiang Kai-shek had wished (IEP, 28 May 1993).

When, on 20 May, Lee Teng-hui took the opportunity of the third anniversary of his presidential term to broadcast his views on the future of Taiwan's politics, he made it quite clear that there were to be no such sacred cows. Instead, he stressed that in party politics the greatest difficulty is to accept that people have different points of view and then to transform those views into a common view. Although the Three Principles of the People remained the belief of the KMT, if the party was to survive in Taiwan, it would need the votes of the people first (IWP, 28 May 1993). In other words, party survival had come to depend on placing the opinion of Taiwan's public above all else. The Lee Teng-hui leadership had moved a long way from the KMT's traditional dogma that it is the will of the Chinese nation that is paramount.

Faced with Lee Teng-hui's growing power, his opponents from three generations began to organise themselves into a caucus aimed at making a last stand on restoring party orthodoxy. They named themselves the New Tong Meng Hui, reviving the nationalist organisation established by Sun Yat-sen as the precursor of the KMT. Their third meeting, on 14 June, was attended by senior figures, including a number of Central Committee members, although their 'spiritual leader', Hau Pei-tsun, only maintained contact by telephone. They dedicated themselves to opposing corruption, opposing dictatorship and opposing advocacy of Taiwanese independence in the KMT. They also made it clear that they were prepared to split the KMT if their calls were not heeded (IEP, 25 June 1993).

Members of the mainly second-generation mainlander New KMT Alliance also realised that they would have to break with the KMT soon, or face being denied candidatures in future elections, as well as being drowned out by the *ex-officio* candidates at the coming party Congress. On 10 August, they finally established a China New Party (CNP). What could well have been in the minds of the breakaway party (although they denied it) was the defeat of the Liberal Democratic Party in Japan's parliamentary elections and the advances made by smaller parties campaigning for clean politics there. At any rate, the CNP hoped to form an effective third political force, dedicated to representing the common people, reviving politics, stabilising the political situation, and holding a balance of power between the two major parties.

Yet on the issue of national identity, the CNP was on the horns of a dilemma. Springing mainly from mainland Chinese backgrounds, and aiming to capture the Chinese nationalist vote of sections of the electorate such as war veterans, the party claimed to be the true heir to Sun Yat-sen's ideology, 'pursuing unity of the nation (*minzu*), democratic politics and equality of livelihood' (IWP, 20 August 1993). On the issue of relations with the mainland, however, there was a degree of obfuscation. Rather than a clear policy on unification, bald proposals were made to 'strengthen the ROC' and 'guarantee the security of the Taiwan Strait'. In fact, the CNP, if it was to continue the tradition of Chinese nationalism, faced the same dilemma that its members had faced when inside the KMT. Their remarkable individual successes at the polls had been achieved on a platform of clean government, while open advocacy of the Chinese nationalist cause could only lose more votes than it might hope to gain. It would ultimately be forced to make the former the party's central theme when it came to establishing a voting base and entering into tactical alliances with the DPP in the Legislative Yuan. Over the following months the word 'China' was quietly dropped from the New Party's title.

THE NEW KMT

When the Fourteenth National Congress of the KMT finally arrived, the New KMT Alliance had been driven out, veteran members of the CSC were on their way out, and voting arrangements were strongly in Lee Teng-hui's favour. The chairman could thus look forward to a transformation of the party and the consolidation of his own power. When he bade farewell to the Thirteenth CSC on 11 August 1993, his remarks were clearly focused on Taiwan and not on China when he remarked that the economy of 'our country', its politics and society were all doing well, as though it had already reached the level of an industrial democracy (UDN, 12 August 1993).

The National Congress itself ran for seven days from 16 August. On the third day Lee was re-elected as party chairman, unopposed, by secret ballot. Over the following days he got what he wanted from the Congress without opposition. The post of vice-chairman was diluted by creating four of them. A new Central Committee of 220 members was approved from a list of 350 candidates drawn up by the party centre. Veteran members were reduced to a few token figures, while representatives of farmers, fishermen, labour, industry and commerce were all increased. Half the candidates on the list were members of the government executive system, while a third were members of the central representative institutions. Serving military commanders were excluded altogether as part of a move towards 'nationalising the army'. As for the CSC, unlike in the past when the chairman had appointed all members of the CSC, Lee Teng-hui now only appointed fifteen of the thirty-one members. The remaining sixteen were elected by the new Central Committee. Opposition to Lee in that body, however, had now devolved on to representatives of war veterans and overseas Chinese, who only made up about a quarter of the total membership. The result was that nineteen members of the new CSC were new blood. Moreover, the introduction of a new system whereby the CSC would be re-elected annually meant that it would be hard for opposition to become entrenched there.

Lee Teng-hui might, then, have successfully removed opposition from the main bastions of KMT power. Yet in the long run his victory turned out to be Pyrrhic, at least so far as party discipline was concerned. With there being no ideological glue to bind the newly shaped party together, delegates to the Congress proved hard to control. Particularly damaging for the KMT's image was the behaviour of Legislative Yuan members attending as *ex-officio* candidates. In the process of bargaining for votes to get themselves elected on to the Central Committee, money changed hands and complex alliances were formed which undermined any appearance of real democratic procedure. During the crucial debates over the new vice-chairmanships, clashes on the conference floor occurred between delegates from different wings of the party, which at times even degenerated into physical brawls.

As the image of the KMT continued to decline through corruption and division, a situation developed in which public support for the president was rapidly becoming divorced from support for the party, as shown by its poor performance at the polls. When local elections were held on 27 November for twenty-three mayors and county magistrates, the KMT share of the vote dropped below 50 per cent for the first time, to a mere 47.47 per cent. The DPP, meanwhile, broke the 40 per cent barrier for the first time, polling 41.03 per cent. The New Party made its debut and polled 3.07 per cent, claiming to have won 16.6 per cent of the votes in the six constituencies where it fielded candidates.

This poor KMT showing was shortly followed by a fiasco when the party went to the polls in elections in January 1994 for small-city mayors, village chiefs and local councillors, and in March for speakers and deputy speakers of city and county councils. As in the past the opposition did not have the resources to field sufficient candidates to form a majority in any of these bodies, but the KMT still saw a decline in the number of seats it had won in the same contests in 1990. More significant was that these elections revealed the intensity of factional conflict at the grass roots. The party centre could now exert almost no control in the localities as factions vied with each other through vote-buying and violence. An investigation into allegations of vote-buying produced charges against 215 people, while cases of alleged election irregularities totalled 136. Those charged included speakers, deputy speakers, councillors, provincial assemblymen and various associates. Moreover, the director-general of the National Police Administration revealed that some 300 of the new councillors had criminal records or underground backgrounds, with many having been involved in past acts of violence.

By the beginning of 1994 a situation had thus developed in which a charismatic president was winning praise at home for his creative foreign policy and charismatic leadership, while presiding as chairman over an unpopular and disintegrating ruling party. Meanwhile, much of his support was coming from an opposition party ostensibly committed to secession from China but with which he had built a working relationship on the matter of domestic reforms. Electoral politics in Taiwan since the DPP debacle of the Second National Assembly elections had focused less on the question of national identity and more on domestic issues of social welfare, the environment and tackling corruption. Not only was the KMT in a poor position to fight on these issues, but even when the will did arise, the factionalism and vested interests upon which the party had built its support under a Leninist system of organisation often prevented any practical measures from being taken.

TOWARDS A PRESIDENTIAL SYSTEM

In this context, what is significant about the constitutional reforms that took place under Lee's leadership after his consolidation of power at the KMT's Fourteenth National Congress is that they put in place a presidential system under which Lee Teng-hui (or his successor) could probably survive as the leader of Taiwan even if the KMT were to lose power. So far no less than eighteen additional articles had been added to the constitution by the National Assembly since 1990. When this body met in the summer of 1994, these were simplified into ten additional articles (FCJ, 24 September 1994), which were promulgated by the president on 1 August.

One of the things that these additional articles achieved was a considerable enhancement of the president's powers. The balancing power of the premier was reduced by removing his authority to countersign the president's personnel appointments. The president also held on to the power to re-establish the much reviled security institutions of the martial law era, namely the National Security Council and its subsidiary organ, the National Security Bureau. Such measures, not surprisingly, raised fears that the debate over the division of powers was no longer about a presidential or a cabinet system but about an 'emperor system' (IWP, 24 December 1993). Lee's response, however, was to maintain that what he was working towards was a French-style presidential system. He had in fact taken advice from French constitutional experts on the introduction of this model, which could result, as it had during the Mitterrand presidency in France, in the president 'cohabiting' with an opposition premier: an interesting prospect in Taiwan's circumstances.

The first step towards realising the possibility of bringing the DPP into government occurred when the ten additional articles enabled the first elections to be held for the mayors of the two main cities of Taipei and Kaohsiung, and for provincial governor in December 1994. A breakthrough was made by the DPP when its candidate, Chen Shui-bian, was elected mayor of Taipei in December. The former secessionist firebrand finally found himself being offered a seat in the cabinet. That Chen stated in his campaign that he would respect the ROC constitution marked just how successful the consensus between the two main parties had become. How far this extended towards collusion is hard to say, although Chen was not alone in expressing 'surprise' at the large number of votes he polled. The KMT's singularly unpopular incumbent, Huang Ta-chou (Huang Dazhou), meanwhile complained in the CSC that a campaign had been launched within the party to drop him and support Chen (UDN, 29 December 1994).

That the elections for provincial governor and city heads were extremely sensitive for Lee had been a matter of discussion in Taiwan for some time.

When it appeared at one point that the elections might be postponed, speculation had arisen about fears at the highest levels of the KMT over a possible 'Yeltsin effect'. A charismatic provincial governor elected by the population of Taiwan would be able to claim more legitimacy than an unelected president supposed to represent China (UDN, 8 April 1994). The victory in the election for provincial governor of the well-established incumbent and confidant of Lee Teng-hui, James Soong, appears to have minimised such a risk.

It would appear, then, that what had been created under Lee Teng-hui's leadership was a strong presidential system which had achieved a wide degree of consensus with the DPP based on its function of steering Taiwan between the Charybdis represented by the dangers of ethnic conflict and the Scylla of mainland policy. How far the KMT had moved from the ideals of Chinese nationalism in this process is perhaps best expressed by the exclamation of the veteran Chinese nationalist and CSC member, Hsu Li-nung (Xu Linong), on defecting to the New Party in November 1993. Lamenting bitterly how the party had degenerated into corruption and power-grabbing and was looking to anybody, including secessionists, for support, he condemned the KMT under Lee Teng-hui as being the party of Sunism in name only, 'hanging up a sheep's head and selling dog's meat'. To emphasise his point, Hsu even quoted the words of the DPP party chairman that, 'It is not the DPP that has a Lee Teng-hui syndrome, it is Lee Teng-hui who has a DPP syndrome' (UDN, 25 November 1993).

THE PRESIDENTIAL ELECTION

As well as concentrating power in the hands of Lee Teng-hui, however, the most important thing that the ten additional articles to the constitution achieved was finally to confront the issue of how the president was to be elected when his term expired in 1996. The second article now stipulated that his election was to be 'by the entire populace of the free area of the Republic of China'. As has been explained above (pp. 74–5), such a formula had been opposed by Chinese nationalists as an infringement of the one-China principle. Moreover, because the most likely winner of the election was Lee Teng-hui, who had little nationalist credibility left, such an election would inevitably have serious repercussions for relations with the Chinese mainland. When the election approached, the fact that the other candidates were Peng Ming-min, who had returned to Taiwan and won the DPP primaries, and Lin Yang-kang (Lin Yanggang) and Hau Pei-tsun who had been expelled from the KMT in December 1995 after they decided to run as a team for president and vice-president, made the election look increasingly like a contest over the issue of Taiwan's identity.

Yet most people expected the incumbent to win, and Lee Teng-hui's true intentions towards the one-China principle had become steadily more suspect. As noted above, for Beijing there had been uncertainty over Lee's true intentions at least since his reappointment as president in 1990. Some solace could be gained from the fact that elections had not led to the victory of the DPP, with the opposition's failure at the polls in 1991, accompanied by the subsequent fall in the KMT's share of the vote, appearing to bear out early conclusions about the factionalisation of Taiwan's politics (Wang 1993: 31–2). By 1994 mainland observers could claim that Taiwan's electoral politics had settled into a fairly clear pattern, with the DPP constrained in its advocacy of Taiwan's independence by its rejection at the polls and the danger of alienating the support of the business community. The KMT was said to be similarly constrained by public opinion in its pursuit of policies such as double recognition and limiting cross-Strait transactions (Li 1994: 36–7). Moreover, the development of the contacts between the SEF and ARATS into a meeting between the chairmen of the two organisations, Koo Chen-fu (Gu Zhenfu) and Wang Daohan, respectively, in Singapore on 27–29 April 1993, had been seen as marking another success of 'peaceful unification'.

Opposed to such optimism, however, the earlier suspicions over Lee Teng-hui's true intentions concerning unification seemed to be confirmed by the general trend in Taipei's mainland and foreign policies. This was evident in the progression from Chiang Ching-kuo's commitment to 'one China', through the Lee administration's idea of 'one country, two governments', and 'one country, two areas', to the idea of two 'political entities' in the *Guidelines*, the recognition of Beijing's rule on the mainland and the increasing flexibility in Taipei's foreign policy. Behind all this lay Taipei's attempts to obfuscate the meaning of 'one China' by redefining it in terms of a vague entity not necessarily related to concepts of sovereignty. This had been made clear in statements by the NUC and by Lee himself in an interview with the Japanese journalist Ryotaro Shiba on 31 March 1994, in which he said that the implications of 'China' are not clear, that 'sovereignty' is a dangerous concept, and that the notion that Taiwan is a part of the PRC is a 'strange dream' (Yan 1995: 22–3).

It is against this background of uncertainty over the impact of democratisation on Taiwan's relations with the mainland that Jiang Zemin attempted to put his personal stamp on Taiwan policy when he made the lunar new year speech with which this work started. Delivered on 30 January 1995, this consisted of a fairly lengthy preamble, followed by eight points defining Beijing's Taiwan policy. Briefly paraphrased (from Jiang 1995a), these are as follows:

1 The one-China principle must be upheld as the foundation and precondition for peaceful unification.
2 Taiwan is free to develop private economic and cultural contacts with foreign countries.
3 Bilateral talks on peaceful unification should be held.
4 'Chinese will not attack Chinese' (*Zhongguo ren bu da Zhongguo ren*) unless there is foreign intervention or secession.
5 Great efforts should be made to develop exchange and co-operation across the Strait to enable economic development in the next century for the benefit of the whole Chinese nation (*minzu*).
6 Chinese culture must be built up and maintained as the foundation for peaceful unification.
7 The population of Taiwan, no matter from which province, are 'all bone and flesh compatriots'. Their wish to be 'masters of their home' will be respected, and views on peaceful unification will be welcomed from all of Taiwan's political parties and individuals from all circles.
8 The 'leaders of the Taiwan authorities' are welcome to visit the mainland 'in the appropriate capacity', and invitations to mainland leaders to visit Taiwan will be accepted.

Although none of these eight points are new, their restatement by the apparent successor to Deng Xiaoping was received with some enthusiasm in Taipei as meaning there would be no dramatic change in Beijing's policy (CDN, 4, 5 May 1995). Yet a report by a mainland affairs working group of the KMT to the party's CSC on 8 February also drew attention to the links of Jiang's initiative with his bid for the PRC leadership in the context of an economy plagued by problems of overheating, loss-making state enterprises, implementing a new tax system and corruption. The report pointed out that achieving unification with Hong Kong, Macao and Taiwan would allow the CCP to claim that it had surpassed the Han and Tang dynasties as unifiers of China. Although Beijing was concerned about secessionist calls in Taiwan, it believed that transactions across the Strait had reached a point at which negotiations would have to deal with political matters, leading to 'peaceful unification'. Jiang's apparently conciliatory moves, the report warned, should thus be seen in the context of the CCP's past record of dealing with weaker opponents, which tended to involve keeping them off balance by taking measures to stabilise them temporarily, then attacking as necessary (CDN, 9 February 1995).

Whatever Taipei's interpretation of Jiang's eight points, however, it is clear that acceptance of them would have left the Lee administration with little room for manoeuvre. In the preamble to his eight points, Jiang had in fact dismissed all of the Lee administration's attempts to raise Taiwan's status in foreign and mainland policy. Although he might have agreed that Taiwan's international economic and cultural links could be developed, there was no suggestion of any flexibility on allowing Taiwan to be represented in international organisations. The invitation for the 'leaders of the Taiwan authorities' to visit the mainland in 'an appropriate capacity' was also a way of ruling out government-to-government negotiations between the two 'political entities'. Moreover, although Chinese would not attack Chinese, any departure from the one-China principle, as Beijing understood it, by people inside or outside the island would still be met by force.

Facing the situation of a dangerous deadlock in the most crucial areas of foreign and mainland policy, then, Lee Teng-hui replied to Jiang's initiative with his own six points. He announced these to the NUC on 8 April 1995 as follows:

i) Under the reality of the political division between the two sides, pursue the unification of China;

ii) Take Chinese culture as the foundation, strengthen exchanges between the two sides;

iii) Increase cross-Strait trade, develop mutually advantageous and mutually beneficial relations;

iv) Both sides take equal part in international organisations, with the leaders of both sides thus meeting naturally;

v) Both sides uphold the use of peaceful means to resolve all conflicts;

vi) Both sides should commonly preserve the prosperity of Hong Kong and Macao, and facilitate democracy in Hong Kong and Macao.

(UDN, 9 April 1995)

The key differences between Lee's and Jiang's positions had thus been thrown into clear relief. Whereas common ground could be found in the issue of developing a common Chinese cultural identity and increasing cross-Strait transactions, Lee still insisted on equal representation in international organisations and meeting Jiang Zemin in an international forum. He also thought that Beijing should renounce the threat to use force against Taiwan, and he linked the issue of democracy in Hong Kong and Macao to Taiwan's future. With the two sides having staked out their bargaining positions for the period ahead, the way should have been open for their diplomats to continue to grope for common ground. In the middle of May it was announced that the SEF and ARATS had reached a provisional agreement that a second Koo–Wang meeting would be held in Beijing in July.

It was at this point, however, that the Clinton administration gave in to bipartisan pressure to grant Lee Teng-hui a visa for a private visit to his alma mater, Cornell University, which he made from 7 to 12 June. From Beijing's perspective, the possibility that events that had appeared to indicate the success of 'peaceful unification' had in fact masked a much longer-term strategy by Lee Teng-hui to break the one-China principle appeared to have been confirmed (Yan 1995).

AFTER DEMOCRACY?

The measures taken by Beijing to raise the cost of this departure by Taiwan and Washington from its version of the one-China principle make up a long list. As far as Washington is concerned this includes, at least, the cancellation of high-level military visits to the USA, the postponement of negotiations on missile proliferation and nuclear co-operation, the withdrawal of Beijing's ambassador to Washington, an apparent favour shown to non-American firms in the awarding of large business contracts, overtures towards Moscow, Pakistan and Iran, and the testing of nuclear devices and intercontinental ballistic missiles. What was interpreted by some as a veiled threat of a nuclear strike against the USA itself might be added to this range of options for warning Washington that loss of co-operation with Beijing due to the Taiwan issue would have serious consequences for Sino-American relations (IHT, 25 January 1996).

The mobilisation by Beijing of its resources against Taiwan, on the other hand, was more directly aimed at influencing the outcome of the election there. First amongst these there was the military option. Between 30 June 1995 and the presidential election the following March, a series of military exercises in and around the Taiwan Strait were held by the PLA. These included repeated missile testing in the seas near Taiwan and combined forces exercises in the Strait on a scale not seen since the crises of the 1950s. Apart from showing how the mainland could disrupt Taiwan's transport links with the outside world, these measures also caused a crisis of confidence resulting in an outflow of people and capital and a dive in the stock market. Meetings between the SEF and ARATS were also cancelled, as was the imminent second Koo–Wang meeting. To clarify who was responsible for this crisis in cross-Strait relations, a propaganda campaign was launched against the person of Lee himself. As the election approached and the tension in the Taiwan Strait escalated, Beijing's spokespersons openly began to link the PLA exercises with Lee's actions, something made clear in PRC premier Li Peng's National Day speech of 1 October.

Whether or not Beijing's strategy worked, it is only to be expected that all sides should have claimed satisfaction with the eventual results of the presidential election. Lee Teng-hui and his running mate Lien Chan could certainly claim a landslide victory with 54 per cent of the vote. Mainland commentators could try to pour cold water on this by drawing on reports in the Taiwan press to back up their interpretation that the result showed a decisive rejection of Taiwan independence. Peng Ming-min had in fact only polled 21.1 per cent of votes, which was less than the combined votes of the openly anti-independence candidates, Chen Li-an (9.98 per cent) and Lin Yang-kang (14.9 per cent).

Perhaps the clearest impact that can be seen of electoral politics in Taiwan on the one-China principle by 1996, though, is that it had not resulted in the kind of direct vote for independence that has characterised many of the secessions from the former Soviet Union. In fact, when elections were held for a Third Legislative Yuan in the December before the presidential election, the DPP proportion of the vote fell back to only 33.2 per cent. In elections for the Third National Assembly held simultaneously with the presidential election, this figure fell to only 29.8 per cent. The divisions in the DPP over what priority to give between the independence platform and domestic reform had left the party as divided as ever. When party chairman Shih Ming-teh had suggested promoting democracy through a coalition with the KMT or the New Party, this had only led to condemnation from more radical members. As for Peng Ming-min, shortly after his defeat the veteran secessionist lost no time in announcing the formation of a National Building Association, which became a formal political party on 16 August, to 'carry the burden' of independence for the DPP (CN, 17 August 1996). By way of contrast, the anti-independence New Party had become a real third force, gaining 13 per cent and 13.7 per cent at the polls in December and March respectively. The KMT, meanwhile, was reduced to a slender majority in the Legislative Yuan and had lost the 75 per cent majority needed in the National Assembly to push through constitutional changes unopposed.

The real significance of the 1996 presidential election, however, cannot be grasped from the number of votes polled alone. As far as the development of the one-China principle is concerned, what the PRC's measures do seem to have more or less achieved is to ensure that if Lee Teng-hui won the election he would not be in a position to break Beijing's version of that principle again. This can be seen in the shift in Taipei's stance on several key points. First of all, concerning the relationship between mainland policy and foreign policy, for example, in early July 1995 it had been stated by the MAC that foreign policy would be given equal weight with mainland policy (UDN, 8 July 1995). By September, however, the deputy secretary-general of the SEF was stating that mainland policy should take priority over foreign policy due to questions of national security (UDN, 10 September 1995). This position was confirmed by Foreign Minister Frederick Chien on various occasions between the end of December and the March elections (UDN, 30 December 1995, 5 February 1996). It was also stated in Lien Chan's new year speech, in which the premier explained that flexibility in foreign policy should not be at the expense of the overall objective for the nation (UDN, 1 January 1996).

The most radical change in Taipei's position, however, was in the changing response to Jiang Zemin's eight points. Lee's initial reaction had been his six-point speech restating Taipei's preconditions which must be met before progress could be made on unification. By the beginning of September 1995, however, he had shifted to stating that his six points and Jiang Zemin's eight points could be taken as the foundation for seeking agreement (UDN, 3 September, 21 December, 23 December 1995, 1 January, 24 February 1996). That Lee did not mention the precondition that Beijing would have to give up the threat to use force before talks could be held was seen by some elements of the Taiwan press as a significant change in policy (UDN, 11 February 1996). Finally, in his inauguration speech, Lee made one of the most dramatic conciliatory gestures to the mainland of his entire administration when he announced a mission there to meet with its top leadership (1996a).

In general, then, rather than Taiwan's democratisation resulting in a clear-cut decision on the island's international status and identity, constraining factors appear to have led to an accommodation with the status quo across the Strait. This appears to have borne out the KMT's position that constitutional reform could be carried out by finding ways to circumvent the issue of the island's relationship with China. It has also shown that mainland observers were right in so far as they expected a weakened KMT to hold on to power by bargaining across the political spectrum, while parties would be constrained from adopting secessionist platforms by the risk of alienating voters. However, the interaction between democratisation and national identity has also shown that satisfying demands for greater access to the mainland and more recognition in international society necessitated a variety of *ad hoc* initiatives by Taipei that have led to a more sophisticated attempt to articulate the meaning of one China than opting for either independence or unification. From this perspective, the events leading up to March 1996 indicate the limits within which this articulation takes place. To properly assess the significance of the impact of democratisation on Chinese nationalism, therefore, a survey is needed to show how political developments in Taiwan impact on the wider relationships the island enjoys with China and with international society. This will be the task of the following two chapters.

5 Forging a post-nationalist identity

If democratisation in Taiwan has resulted in attempts to reinterpret the one-China principle, this raises the question of what kinds of links the island can maintain with China in the pursuit of its own interests. This question needs to be addressed both within Taiwan's domestic politics and in terms of the relationship between Taiwan and those communities of people in the world who define themselves as 'Chinese'. Concerning the debate inside Taiwan, what democratisation has resulted in has been the breaking of the nationalist link that binds Chinese identity with the single Chinese state. Yet it is important to note that, even as the reforms to the ROC constitution were getting into full swing, Lee Teng-hui made a point of emphasising that the people of the island could not break their relations with the rest of the Chinese people. Nor could they break their links with Chinese culture (Lee 1991b: 133).

To understand why Lee should wish to emphasise that reform in Taiwan should not imply separation from China, it is necessary to locate the island's interests within the global relationships between people who consider themselves to be Chinese. No matter what secessionists might demand in terms of *political* relations with the PRC, the people of Taiwan may not wish to turn their backs on the benefits of being located in what Tu Wei-ming has called this 'living tree' of Chineseness (Tu 1991). From this perspective, the Lee administration's policies have been characterised by attempts to maximise the benefits of Taiwan's being a branch on this tree while not compromising the island's political independence from the mainland more than is necessary. This has resulted in what might best be called Taiwan's 'post-nationalist' identity.

NATION AND STATE: BREAKING THE LINK IN TAIWAN

If at the heart of Chinese nationalism there lies the imperative that the national unit and the political unit should be congruent, democratisation in

Taiwan had to call this into question. When Lee Teng-hui reminded the KMT Congress that, although the party should not lose sight of its ideal of uniting China, Chiang Ching-kuo himself had stressed that anything going against democracy had to be expunged (UDN, 23 August 1993), he was drawing attention to the fact that sovereignty was now going to be exercised by the population of Taiwan. When he addressed the National Assembly on 26 May 1994, he began to clarify the ideological implications of such a departure when he advocated the doctrine of popular sovereignty, or 'sovereignty in the people' (*zhuquan zai min*). The problem with such a doctrine in the context of Chinese nationalism, of course, is that 'the people' here must mean not the Chinese nation but the voters of Taiwan. That this was what was in Lee's mind was made clear when he stated that if sovereignty was located in the people and Taiwan continued to be modernised, the twenty-one million residents of the island could unite against the Chinese Communists and stand up with pride in the world (UDN, 27 May 1994). That 'the people', for Lee, refers to the population of Taiwan was further indicated when, in an interview with the Japanese journalist Ryotaro Shiba on 31 March 1994, he used the formula in the same context that he referred to the KMT as a 'foreign authority' (*wai lai zhengquan*) and insisted that the notion that Taiwan belongs to the PRC is 'a strange dream'.

For Chinese nationalists, these words were interpreted as an attempt to say that China does not exist and that Lee Teng-hui lacked 'Chinese feelings' (RRB, 16 June 1994; *Wen Hui Bao*, 16 June 1994). The point that Lee was making about popular sovereignty, though, was that there is no necessary linkage between one's ethnic identity and the political community one wishes to belong to. As has been noted above, the seeds of this idea can be traced back in opposition thinking at least as far as Peng Ming-min and the Dang Wai writers, who saw that there could only be stability in an ethnically divided society such as Taiwan's if everyone identified themselves politically with Taiwan's destiny. Until 1990, however, most of the actions of the state in Taiwan had resulted in the opposite effect by imposing the distinction between 'native' (*ben sheng ren*) and 'outsider' (*wai sheng ren*) on individuals in a number of ways. This was done not only through the alienation of the pre-1945 population by the imposition of the state version of a Chinese identity; it was also maintained down the generations through identifying individuals according to where their father was born. Thus, while an independent survey in 1985 put the proportion of those who were actually born on the Chinese mainland at a mere 5.7 per cent of the population (Tien 1989: 36), the official 1990 census identifies 13 per cent (2,645,000) of the population as having their origins in mainland provinces (IMP, 18 November 1992).

In a society suffering such a cleavage of identity there is always the danger that democratisation will spill over into ethnic conflict. In Taiwan, as frequent elections repeatedly raised questions over what community individuals should attach their loyalty to, fears of conflict between 'natives' and 'outsiders' inevitably arose. They appeared to be becoming reality when, during elections for provincial and city mayors at the end of 1994, a spate of violent attacks against mainlanders and their property occurred (UDN, 2 December 1994). The complex nature of the politicisation of identity that was occurring here is made clear from the letters pages of the daily newspapers. One particularly telling case is that of the 'middle-class', female 'floating voter' whose family has been in Taiwan for eight generations and whose Hakka grandmother was ejected from a taxi because she spoke Taiwanese with 'an accent' she picked up from her mainlander husband. This kind of problem in Taiwan's society is something that politicians of both the mainstream of the KMT and the moderate wing of the DPP do not want to see. Broader public opinion is certainly against going down such a road, as evidenced by the letters pages and editorials of newspapers, including those which traditionally lean to the side of independence ('Yi ren . . .' 1994, 'Taiwan renmin . . .' 1995).

If dissident writers had realised the danger of ethnic division relatively early on, by the early 1990s their thinking on the relationship between political and ethnic identity was becoming mainstream. Scholarly analyses were pointing out that the idea of a Chinese race was too big and too remote to be of significance to Taiwan's 'community of shared destiny' (Lin Zhuoshui 1992). Veteran opposition writers were claiming that a national identity depends not only on blood, language and culture but also on subjective loyalties to a 'community of shared destiny' (Li 1991). With support for the DPP on the rise, warnings were also being voiced that a confusion of ethnic nationalism with civic nationalism (*guomin zhuyi*) had to be overcome to stop Taiwanese nationalism going down the road of super-nationalism (Wu 1991). When the DPP drew up its charter, it thus made the development of a civic society as the foundation for statehood one of its three main principles (DPP 1993: 13).

It is in this context that Lee Teng-hui told a group of university professors, in August 1991, that there was a need to graft the concept of '*Gemeinschaft*' (*shengming gongtong ti*)[9] on to traditional family ethics and morality (Lee 1992b: 117). Of course, Lee Teng-hui could never accredit his use of the idea of *Gemeinschaft* to opposition thinking, but traces its origins to Goethe and Kant. However, when rendered in Chinese, Lee's '*Gemeinschaft*' (*shengming gongtong ti* is literally 'living community') and Peng's 'community of shared destiny' (*mingyun gongtong ti*) are easy to associate. Peng himself has certainly made political capital out of claiming to be the inspiration behind Lee Teng-hui's thinking on *Gemeinschaft* (Peng 1994: 29). There are also no doubts about the relationship between the two concepts amongst Chinese nationalists. When Lee suggested to the KMT's Thirteenth CSC that the ideal of creating a *Gemeinschaft* should be included in a revised KMT charter, Hsu Li-nung insisted that the concept be rejected as having its origins in Peng (UDN, 20 June 1993). Mainland critics of Lee also make the connection and see it as contributing to secessionist attempts to be accepted internationally as a 'political reality' (He 1993: 6–7).

Whatever the origins of Lee's idea of *Gemeinschaft*, it certainly parallels Peng's belief that a political community is built by the subjective identification of individuals, rather than objective criteria imposed by ethnicity. In this respect, it is intimately linked by Lee to the idea of popular sovereignty. In a speech to a KMT conference on 30 December 1994, Lee thus juxtaposed the two concepts, explaining that the function of popular sovereignty is to stir up the consciousness of every citizen to be 'master of his own country' (*guojia*), while the cohesion of the *Gemeinschaft* arises from integrating the free will of the individual with the wealth and good of society (CT, 31 December 1994).

Working against social cleavages are the natural tendencies for individuals with different origins to overcome their prejudices. As new generations have grown up without the experiences of the Chinese civil war or the first years of the ROC occupation of Taiwan, such natural tendencies can be seen in phenomena such as the increase in marriages between 'natives' and 'outsiders'. This has been especially true amongst those receiving higher education (Wang 1993).[10] As for language, whereas in the past native Taiwanese who reached the level of higher education were more likely to identify with China and speak Mandarin, the process has gradually become less unidirectional. Younger 'outsiders' have also felt a natural need to use the Taiwanese dialect for everyday living and work purposes. Ambitious 'outsider' politicians, such as James Soong, have even mastered the Southern Fujian dialect for use when addressing the public.

Rather than develop any kind of exclusive conception of Taiwanese nationality according to origins, there has been an effort by the two main parties to encourage these tendencies towards social integration. Among other measures taken by the state to prevent the perpetuation of provincial divisions down the generations has been the end of recording the provincial origins of individuals in the census since 1990. Identity cards and passports have also been changed to record the actual province where one was born as one's place of birth, rather than the previously used 'China'. Second-generation mainlanders thus have 'Taiwan' as their place of birth, rather than a mainland province listed as place of origin. State resources have also been directed away from cultivating Chinese nationalism and directed more towards sponsoring a cultural identity that, although native to Taiwan, is pluralistic and creative. An important element of this has been a catharsis of the divisive mythology of the first years of ROC rule in Taiwan. In early 1992 a report on the 228 Incident was delivered by a committee set up by the president to research newly released documents. This was followed by an apology to relatives of victims of the incident by Hau Pei-tsun as premier, and a competition for the erection of a 228 Memorial in Taipei's New Park, since renamed '228 Park'. The resulting edifice consists of three juxtaposed cubes surmounted by a high pinnacle which represents 'Taking a spirit of independence to identify with the land, constructing a *Gemeinschaft*, so as to avoid tragedy occurring again' (EY 1995: 6). When Lee Teng-hui unveiled this monument on 28 February 1995, he announced that the country (*guojia*) had entered a completely new era and defined the tasks of the future as developing *xiangtu* culture, identifying with and loving 'this piece of land', and 'managing great Taiwan', so as to 'bring together a *Gemeinschaft* of shared sorrows and joys' (Lee 1995a).

The mass media have also played a part in this process of coming to terms with the past. Soap operas and films replaying the events of 1947 have been produced, while cultural policy has been further adjusted so that sponsorship of television, film, opera, puppet theatre and the fine arts has come to focus much more on Taiwan's history, traditions and innovations. Exhibitions and performances sponsored by the CCPD now aim to stimulate interest in what remains of Taiwan's aboriginal cultures and in the arts and crafts of Taiwan. Such developments are mirrored in the private sector, where the 1995 centenary of the Treaty of Shimonoseki provided the occasion for a reassessment of the past, with a flood of books and articles celebrating and analysing the contributions of Taiwanese intellectuals to local culture under the Japanese occupation.

If state policy is now to encourage the development of an integrated society for Taiwan, there are also factors which militate against the growth of an exclusive and narrow definition of what it means to be 'Taiwanese'. Important amongst these is the voice of what the authorities have categorised as the nine non-Han 'tribes' said to be the descendants of aboriginal peoples who preceded settlers from the Chinese mainland. The largest of these is the Ami, numbering 122,800, while the smallest are the Saisiyat and the Yami, both numbering 4,200 (*ROC Yearbook* 1993: 34). Under the state's previous policy of cultural homogenisation, these peoples were identified by anthropologists as culturally inferior and in need of 'assistance' to establish national bonds and to prepare them for the recapture of the mainland. The resulting alienation led to poor living conditions, bad education, urban drift, widespread alcoholism, prostitution and cultural commodification for the satisfaction of tourist voyeurs.

When the issue of minority representation in parliamentary bodies came before the National Assembly in 1991 and 1992, the tribes formed a 'Taiwan Aboriginal Rights Promotion Association'. One of their major demands was to insist that their collective name should be 'rectified' from the pejorative 'mountain compatriots' (*shan bao*) to the more acceptable 'aboriginals' (*yuan zhu min*) (IMP, 9 May 1992). When the KMT, after some prevarication, finally conceded to this demand, it revealed a new confidence and flexibility over defining Taiwan's identity in terms of plural historical and ethnic origins. Equally significant, however, was that the DPP supported the campaign, indicating that it too is committed to a pluralistic vision of society rather than a narrow Taiwanese nationalism. For the aboriginal peoples, Taiwanese chauvinism is as much of a threat as Han chauvinism (Fu 1993). By allowing a shift to take place in the mythological origins of Taiwan away from the Fujianese and towards those who now live on the absolute margins of society, the DPP was signalling a healthy decentring for Taiwan's rising, but not necessarily pluralistic, opposition culture.

By the early 1990s, then, the mainstream factions of both the KMT and the DPP had come to accept that the nationalist linkage of ethnicity with the state was not desirable for Taiwan's developing democracy. What defines one's membership of Taiwan's *Gemeinschaft* is not when you came to the island, nor what ethnic group you belong to, but whether you yourself want to identify with Taiwan (Lee 1994). It was thus that, in his new year speech for 1995, Lee Teng-hui added the soothing of ethnic tensions to his list of achievements, along with raising Taiwan's international status and locating sovereignty in the people. Yet if an alternative, post-nationalist, conception of Taiwan's political community has been generated by this policy combination, this has important implications for how China itself is to be identified. This is because, by breaking the political link between Chinese identity and the state, the way is left open for cultural, ethnic and economic ties with China to be developed without entailing the imperative for political amalgamation between the two sides of the Taiwan Strait.

THE LIVING TREE

Rather than the nation-building activities of Chinese nationalists having resulted in the kind of monolithic nation-state intended, attempts to cultivate loyalty to the Chinese nation have resulted in a complex identity which can be categorised into at least four 'nations'.[11] First, there is the nation which is composed of all the individuals living under the PRC's jurisdiction, which includes those identified by Beijing as Han, as well as those categorised as 'national minorities'. Second, there is the nation as defined by unofficial Chinese ethnic nationalism, which excludes the 'national minorities' and only extends to the Han (Gladney 1990). Third, there is the population of the PRC plus the 'compatriots' (*tongbao*) of Taiwan, Hong Kong and Macao, which will be called 'Greater China' below. Finally, there are people of Chinese descent who live in other states. These are the 'Chinese overseas' who do not think that foreign citizenship precludes political and cultural attachment to China (Wang 1981).

Within this ramification of relationships a good degree of latitude can be found for forging a post-nationalist identity for Taiwan. The first step, however, is to work towards making it clear that Taiwan is not under the legal jurisdiction of Beijing. This can be seen in Taipei's attempts to define the meaning of 'China' in a way that is compatible with the island's domestic developments and its foreign policy aims. The first formal step in this process was the struggle to define 'China' for official use when the NUC was called on to clarify the concept during the split in the KMT over the call for a 'one China, one Taiwan' policy. The resulting document, 'The Meaning of "One China"', consists of three paragraphs. In effect, these do not do much more than elaborate on Huang Kun-huei's ambiguous 1991 interpretation of the *Guidelines for National Unification*, as meaning that Taiwan and the mainland are 'one country, two areas' (Huang 1991: 3). First, that there is only one China is argued on the grounds that such is the claim made by the two contending states:

> Both sides of the Taiwan Straits agree that there is only one China. However, the two sides of the Straits have different opinions as to the meaning of 'one China'. To Peking [Beijing], 'one China' means 'the People's Republic of China (PRC)', with Taiwan to become a 'Special Administrative Region' after unification. Taipei, on the other hand, considers 'one China' to mean the Republic of China (ROC), founded in 1911 and with *de jure* sovereignty over all of China. The ROC, however, currently has jurisdiction only over Taiwan, Penghu, Kinmen and Matsu. Taiwan is part of China, and the Chinese mainland is part of China as well.
>
> (NUC 1992: Par. 1)

It is then argued that China is, in fact, politically divided, but that this need not militate against its ultimate future oneness because this division is only a 'temporary' historical phenomenon:

Since 1949, China has been temporarily divided, and each side of the Taiwan Straits is administered by a separate political entity. This is an objective reality that no proposal for China's unification can overlook.

(NUC 1992: Par. 2)

The final paragraph deals with what is to be done about this division of China by referring back to the three-stage process encapsulated in the *Guidelines for National Unification*.

What 'The Meaning of "One China"' achieves, then, is to reiterate that China can be divided, at least temporarily, into distinct 'political entities'. This is a far cry from the former ROC position that only one state can be recognised as the Chinese state. It can also be contrasted with Beijing's position as restated in the White Paper *The Taiwan Question and Reunification of China*, issued by the State Council of the PRC. This document is vehement that:

There is only one China in the world, Taiwan is an inalienable part of China and the seat of China's central government is in Beijing. This is a universally recognised fact as well as the premise for a peaceful settlement of the Taiwan question.

(Taiwan Affairs Office 1993: 13)

Taipei's response to this document reveals just how divergent the visions of China promoted by both sides have become. In a document released by the MAC under the title *There Is No 'Taiwan Question' There Is Only a 'China Question'*, 'China' is defined in a woolly fashion as a term that 'connotes multifaceted geographical, political, historical, and cultural meanings' (MAC 1993: 4). This amorphous entity is then clearly distinguished from the 'political entities' that have come to exist within it, when it is stated that: 'The Republic of China was founded in 1912. It maintained sovereignty over the territories that had been governed by a succession of Chinese governments down through the ages. The international community in general called these territories simply "China"' (MAC 1993: 1).

Within this loosely defined China, it is held that Taiwan and the mainland are indeed both 'Chinese' territory. But it is also emphasised that, 'It is an undeniable fact that the two have been divided and ruled separately since 1949' (MAC 1993: 4).

What is crucially important about making this distinction between China and the political entities that exist within it is the implication that there can be two legitimate governments within China. This is implied most clearly when it is stated that: 'Although the Chinese communists have enjoyed jurisdiction over the mainland area, they cannot be equated with China. They can in no way represent China as a whole, much less serve as the "sole legal government of all Chinese people"' (MAC 1993: 4). The Communists, then, can serve as a legal government, but only over a part of the Chinese people. A subtle shift has occurred so that the argument is no longer concerned with the right of the PRC to represent China in international society. It is now about the right of the PRC to represent the *whole* of the Chinese nation, of which Taiwan is a part. The implication is thus that there can be one China and two Chinese states.

Having loosened up the concept of China and accepted that the PRC and the ROC may have equal rights to represent parts of the Chinese nation, the imperative of national unification is then most blatantly shed when the document states:

> We believe that the value of national unification lies not in a single jurisdiction over China's territories but in enabling the people on the Chinese mainland to enjoy the same democratic, free, and equitably prosperous lifestyle as is enjoyed by the people in the Taiwan area.
>
> (MAC 1993: 14)

In other words, the principle of a single Chinese state becomes of secondary importance to the nature of the body politic as judged by the quality of life it can deliver.

Right at the beginning of Taiwan's reforms, Chiang Ching-kuo made a similar point about the need for the mainland to become more like Taiwan as a precondition for unification when he insisted that unification could only take place under the Three Principles of the People (Jiang 1986: 17). As democratisation got under way in Taiwan, however, this began to take on increasingly radical implications. By the time of Lee Teng-hui's reappointment as president in 1990, a stark contrast existed between the 'Taiwan experience' and the post-Tiananmen conditions of the mainland. It was in this context that his inauguration speech made the implementation of political democracy and a free economic system two of the conditions Beijing would have to meet before the process of unification could begin (Lee 1990b: 8). In March 1991, these preconditions for unification were enshrined in the first comprehensive statement of Taipei's position on unification, the *Guidelines for National Unification* (EY 1991: Sec. 2, Art. 1, Clause 3). The premise that people would only be loyal to a state if it offered the right political and social conditions had once been used by Dang Wai writers to lambast the KMT's Chinese nationalism. By the early 1990s it had come to lie at the heart of the KMT's mainland policy.

That what amounts to a theory of self-determination has to be hidden by such vagaries is in the main due to the constraints imposed by the PRC's attachment to the one-China principle. Yet it would be wrong to understand the idea of a Chinese entity behind the various political entities proposed by Taipei on this basis alone. It rather draws our attention to the fact that many people in Taiwan do perceive there to be considerable benefits that they can accrue from exploiting their links with a supra-state Chinese community, while maintaining the political independence of their government in relationship to the PRC. The administration, business people eager to exploit the economic reforms of the PRC, and individuals with family or sentimental connections with China, do not wish to forgo these benefits. An example that indicates the existence of such sentiments is the indignant reaction to a move by Beijing, in 1992, to introduce a rule that household registration certificates had to be shown by Taiwan residents when applying for permits to visit the mainland. The reaction in Taiwan was characterised by complaints not only from ROC officials, but also in the press and media, that the *mainland* authorities were departing from the one-China policy by treating residents of Taiwan 'like foreigners'.

It seems that the consolidation of different political systems on each side of the Strait was not supposed to put in jeopardy the special place of Taiwan within a wider Chinese identity. It will be shown below how the Lee administration has attempted to preserve the links with the various communities within this identity while maintaining the political independence of Taiwan.

THE ROC AND THE CHINESE OVERSEAS

The relationship of the ROC with people of Chinese descent living outside Chinese territory has always been one of great political and emotional significance. Chinese nationalism first took root in the communities of emigrants from the Qing dynasty, and it was among such communities in Japan and the United States that Sun Yat-sen established his first revolutionary power base and organisation. It is thus that, even today, people of Chinese descent living overseas are still acknowledged by the KMT to be the 'mothers of the revolution'. Arising out of the ethnic criteria of early Chinese nationalism, anyone whose ancestry can be traced back to China is referred to as one of the 'overseas Chinese' (*hua qiao*). Moreover, anyone who is of direct Chinese descent was considered a citizen of the ROC entitled to representation in parliamentary chambers. It is according to this criterion that the ROC can claim that there are some 35.5 million 'overseas Chinese' in the world, 86.27 per cent of them in Asia, 10.51 per cent in the Americas, and the rest scattered over the globe (*ROC Yearbook* 1994: 185).

With great financial resources and extensive business networks people of Chinese descent living overseas continue to be seen as an important economic and political resource by both Taipei and Beijing. For the former, international isolation gives the Chinese communities throughout the world an added significance in the process of building international links and putting indirect pressure on other states to alter their attitudes towards Taiwan. It is not then surprising that Lee Teng-hui has repeatedly signalled that he intends to continue to struggle for their support and has insisted that the relationship between the ROC and the 'overseas Chinese' is unbreakable (UDN, 2 April 1992).

In addition to the economic potential of people of Chinese descent living throughout the world and the emotional appeals of Chinese nationalism, their political representation in the ROC is also central to maintaining the constitutional appearance that the government in Taipei is more than just the government of Taiwan. During the process of reform, the issue of their representation thus became central to the constitutional debate and emotional appeals were made for the privilege to be maintained. One 800-name petition from eighty-six groups in Hong Kong and Macao, expressing scepticism about Lee Teng-hui's anti-independence stance, was even presented written in blood.[12] One article in the KMT organ, the *Central Daily News*, went so far as to point out that the Chinese overseas never forget their roots, even using chopsticks to eat hamburgers and ice cream. Such people, it argued, identify so strongly with China that some thirty million of them should be more entitled to political participation in the ROC than those who advocate Taiwanese independence ('Kuaizi Wenhua' 1992).

As well as being anathema to the DPP, however, the idea that all people of Chinese descent should have political rights in the ROC presents a number of practical problems for Taiwan. How, for example, can a consistent concept of citizenship for individuals overseas be arrived at when ROC law says that all citizens must pay taxes and do military service? Moreover, revisions to the Election and Recall Law made in 1991 state that voters must live in a constituency for at least six months before gaining the right to vote there. Then there is the theoretical possibility that a tacit recognition of dual nationality in ROC law (which allows any 'Chinese' person to become a voter in Taiwan) could result in an unmanageably large overseas electorate outnumbering the population of Taiwan itself. This could even be manipulated by the PRC to interfere in Taiwan's domestic affairs. Last, but by no means least, there is the problem of arousing suspicion and hostility among the governments of countries possessing large Chinese populations, especially many South-east Asian states. Despite vocal support for overseas Chinese representation in

Taiwan, therefore, there was also much strong opposition to attempts to enshrine their rights during the reform process. The DPP was bitterly opposed to allowing them to vote in elections.

One solution for the Lee administration would have been to make a clean break and annul overseas Chinese representation. Instead, the principle of overseas Chinese political representation was put into law under the articles added to the constitution in 1991. According to these articles, twenty overseas Chinese nationals shall be elected to the National Assembly and another six shall be elected to the Legislative Yuan. This commitment was again reaffirmed by the National Assembly in 1992, when it adopted the eighteenth additional article, which stipulated that the state shall accord to Chinese nationals abroad their rights to political participation. These rights are again reiterated by the first and third of the final ten additional articles. However, what distinguishes the rights of the overseas Chinese from those of residents of the 'free area' is that, just as with members of the 'nation-wide' (i.e. mainland) constituency, they are not actually entitled to vote. Instead, they have representatives appointed according to the proportion of votes gained by parties contesting elections held in Taiwan itself.

Because this representation of the overseas Chinese is more symbolic than real, the DPP can live with it. Because it also maintains the appearance that parliamentary institutions represent the will of all 'China', it can be used to smooth the ruffled feathers of Chinese nationalists, wherever they might be located. Such a device cannot be used, however, when it comes to the rights of the overseas Chinese to vote in presidential elections. In this case, individuals are either enfranchised or they are not. Because direct election of the president has the additional significance of being a symbolic reaffirmation of Taiwan's *de facto* independence for the DPP, the issue of overseas Chinese participation became particularly controversial when enmeshed with the domestic debate over whether an elected president will be a 'president of Taiwan' or a 'president of China'.

The compromise solution to this issue was proposed in 1994 by the KMT working group on constitutional reform, central to which was a redefinition of what 'overseas Chinese' means. This involved moving away from a definition in terms of purely ethnic criteria in favour of a legal conception which only enfranchises people of Chinese descent overseas who have previously been residents of the Taiwan area and who have registered their household in Taiwan at the time of voting (UDN, 14 May 1994). As the Ministry of Foreign Affairs claimed that only around 180,000 Chinese people overseas actually carry ROC passports, this would reduce the number of voters to an acceptable figure (UDN, 14 May 1994).

Article 3 of the ten additional articles finally enshrined this legal status by stating that 'citizens of the free area of the Republic of China residing abroad' could return to vote in elections. The legal definition of 'overseas Chinese' that was arrived at thus brings their status closer to that of expatriates from western democracies.

Yet this legal redefinition of the status of the overseas Chinese does not preclude the cultivation of other kinds of relationships. For many years both the ROC and the PRC have had special agencies to cultivate links with people of Chinese descent living overseas, and these continue to operate. The ROC's Overseas Chinese Affairs Commission (OCAC) was established in 1926 to serve this purpose, and under Lee Teng-hui this organ has continued its work of fostering cultural and economic ties, and providing information and consular services for people of Chinese descent wishing to visit and engage in activities in the ROC. The OCAC claims to reach out to 9,134 registered overseas Chinese associations throughout the world, holds world conferences and facilitates travel to the ROC for educational, cultural, political and business purposes. In fiscal 1993, it provided US$7.7 million to its cultural and educational branch (*ROC Yearbook* 1994: 184), as well as subsidising various television and radio broadcasting stations overseas, and publishing and distributing journals and newspapers.

In competing with the PRC for the loyalty of people of Chinese descent living overseas, financial aid and other forms of assistance are offered by the OCAC. Donations and loans are made to help victims of natural and man-made disasters, such as the Los Angeles riots of 1992 and typhoons in the United States. The ROC constitution in fact stipulates that the state has a duty to foster and protect the development of the economic enterprises of the Chinese overseas. To further this aim, in 1988 the OCAC joined with the Ministry of Finance to establish the Overseas Chinese Credit Guarantee Fund with a sum of US$35.3 million. Between the end of May 1989 and the end of December 1992, 323 guaranty projects requiring total security deposits of US$48 million were approved.

Encouraging investment by the Chinese overseas in Taiwan is also a priority task for the OCAC. It claims that between 1952 and 1992 some 2,326 overseas Chinese investment projects in Taiwan were approved, totalling US$2.49 billion. In the early 1990s the pace of this investment was increasing dramatically, reaching a peak of US$1.6 billion in 1994 (GSB, 4 June 1996). Visits, seminars and conferences are frequently held by the OCAC to promote economic development in Taiwan and trade with the Chinese overseas. The World-wide Overseas Chinese Economic and Trade Conference in May 1992 was attended by 893 Chinese from overseas, originating from forty-nine countries and regions. The United

World Chinese Commercial Bank has an overseas service department which helps the Chinese overseas to apply for investment and to provide assistance for purchasing real estate (*ROC Yearbook* 1994: 192).

Although the overseas Chinese have been disenfranchised in Taiwan's domestic politics, then, the state machinery set up to cultivate links with a world-wide Chinese community is maintained and expanded. What holds this identity together is hard to define. That there is a sense of Chineseness which extends beyond political borders, though, is certainly a sentiment shared by other Chinese statesmen in the region. As Singapore's Lee Kuan-yew asked a conference of Chinese entrepreneurs from all over the world in Hong Kong in November 1993, the Anglo-Saxons network, so do the Jews, the Hindus and the Muslims, so why not the Chinese? Moreover, those who see themselves as Chinese have certain advantages when operating within the PRC where personal connections are often a substitute for rule and regulation (FEER, 2 December 1993: 17). Perhaps Lee Teng-hui and Lien Chan were responding to such overtures when they visited Singapore for their 'holidays' in early 1994, and, among other things, discussed the joint development of the PRC's Hainan Island with Lee Kuan-yew. Such economic transactions between Chinese states draws attention to another of the Chinese 'nations' that have come to exist, that of 'Greater China'.

TAIWAN AND GREATER CHINA

That the idea of a Chinese community beyond the state holds advantages for both the ROC and the PRC is particularly evident in the development of what has come to be called 'Greater China'. Alluding to the development of economic ties between the Chinese mainland, Hong Kong and Macao, Taiwan and sometimes even Singapore, the idea of a 'Chinese Common Market', a 'Chinese community' and a 'Chinese economic grouping' began to be floated in Taiwan and Hong Kong from 1979 onwards. Since then, the wider implications for economic integration have been explored in English- and Chinese-reading circles, through journals, conferences, and academic and business groupings (Harding 1993).

Underlying the development of the idea of a Greater China has been the rapid increase in trade and investment between its constituent economies during the period of post-Mao economic reforms in the PRC. Because economic links between Taiwan and the Chinese mainland have had to be conducted through a third territory, Hong Kong has come to play the role of entrepot in a dynamic triangular relationship. This started to develop when private individuals from Taiwan began to trade with the mainland in

1979 through Hong Kong. A small number of Taiwan business people also broke the law to make direct investments on the other side of the Strait. When Taipei lifted the ban on residents from Taiwan visiting the mainland, a surge of business activity followed.

At the start of the 1980s exports to the Chinese mainland accounted for only 1.22 per cent of Taiwan's global exports and 0.5 per cent of imports. After indirect travel between the two sides of the Strait was liberalised, the resulting pressure led to a gradual relaxation by Taipei of its restrictions on doing indirect business in the mainland. In June 1989, a process of liberalising the indirect importation of goods from the mainland into Taiwan was initiated, and in October 1990 the go-ahead was given for Taiwan's businessmen to register with the ROC government their investments and operations on a list of approved items. In December 1991, banks in Taiwan were allowed to conduct financing arrangements for exports originating from the mainland, and in January 1993 guidelines were drawn up to liberalise the import of industrial technology to Taiwan from the mainland (Kao 1993). By the end of 1992 only 103 items (1.3 per cent of the total) were under control for export to the mainland, being mainly high-technology products restricted by COCOM, and rare plants and animals.

According to statistics from the Hong Kong customs and the ROC Ministry of Finance, the proportion of Taiwan's exports going to the mainland market rose from 2 per cent in 1987 to 16.34 per cent in 1993 (UDN, 28 January 1994). The figures began to soar in the early 1990s. According to the ROC's own figures, aggregate trade between Taiwan and Hong Kong rose from US$14.37 billion in 1991 to US$17.2 billion in 1992, around 40 per cent of which constituted indirect cross-Strait trade (MAC 1993a: 5–6). By 1994, Taiwan's trade surplus with Hong Kong had reached US$19.7 billion. The process of economic integration was also rapid in terms of investment flows. PRC officials estimate that by the end of 1992 a total of US$8.9 billion of intended investment by 10,000 Taiwan businesses in the mainland had been approved (Kao 1993: 8). By the end of 1992, Taiwan had overtaken Japan to become the second largest source of foreign direct investment (FDI) for the PRC, following Hong Kong (Ash and Kueh 1993: 730). The total flow of capital from Taiwan to the Chinese mainland, including purchase of property and type-B stocks, expenditures by Taiwan residents in the mainland and remittances to relatives and wages paid to mainland workers in Taiwan (illegal and legal) was estimated to be US$20 billion as of November 1992.

This was offset by a US$17 billion trade surplus to make a total capital deficit of US$3 billion. Amongst this capital flow, investment in manufacturing has grown rapidly. By the end of April 1996 Taipei had given permission for 11,392 investments in the mainland, at a total value of US$6.1 billion. The PRC puts the figure much higher, at US$24.3 billion (GSB, 15 May 1996). With many investors obviously preferring to circumvent restrictions and red tape by not bothering to register with Taipei, and allowing for the likelihood of inflation of the PRC statistics for propaganda purposes, the true amount is probably somewhere in between. Another trend in this investment flow has been an expansion northwards from the originally favoured southern coastal provinces of Guangdong and Fujian, to give Shanghai the highest concentration (US$90 million) and Zhejiang province the highest overall total (US$180 million) by the middle of 1996 (GSB, 15 May 1996).

A number of factors underlie this synergy between the economies of Taiwan and the Chinese mainland. First of all, with labour and land costs soaring in Taiwan, the island's businesses have been attracted to the mainland by its abundance of cheap labour and land, and the freedom from environmentalist pressures that are mounting in Taiwan (Ash and Kueh 1993: 711–12). Moreover, many alternative local sites for investment have become less attractive as the scale of Taiwan investment in ASEAN economies has meant that wages have risen there too (Luo and Howe 1993: 753). Anti-Chinese sentiments also remain a negative factor for doing business in such countries. There has thus been a wholesale transfer of labour-intensive and light industries, such as electrical engineering, footwear, plastics and textile production, from Taiwan to the mainland (Ash and Kueh 1993: 738). Not only are Taiwan's entrepreneurs attracted by the prospect of doing business in the environment of a familiar culture and language, but companies can make profits 10–15 per cent higher than they would be able to reap in Taiwan (Luo and Howe 1993: 757).

On the grounds of complementarity, economic integration could indeed lead to great benefits for all sides. Not only would Taiwan's entrepreneurs enjoy access to unlimited cheap labour and primary resources, but they might also gain from access to the PRC's lead in fields such as space technology, microbiology, medicine, optics and nuclear engineering, as well as the mainland's heavy industrial base (Kao 1993: 25–6; Luo and Howe 1993: 765). Taiwan's lead in areas such as computer manufacturing, electrical appliances and information technology, and its expertise in industrialisation and distribution, might be of use to the PRC in developing fields such as electronics, telecommunications and engineering (Luo and Howe 1993: 765).

The ties that are developing between the economies of Greater China are not analogous to those of common markets such as the European Union and ASEAN, however. Trade and investment activities are rather the result of the internationalisation of manufacturing production and are geared towards re-export to third countries (Ash and Kueh 1993: 742).

This can be seen in the underlying structural transformation of the pattern of Taiwan's overseas trade as a whole. This originally took the form of a triangular relationship in which Taiwan imported essential components from Japan and assembled them for the US market. Liberalisation of cross-Strait relations enabled this to develop into a double triangle. In this configuration, essential components are still imported from Japan, only now they are re-exported to the mainland market via Hong Kong, many for finishing and re-export to world markets, especially the USA. In 1993, Taiwan's trade surplus with Hong Kong thus stood at US$16.7 billion, the highest ever with any single trade partner, while its deficit with Japan had boomed to a record US$14.2 billion (UDN, 11 January 1994).

In this respect, the resources of the Chinese mainland have proved to be useful for Taiwan's investors and traders as a target for FDI aimed at processing materials from Taiwan for re-export to world markets. This movement of manufacturing and investment amounts to a tactic which enables Taiwan's exporters to avoid the handicaps imposed on their exports by the high value of the New Taiwan Dollar, which between 1985 and the early 1990s had risen by 40 per cent against the greenback. Businesses are also keen to make use of PRC export quotas and preferential tariffs under its most favoured nation status, especially for exporting to the European and North American markets. It is thus that Taiwan's investors in the mainland even began to join their counterparts in Hong Kong to finance lobbying activities to secure MFN status for the PRC's trade with the United States (Kao 1993).

With Taiwan being under heavy pressure from the United States to reduce its trade surplus, and with its domestic costs on the increase, it is not surprising that the idea of a Greater China has at times been enthusiastically floated in the ROC. In December 1991, Hsui Sheng-fa (Xu Shengfa), a member of the KMT's CSC and chairman of Taiwan's National Federation of Industries, told a conference on the East Asian economy that the tendency of the times is for Taiwan, Hong Kong and mainland China to form a Greater China natural economic zone (*da Zhongguo ziran jingji qu*). Looking ahead to what he saw as inevitable direct contacts between the two sides of the Strait after Hong Kong falls under PRC sovereignty in 1997, he recommended speeding up joint development of the southern coastal region of the mainland before that time. He even went so far as to suggest that the Chinese overseas could be brought into this entity, thus extending it to Vietnam, Thailand, Malaysia, Singapore, Indonesia and the Philippines ('Zhenghe . . .' 1991).

Although high-level sources in the KMT have been reported as claiming that a Greater China economic zone is still only an ideal, they have not ruled out the possibility of such a formation under stage two of the

Guidelines for National Unification (UDN, 7 December 1991). An annual report by the Mainland Economy Research Institute of the Ministry of Economic Affairs in March 1992 went much further by claiming that a Great Chinese Economic Sphere (*da zhonghua jingji quan*) does in fact already exist. The report recommended that Taiwan's businessmen should concentrate their activities in the southern coastal area of the mainland with its ports facing Taiwan, thus enabling a rapid pull-out if necessary. It was optimistic that such economic development would speed up the process of change in the PRC, which in turn would lead to the reforms necessary to complete stage one of the *Guidelines* (CT, 24 March 1992). This strategy came to be called the 'westward policy' (*xi jin zhengce*).

It was in the same month as this report that Lee Teng-hui told the Third Plenum of the Thirteenth Central Committee of the KMT that he was impatient to get constitutional reform completed and take a new direction in mainland policy. He hoped that this could go beyond both the two sides of the Strait and the KMT and CCP, and open up the possibility of co-operation and mutual assistance between Taiwan, Hong Kong, the Chinese mainland, and 'Chinese people the whole world over', so as to 'improve the lives of the whole body of the people of the Chinese race' (CT, 14 March 1992). In May the following year, Lee told a conference of lawyers that, following the international flourishing of Taiwan's private enterprise, the mainland's adoption of an open development policy, and the intermediary trade activities of Hong Kong between the two sides of the Strait, a Chinese people's (*hua ren*) mutually interdependent trade co-operation relationship was in formation (UDN, 4 May 1993). Again, in the same month, a meeting between the ROC National Federation of Industries and the Hong Kong General Chamber of Commerce in Taipei saw the signing of a memorandum of understanding on bilateral co-operation and announced plans to invite PRC officials to their future meetings (in Hong Kong). This was greeted by the local press as a great step forward in forging a Chinese common market (FCJ, 7 May 1993).

Lee's enthusiasm for the concept of a community of co-operation among Chinese people, despite political divisions, was echoed in November 1993 by presidential adviser Tao Pai-chuan (Tao Baichuan), who expressed his enthusiasm about the future of a Chinese 'community of shared destiny' (Tao 1993). For Tao, this would not only be good for Taiwan but would even 'save the country, save the people' (*jiu guo jiu min*) by extending membership to all the 'countries' and 'political entities' of the Chinese nation (*zhonghua minzu*). While these entities would retain their sovereignty and territorial integrity, they could hold regular meetings and create a permanent secretariat to resolve problems and bring members closer towards unification. Tao envisioned that this could happen on the hundredth anniversary of division and claimed the support of Singapore's Lee Kuan-yew for such a plan (UDN, 3 November 1993). For the ROC, then, the prospect of co-operation between Chinese which will give the region 'a place among the world's major economic powers' is an economically attractive proposition. In the eyes of the Mainland Affairs Council, 'from a long-term point of view, such a proposition has considerable advantages' (MAC 1993a: 10).

THE LIMITS OF FLEXIBILITY

To understand the limitations of the Lee administration's policy towards the evolving Chinese identity, it is necessary to assess how the political implications of the pull of the mainland Chinese economy can be balanced by the development of Taiwan's own sense of identity, or *Gemeinschaft*. From what integration theorists call a functionalist perspective, it might be expected that increasing transactions between the two sides will lead to a qualitative change in the political relationship through a number of processes. First of all, there is the possibility that Taiwan could become over-dependent on the booming PRC economy and thus be forced to make political concessions through economic pressures of some kind. Then there is the possibility that there could be some kind of 'spill-over' effect from commercial and social transactions into areas of bureaucratic and ultimately political co-operation.

The fear that Taiwan might be becoming over-dependent on the mainland economy arises from suspicions that the island's industries are being 'hollowed out'. This is supposed to be caused by the relocation of firms to the mainland, leading to a possible transfer of sectors of industry and a neglect of research and development activities in Taiwan (Kao 1993: 9). Moreover, investment in the mainland could help the PRC economy surge ahead of Taiwan's in world markets as Taiwan-based companies enjoy the cheap costs of the mainland (Kao 1993: 18–19). Evidence that this is happening includes the fact that the volume of PRC exports to the United States in 1992, at US$25.7 billion, took the edge over Taiwan's US$24.6 billion for the first time (GATT 1994). That Taiwanese dependence is likely to be a one-way affair is also supposed to be evidenced by the island's increasing trade surplus with the mainland, its relatively small size as the mainland economy continues to boom, and the ability of mainland firms to procure its imports from Taiwan from other sources (Kao 1993: 7). In the words of the MAC's Kao Koong-lian (Gao Konglian), 'It is clear, therefore, that both politically and economically, the Chinese Communists have everything to gain and nothing to lose from cross-Strait trade' (Kao 1993: 8).

Faced with this shifting economic balance, the Lee Teng-hui administration appears to have accepted fairly early on that it would be impossible,
and probably economically undesirable, to stop trade and investment in the
mainland. As Lee put it in 1991, 'In terms of actual interests, the future
development of Taiwan's economy cannot be confined solely to this small
island. We need the mainland as our hinterland to preserve and support us'
(Lee 1991b: 133). Even when the administration has made signals that it is
considering taking measures to restrict investments, the resulting
confusion and loss of confidence in business circles in Taiwan have led
to rapid backtracking. This was seen most clearly in August 1996 when,
during the crisis in political relations following the ROC presidential
election in March, Lee Teng-hui made a speech suggesting that quotas
should be placed on investments in the mainland (GSB, 15 August 1996).
Within a week the stock market had fallen 181 points, confusion reigned
within conglomerates such as Formosa Plastics and United Enterprises
over the future of massive infrastructure projects already agreed with
mainland partners, and economics experts asked why international
investors should bother to locate in Taiwan if links with the mainland
were going to be constricted. It was not long before Lee backtracked on his
earlier pronouncement about taking concrete measures, explaining that he
was just alerting investors to the risks to national security posed by their
activities (CT, 21 August 1996).

What such events show is that economic transactions across the Strait do
inevitably shape the actions of policy-makers in Taipei. Whether or not this
will lead to the kind of political spill-over that will result in political
integration between the two sides is another matter, however. Proponents of
functionalist theories of integration looking at the case of Europe concluded
some time ago that their assumptions had overlooked the fact that political
integration does not proceed by interaction between economic and
bureaucratic actors alone. It requires the addition of a deep philosophical
and ideological commitment to integration (Deutsch 1988: 277; Dougherty
and Pfaltzgraff 1990: 439–42; Haas 1967: 324). According to Deutsch,
before such a political 'take-off point' for integration can be reached, there
needs to be an unlikely congeries of conditions present, such as the
expectation that integration will lead to a better way of life, the presence of
an external threat, the arrival of a new generation on the scene, and a
coalition across society in favour of integration (Deutsch 1988: 277–9).

For integration theorists in mainland China, the formula 'one country,
two systems' can surmount the kinds of obstacles raised by western
integration theorists. Although by 1990 they were expressing doubts about
the political direction Lee Teng-hui was taking, they still proposed that
Beijing's overall policy was flexible enough to overcome unwillingness for

political integration in Taiwan (Guo 1990: 5–17). Even in early 1995, when low-level transactions began to falter, mainland experts were optimistic that negotiations would be able to take up the slack and continue to promote unification (*Qiushi* 1995: 9). Evidence to indicate a growth of sentiment in favour of political co-operation between the two sides of the Strait could always be found in phenomena such as pressure from inside Taiwan on the ROC government to permit direct links across the Strait or Taipei's moderation of its position on the one-China principle. It does in fact appear that, during the Strait crisis prior to the ROC presidential election, representatives of Taiwan businesses in the mainland did urge restraint. However, it is equally important to note that this was directed not only at Taipei but also at Beijing. If the Taiwan business community in the mainland is to have any role in cross-Strait political relations it may just as well be one constraining Beijing as one encouraging Taipei to develop direct links.

The double-edged political role of Taiwan businesses in the mainland can be seen through a closer analysis of how they are organised and what kind of relationships they have with the mainland authorities. Beijing actually passed regulations allowing Taiwan businesses to form associations in the mainland in 1988. The first one was not established until 24 March 1990, in Beijing, but by 1996 there were no less than thirty-two spread throughout the mainland. They enjoy close relationships with the Taiwan Affairs Office of the State Council, the security services, local government and party units. Their secretariats are even drawn from these sources. It might be expected, then, that such organisations would be increasingly subservient to Beijing's dictat. However, according to the PRC's own statistics, out of around 30,000 Taiwan enterprises in the mainland, only 10,000 are actually members of the associations. While reasons for membership include security, obtaining information and networking, one of the main reasons for not joining is precisely the fear held by business people of getting caught up in sensitive political matters. Most significant, however, is the fact that while Beijing is keen to have Taiwan businesses under the wing of its own organisations, when some entrepreneurs announced a plan to establish their own mainland-wide Taiwan business association in December 1994, this was opposed by the Taiwan Affairs Office and had to be dropped (Wang 1996). What such observations indicate is that rather than business transactions between the two sides of the Strait leading to a political will for integration, the business community could equally well be seen as a force for the exercise of constraint by all sides.

Further evidence for this can be seen in attempts by Beijing to mobilise the Taiwan business community in the mainland in the period just before the 1996 presidential election in Taiwan. While the PLA was shooting missiles and holding war games off the coast of Taiwan, Wang Daohan and Tang Shubei of ARATS toured Taiwan business associations throughout the mainland to explain that these actions were not aimed at Taiwan compatriots (UDN, 30 October 1995). Heads of all associations were invited to meetings at which the safety of investments was guaranteed and the link between Lee Teng-hui's ambitions and risks to their life and property was stressed (UDN, 2 September 1995). Statements by other spokespersons also made a point of specifying that military measures were being made necessary only by Lee Teng-hui's visit to Cornell and were not directed against the population of Taiwan, with whom relations would continue to be strengthened (Qian 1995; Shen 1996).

Throughout the period of greatest tension captains of Taiwan industry such as Hsui Sheng-fa, chairman of the China National Federation of Industry, continued to visit state organisations in the mainland, for example the Taiwan Affairs Office of the State Council. Head of Formosa Plastics Wang Yung-ch'ing (Wang Yongqing) and his brother Wang Yung-tsai (Wang Yongzai) continued to be wooed by the offer of beneficial investment conditions for large-scale projects at the height of the tension. The head of the Supreme People's Court, Ren Jianxian, urged courts to protect the rights of Taiwan investors and businesses in the mainland for the sake of unification, and the NPC expressed an intention to pass a law giving Taiwan investors the same treatment as natives of the mainland in areas such as buying tickets and accommodation.

That Beijing's efforts may have had some results was shown when, at the end of February 1996, lower-level representatives of Taiwan businesses who returned from the mainland for the Spring Festival felt the need to appeal to the ROC government to stop verbally provoking Beijing and urged whoever was going to be the new president to come up with a timetable for direct transportation and peace negotiations. Such figures appeared to be sympathetic to the constraints within which Beijing policy-makers had to work, including the possible challenge to Jiang Zemin from radicals and the military and the problem of reining in the increasingly autonomous provinces (UDN, 28 February 1996).

By the beginning of March, business leaders in Taiwan were increasingly vocal in their appeals for Taipei to exercise more restraint in its mainland policy. The director of the Nanchiao Chemical Company, for example, pointed out that Taiwan would have to be reasonable if it expected the mainland to be, and that US intervention would complicate the problem by provoking the mainland and making Taiwan a chip between the big powers. The chairman of the Taipei Chamber of Commerce felt the need to point out that the mainland would not need to use force so long as Taiwan did not declare independence. The president of Dah An Commercial Bank reminded the authorities that what the markets fear most is a lack of confidence. He also complained that careless talk by politicians could harm Taiwan's economy and asked how long the Central Bank of China could prop up the New Taiwan Dollar (UDN, 10 March 1996).

Such phenomena may indicate that Beijing can use the Taiwan business community to exert pressure on Taipei not to depart from the PRC interpretation of the one-China principle, but this is still a long way from the formation of the kind of political movement needed to achieve political integration between the two sides. On the contrary, such tactics could turn out to be a two-edged sword for Beijing. For example, during the meetings between the Taiwan business associations and the mainland authorities, members of the former also pleaded for Beijing to change its own policy. Military exercises had disrupted Taiwan's fishing industry and unsettled the island's markets, they complained, while it had become impossible to work while worrying about the safety of their families back home. They also reminded their hosts that because much of Taiwan's investment in the mainland is for the production of goods to be finished and re-exported from Taiwan to world markets, any threat to Taiwan's security would ultimately rebound on mainland exports (UDN, 16 March 1996).

These negative results of the campaign of intimidation led Beijing to try to clarify again that the mainland's actions were not actually aimed at the general population of Taiwan. A speech by Li Peng to the National People's Congress which praised the development of economic and cultural links across the Strait, for example, was seen in Taiwan as an attempt to establish a new sense of order (UDN, 6 March 1996); so were his remarks to the press conference afterwards, in which he held that the PLA exercises were only routine and that Beijing wants the people of Taiwan to live in peace and security (UDN, 18 March 1996). It was also at this time that Chinese and western officials began to reveal assurances that Beijing was not intending to attack or invade Taiwan (UDN, 13 March 1996). Perhaps there can be no more graphic illustration of the fundamental contradiction in Beijing's policy of 'peaceful unification' than these belated gestures of goodwill made to the people of Taiwan while the PLA forces were massing in the Strait.

Against functionalist understandings of cross-Strait integration, then, it can be argued that without the political will, unification is not likely to occur through a process of 'spill-over'. It can even be argued that transactions have led to anything but a meeting of hearts and minds. Some analysts have gone so far as to claim that visits by Taiwanese to the mainland have actually strengthened Taiwanese consciousness. As Chang

Mao-kuei (Zhang Maogui) of the Ethnology Institute of the ROC's Academia Sinica points out, this process is only encouraged by PRC policies that categorise all residents of Taiwan, whether of mainland or Taiwanese origin, as 'Taiwan compatriots' (*taibao*). Moreover, the experience of the gap in living styles and conditions between the two sides only serves to feed a belief that unification would bring disaster on the heads of the islanders. According to this view, visitors to the mainland are left with only one choice, to go back and identify with Taiwan; or, at the very least, to recognise that a deep division exists between the two sides (Zhang 1992).

The same negative effects may also result from better communications between the two sides. When, for example, Taipei's finance minister, Shirley Kuo, attended the May 1989 meeting of the ADB in Beijing, any propaganda coup hoped for by the mainland was quickly dissipated as images of a disordered and dissatisfied Chinese capital were broadcast throughout Taiwan. When the demonstrations came to their climax, a direct sound link between the demonstrators in Tiananmen Square and Taipei's Chiang Kai-shek Memorial Plaza was established. The crowd of mainly young people who gathered there could follow the events in Beijing right up to the traumatic moment when the movement was crushed.

If transactions do not automatically lead to political integration, then, the preservation of Taiwan's political autonomy in the sea of shifting Chinese identities will depend on the development of its own sense of community, or *Gemeinschaft* as Lee Teng-hui calls it. This, in part, can be understood as insuring against the possibility of the crystallisation of pro-integrationist tendencies into a movement in favour of some kind of political amalgamation across the Strait. Again, the events leading up to the 1996 presidential election in Taiwan provide some indication of how likely this is to occur.

The attempt to constrain Taipei's policies through the manipulation of public opinion in Taiwan is, of course, central to the policy of 'peaceful unification' with its origins in the united front doctrine. As early as 1984 Deng Xiaoping had expressed fears that Beijing was not doing enough to appeal to opinion in Taiwan outside the KMT (Deng 1984: 83–93). Following the reappointment of Lee Teng-hui in 1990, State President Yang Shangkun even told a Taiwan newspaper that the DPP should visit the mainland (CT, 25 September 1990). Around the same time, Jiang Zemin made a speech to the National United Front Work Conference which put new emphasis on giving access to non-KMT organisations in any negotiations between the two sides. This was heralded in the mainland press as an attempt to acknowledge Taiwan's social pluralisation and to deal with Lee Teng-hui's diplomacy (Dong 1990; Jiang 1990; *Liaowang*, 2 July 1990). That the DPP was to be included in negotiations was also stated by Jiang in secret conversations with Shen Jun-shan of Taipei's NUC, the transcripts of which have been obtained and published by the Hong Kong magazine *Jiushi niandai* (*Jiushi niandai* 1996: 8).

If Beijing was becoming increasingly aware that democratisation in Taiwan would mean that it would have to mobilise its resources to manipulate public opinion in the island in such a way as to exercise constraint against departures from the one-China principle, following the Cornell visit this developed into an attempt to drive a wedge between Lee Teng-hui and the voters through a combination of military actions and a propaganda barrage focused on Lee himself. If the aim of these tactics was to alienate public opinion from Lee Teng-hui, it certainly provided ammunition for the campaigns of Lee Teng-hui's rivals. Lin Yang-kang criticised Lee's response to Jiang Zemin's eight points on the grounds that he left the PRC no room to manoeuvre and began to call for an early thaw in cross-Strait relations for the sake of avoiding a military conflict (UDN, 10 April, 23 July 1995). New Party candidate Wang Chien-shien said that Lee's actions had revealed his true intentions of working towards rapid Taiwan independence (UDN 25 May, 7 October 1995).

Such views were repeated by the New Tong Meng Hui (see p. 83) (UDN, 28 August 1995), which held an 'I Am Chinese' march on 13 August 1995 to celebrate the fiftieth anniversary of the defeat of Japan and Taiwan's retrocession to China. The growing atmosphere of external threat and internal division provided the opening for an independent candidate, Chen Li-an, to join the race on a platform of reaching compromise between the two sides of the Strait. During the television presentations and debates held by the candidates in March 1996, the crisis was entirely attributed to Lee Teng-hui, and appeals were made to Beijing not to make the whole island suffer for his actions. The problem with this kind of tactic, however, is that while PRC support for domestic criticism of Lee Teng-hui may have scared some voters in the presidential election, it also allowed him to discredit his rival candidates by accusing them of being fellow travellers of Beijing (UDN, 14 February, 6, 7, 10 March 1996). The results of the election speak for themselves about the limitations in electoral politics of any possible alignment between Beijing and opponents to Lee Teng-hui within Taiwan.

SOVEREIGNTY IN THE KOO–WANG TALKS

Perhaps the breakdown of the functionalist model of integration is most clearly visible in the constraints at work when economic interaction has actually spilled over into political activity. The most prominent case here is the negotiations between Taiwan's SEF and its mainland counterpart, ARATS. These are the 'unofficial' organisations set up to resolve problems arising from the increasing economic and social activity between the two sides.

Rather than being a classic case of functional spill-over from bureaucratic transactions into political co-operation, the Koo–Wang negotiations seem instead to have borne out the sceptical view that when the political will is absent, functional activity is unlikely to lead to political amalgamation. From the start, preparatory talks had already put down guidelines to define the negotiations as 'unofficial' contacts. This involved stating that both sides considered the talks to be 'non-governmental, practical, economic and functional in nature' (SEF 1993: 40), and an agenda was drawn up which limited the discussion to 'practical' issues. These included cultural, academic, scientific and press exchanges, trade and commercial visits to Taiwan by individuals from the mainland, co-sponsorship by the SEF and ARATS of non-governmental economic exchange meetings, and discussions on joint efforts to exploit energy and natural resources (SEF 1993: 17–18).

Although some advances were made on all these fronts, the limits of co-operation became clear with the inclusion of four issues which inevitably would involve a compromise by at least one side over the issue of legal jurisdiction. These are guarantees for the security of Taiwan investments in the mainland, the repatriation of illegal immigrants, co-operation to suppress marine smuggling and piracy, and the handling of fishing disputes. On all these issues the achievement of some kind of *modus vivendi* is a matter of some urgency for Taiwan. Piracy and the security of the massive flow of investment to the mainland from Taiwan have naturally been causes for concern. As for illegal immigrants, between 1987 and 1993 the ROC authorities detained a total of 27,261 individuals from the mainland (MAC 1993b). Fishing disputes, tangled nets and collisions often gave rise to conflicts, sometimes leading to extortion, robbery and kidnap (MAC 1993c).

Koo Chen-fu hoped to be able to resolve these issues by creating a climate conducive to compromise on the issue of sovereignty by encouraging the PRC to develop a 'double-win' rather than 'zero-sum' relationship (SEF 1993: 51). Although Taipei may have been somewhat optimistic about the popularity of game theory in Beijing, the hope was that this would encourage the mainland team to 'put aside' (*ge zhi*) the issue of sovereignty. In effect, this meant that Taipei hoped to arrive at binding legal agreements between two bodies which had not yet recognised each other as legal entities, on the grounds that certain issues can be treated as 'non-political'. Aware of this fundamental contradiction in the SEF position, Wang Daohan could easily turn his opponent's argument back on itself by making it clear that if Taiwan wants to increase its enjoyment of the mainland market, then it should consider the 'non-political' question of what Beijing calls the 'three contacts', namely direct transportation, direct mail and direct trade.

Wang's point must be admitted as having validity in so far as it is inconsistent to argue that when issues are important to the PRC they are 'political', but when they are pressing for Taiwan, then sovereignty can be put aside. Yet this is what Koo Chen-fu insisted on, holding that transportation across the Strait would involve negotiations on navigation rights and the signing and implementation of air and sea transportation agreements. As such agreements would be difficult to accomplish without 'official' representation by both sides, agreements on a legal framework to open up the 'three contacts' would be impossible before Beijing recognised the government in Taipei as an equal 'political entity' with its own legal jurisdiction (MAC 1992).

These, then, are the bounds within which the following rounds of talks between the SEF and ARATS took place. When the two sides met on 2–7 November at the Fujian city of Xiamen, an attempt was made to sign a draft agreement on setting up agencies to resolve disputes and on each side accepting civil judgements made by the other side's courts. This failed when the mainland representative insisted that the PRC could not recognise the judicial sovereignty of Taiwan, and insisted on beginning direct flights (MAC 1993d: 1; UDN, 4, 5 November 1993). Although agreement was reached at the round of talks beginning on 31 January 1994, that 'political' issues should not be raised when practical issues are discussed, this formula proved of little use as definitions of 'practical' and 'political' continued to differ. The SEF took the position that talks on practical issues cannot avoid questions of legality. ARATS, however, insisted that because legality cannot be separated from political issues, the question of law should be avoided altogether (UDN, 2 February 1994).

When the two organisations met again in Beijing in the last week of March 1994, progress again stalled amidst sharp verbal exchanges between the two sides over issues of sovereignty and jurisdiction (FCJ, 1 April 1994). An idea of the strength of this deadlock over the implications of jurisdiction can be gained when it is realised that when the two sides were in discussion at Xiamen, there had been no less than five cases of air hijacking from the Chinese mainland to Taiwan that year alone. Even as the talks were taking place, this number was raised to six as a Xiamen Airlines Boeing 737 was hijacked to Taiwan's Chiang Kai-shek International Airport. No less than five similar incidents were to follow before the year was out. Yet both sides still failed to give way on the issue of jurisdiction.

As an example of political spill-over from the process of economic integration, then, the Koo–Wang talks were significant in so far as they set an agenda for future negotiations, established regular communications between the two sides of the Strait, and resolved a number of consular issues. However, despite these breakthroughs, the two sides had marked out the distance between their different positions on the political issues of sovereignty and jurisdiction. Here, each side accused the other of using issues of urgency as bargaining chips to gain concessions for political claims. Kao Koong-lian of the SEF thus laid the blame for the lack of progress in Singapore on the ARATS refusal to acknowledge his government's jurisdiction and the fact that Taiwan is a 'political entity' (UDN, 8 November 1993). Legal authorities in the PRC, meanwhile, claimed that the Taiwan side was politicising what should be non-political matters (Liu 1993).

HONG KONG 1997

Faced with such a stalemate, it would seem that only some external factor might break the political deadlock and lead to amalgamation across the Strait. The most obvious candidate is the transfer of Hong Kong to PRC sovereignty in July 1997. As well as being an entrepot for indirect trade and investment between the two sides of the Strait, Hong Kong has also become an important site for the overseas development of ROC banks. Moreover, as a transport hub, by 1993 there were on average 184 passenger flights per week between Taipei and Hong Kong, and also 100 cargo flights and fifty-two cargo freighter voyages per month. The number of individual travellers from Taiwan to Hong Kong had increased to 1.74 million in 1992. Hong Kong had become the most popular overseas destination for Taiwan's travellers, and ROC nationals the largest number of visitors to Hong Kong (MAC 1993a: 6).

Yet with there being little enthusiasm in Taiwan for political integration with the PRC, the prospect that dealing with Hong Kong will in future mean dealing with Beijing has only added impetus to the search for innovative devices to surmount the rigidities of statehood, rather than any acceptance of this *fait accompli*. From this perspective, the reliance of Taiwan on Hong Kong as an entrepot for indirect trade with the PRC has driven Taipei to develop a special relationship with that territory in which an interesting convergence begins to take place with the PRC concept of 'one country, two systems'. As Yahuda points out, this is implicit in Taipei's acceptance of the Sino-British Joint Declaration on Hong Kong and Governor Patten's proposals for democratic reform (Yahuda 1993: 703–4). There is, moreover, a conceptual parallel between the PRC's 'one country, two systems' and the division of China into four constituencies in the reformed ROC constitution. This parallel comes out clearly in the guidelines drawn up by the ROC's Mainland Affairs Council for future relations with Hong Kong and Macao:

> Hong Kong and Macao will revert to Chinese Communist control in 1997 and 1999, respectively, after which time they will be part of the 'mainland area'. The Chinese Communists claim that a 'one country, two systems' approach will be employed in the two areas whereby Hong Kong and Macao will be treated as 'special administrative regions'. In order to protect its interests in Hong Kong after 1997, the international community, including major nations of the Americas and Europe, will distinguish between mainland China and Hong Kong, and treat the two areas separately and look upon Hong Kong as an independent economic entity. If, after 1997 and 1999, cross-strait relations are still at the initial stage of the 'Guidelines for National Unification' – no postal, transport or commercial links – then the government will view Hong Kong and Macao as 'special areas' distinct from other areas of mainland China on the condition that the two areas are able to maintain their present free economic systems and high degrees of internationalisation.
>
> (MAC 1993a: 4)

In short, the treatment of Hong Kong and Macao as 'special areas' of China will mean that the people of those territories will be able to have a different status in ROC law from residents of the Chinese mainland. Moreover, the 10,000 or so Taiwan entrepreneurs who use Hong Kong as their base for doing business with the PRC will not be breaking the law under the *Guidelines for National Unification*. Instead, special laws will be drawn up to deal with relations between Taiwan and the 'special areas'. Granting special status to Hong Kong and Macao will also enable the ROC to justify not withdrawing its institutions from those territories when they fall under PRC sovereignty, and for direct transportation links to be maintained. Going further than this, substantive efforts are to be made to develop relations with Hong Kong and Macao, with the various ROC institutions there being integrated to enable them to combine their strengths and offer broader levels of contact services and to implement ROC policies (MAC 1993a: 5–11).

What we see in the Hong Kong dilemma, then, is a case of what might be called, in Kuhnian terms, articulation of the sovereignty paradigm (Kuhn 1970). Although this process of articulation is undertaken by both sides, there are of course important differences between their ultimate visions. For Beijing the idea of 'one country, two systems' is an attempt to integrate Taiwan and Hong Kong into the PRC by extending the Leninist principle of peaceful coexistence with capitalist states to that of coexistence between different systems within one China (Deng 1985a; Guo 1990; Jin 1989), while maintaining the claim that it is Beijing that represents China in the world. From Taipei's perspective, however, the danger that economic convergence might lead to political amalgamation is offset by a variety of *ad hoc* legal and technical devices which avoid implications that Taiwan is under Beijing's sovereign rule. This formula is given practical substance by an aggressive push to consolidate an international status for Taiwan by embedding it in the world economy and arguing for greater representation on the strength of its political and economic achievements. As can be seen from a comparison of the role of the economies on the two sides of the Strait in the global economy, although mainland China has taken a lead over Taiwan in terms of merchandise trade, Taipei has a solid foundation out of all proportion to its relative size upon which to base its arguments (see Figures 5.1 and 5.2).

This two-pronged approach by Taipei can be seen quite clearly in the measures formulated to maintain the efficacy of Taipei's policies after Hong Kong's reversion to PRC rule. The most advanced of these is the establishment of certain ports in Taiwan as 'off-shore' zones from which direct transport across the Strait will be permitted on the grounds that this will not be conducted from within the ROC customs area. In many ways such a concept harks back to the device of the export-processing zone which began with the erection of a man-made harbour in the southern port city of Kaohsiung in 1965 to segregate foreign firms from the island's economy both physically and symbolically (Cullather 1996: 23). Regulations for adopting such a scheme to enable more direct links with the mainland economy were finally approved by the Executive Yuan on 4 May 1995, and four days later Kaohsiung became the first port to begin to put the regulations into effect. The creativity of this measure lies in its circumvention of the policy of no direct contacts through stipulating that transshipments between the mainland and Taiwan are permitted so long as they originate from, or are destined for, third areas and do not pass through ROC customs, while routes between the two sides are designated as neither domestic nor international, but by the new category of 'special' (FCJ, 17 March, 12 May 1995).

What is highly significant about the timing of this development is that it took place in May 1995, just as intense lobbying of the United States Congress to pressure the Clinton administration to allow Lee Teng-hui to make a private visit to Cornell University came to fruition. The essential element of offsetting the danger of socio-economic integration with the

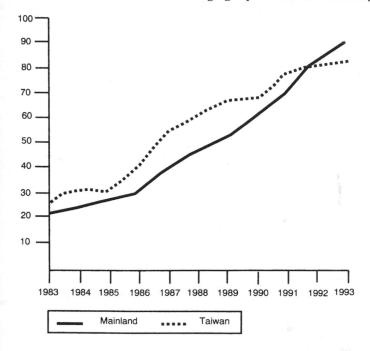

Figure 5.1 World merchandise exports from Taiwan and the mainland, 1983–93 (US$ billion)

Source: GATT, *1994 Trends and Statistics International Trade*, Geneva.

Chinese mainland by an extremely active drive to raise Taiwan's international profile as an independent political entity is here plain to see. That Beijing failed to respond to the transportation initiative, despite having advocated direct contacts for many years, seems to indicate that mainland policy-makers were caught somewhat off-balance by such a tactic. While the PRC may like to see transactions as drawing Taiwan into some kind of integration with the mainland, in Taipei the development of links with the mainland is seen as part of a broader policy of embedding Taiwan in international structures through initiatives such as becoming an Asia-Pacific business operations hub. This would not be feasible without easy transactions with the region's key economy.

In general, then, the functionalist assumptions that seem to lie behind fears that doing business in the PRC will create an 'interest group' of entrepreneurs to serve the interests of the PRC state (Kao 1993: 9–10) seem to fall short of reality when account is taken of the complex relationships that exist within the diversity of Greater China. In fact, what

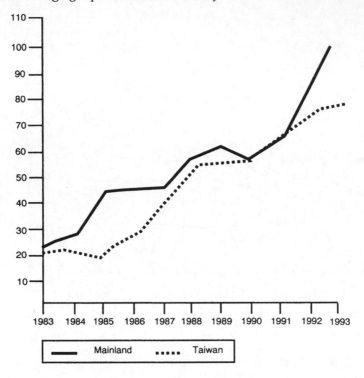

Figure 5.2 World merchandise imports to the mainland and Taiwan, 1983–93 (US$ billion)

Source: GATT, *1994 Trends and Statistics International Trade*, Geneva.

is most marked about economists' and business people's observations about this economic area is that their views tend towards visions of 'a network of overlapping and interlocking economic territories, some large and some small, rather than a single unified economic block' (Harding 1993: 671). In such a vision, the economic sphere of Guangdong, Fujian, Taiwan, and Hong Kong and Macao would be one among as many as eight economic spheres extending into various neighbouring states and into larger economic regions, such as the Asia Pacific Economic Co-operation forum (APEC) (Harding 1993: 672; UDN, 27 November 1993).

This conception of multiple economic areas may in fact be a better reflection of socio-economic realities than the assumption that economic integration will spill over into the kind of political co-operation that will lead to integration. Pressures for better communications between the three territories of Greater China, such as the establishment of ties between the

Hong Kong General Chamber of Commerce and the Chinese National Federation of Industries in Taiwan, might be seen as examples leading towards some kind of co-operation that could spill over into politics. However, when Paul Cheng, chairman of the Hong Kong organisation, proposed discussing with Lee Teng-hui how to help the PRC to maintain its MFN status with the United States in 1993, he also described how his own company had divided the Chinese mainland into no less than five separate areas for management due to the diversity of languages and customs to be found there (FCJ, 7 May 1993; UDN, 4 May 1993). If such diversity of market and socio-cultural conditions between the areas of Greater China is held by observers to be a serious constraint on the deepening of economic integration (Ash and Kueh 1993: 743), the same could presumably be said of its implications for political integration.

In fact, that the satisfaction of pragmatic expectations through economic integration might actually reduce any latent desire for political integration is something that Haas has observed in the case of Europe. It is a finding which tends to undermine functionalist assumptions in general (Dougherty and Pfaltzgraff 1990: 439–42; Haas 1967: 324). With the development of a strong sense of shared destiny in Taiwan, and the satisfaction of economic requirements by liberalising trade and investment in the mainland, the natural processes of economic integration can be allowed to take their course. In this sense, observers like Gerald Segal would seem to be right in noting that economic interdependence buys greater political independence for Taipei (Segal 1994a: 43). If it is true that the great disparities between the political, cultural and economic systems of the two sides of the Strait are more likely to steer people away from any desire for political amalgamation (Scalapino 1993: 226–7), then putting economic and cultural flesh on the bones of Lee Teng hui's depoliticised 'China' is just as likely to make the possibility of political amalgamation recede as it is to make it advance.

TAIWAN'S POST-NATIONALIST IDENTITY

It was argued in Chapter 4 that the political link between Chinese national identity and the state in Taiwan has been broken by democratisation. In this chapter it has been explained how alienation from the various Chinese communities in the world has been prevented through encouraging reciprocal transactions, especially in the economic sphere. The purpose of this with respect to the Chinese mainland has been to allow the population of Taiwan to enjoy the benefits of integration while avoiding acceptance of the PRC's claims to sovereignty over the island.

The result of these two developments for Taiwan's identity and status in the context of the island's relationship with the PRC has been a new articulation of the meaning of 'one China'. At a minimum, this has had to be an external reflection of the new domestic dispensation in Taiwan. That is to say, while Taiwan is located economically and culturally within China, the source of sovereignty over its state is said to lie in the population of the island. Taiwan's government is thus conceived of as *a* Chinese government, rather than *the* Chinese government (Yahuda 1993: 704). Although this is a departure from Chinese nationalism, the resulting identity can be said to be 'post-nationalist' rather than 'anti-nationalist'. This is because it still bears some of the imprints of the history of Chinese nationalism and nation-building, in the form of ethnic, cultural and economic relationships with Chinese communities outside the island. Yet if the development of this post-nationalist identity has been driven largely by domestic forces for democratisation, it remains to be explained how international society can respond to this unique configuration of identity and status.

6   Taiwan's intermediate state

When Lee Teng-hui gave his report on the state of the nation to the National Assembly on 19 May 1994, he stressed not only that the ROC cannot cut itself off from the Chinese mainland, but also that it cannot cut itself off from the world (Lee 1994a). The careful balance between mainland and foreign policy that he was emphasising was essentially a continuation of the strategy initiated by Chiang Ching-kuo. By the mid-1990s, this had come to be developed into a fine balance between exploiting Taiwan's links with a trans-state Chinese ethnic identity on the one side, while devising various diplomatic methods to establish an international status for Taiwan on the other.

While such methods have had much success in raising Taiwan's international profile, they have ultimately been limited by the structure of an international society that recognises the sovereign state as its most basic actor. So long as states have been forced by the PRC to make a choice between recognising either Beijing or Taipei, Taiwan has been left in a condition between the two possible statehoods: unification with the PRC on one hand, or an independent Taiwan on the other. So long as neither of these conditions can be achieved, Taiwan's status might best be described as that of an 'intermediate state'.

The term 'intermediate state' is, in fact, borrowed from Hedley Bull. When Bull coins the term, however, it is to remark that the appearance of entities that remain transfixed between two statehoods might signal the decline of the international society of states (Bull 1993: 267). The term is here applied to Taiwan but does not suggest that the island's intermediate state poses a threat to international society. It is rather to draw attention to the difficulty posed for the foreign policy of such an entity when it has to deal with an international society whose institutions are designed to deal with states alone. Below it will be shown how, although that policy has had many successes in raising Taiwan's international profile, the balance between domestic demands, Chinese nationalism and the requirements of international society prevent it from achieving any kind of recognisable statehood.

PRAGMATIC DIPLOMACY AND FLEXIBLE IDENTITY

Taipei's foreign policy can best be understood as the result of numerous innovative diplomatic practices which have established a variety of foreign relations. The range of these foreign relations can be envisioned as lying along a scale. At one end are states which have established full diplomatic relations with the ROC, and number around thirty. All of these, except the Republic of South Africa, are either geographically small, economically less developed, or both. They are concentrated in Central and South America, the Caribbean, Africa, the Pacific islands, and the Holy See. At the other end of the scale of recognition are states which have no relations with Taiwan: these used to comprise the Communist states, but since the collapse of Communism in the Soviet Union and Eastern Europe, most of them have joined the majority of states in between the two extremes, swelling the number enjoying what Taipei calls 'substantive' relations with the island to around 140 (*ROC Yearbook* 1994: 174).

What is important to understand about the notion of 'substantive' relations is that Taipei has had to accept that establishing relations with other states is more of a gradated process than a clear-cut act of recognition. This makes it worth trying to maximise the degree of recognition, even if the ultimate step of establishing full diplomatic relations cannot be accomplished. The result is a constant testing of the limits of the one-China principle which has had a variety of results. The first model for these was established when Japan terminated relations with Taipei in 1972 and the ROC established a representative office under the title 'Nationalist China's Association of East Asian Relations in Japan'. Tokyo reciprocated with a 'Japan Interchange Association' in Taipei. Staffed by officials on leave or retired from government office, such institutions could keep economic, cultural and consular concerns separate from political affairs. They thus provided a convenient model for other states wishing to have some kind of relationship with Taiwan short of recognition, in particular the United States after it terminated diplomatic relations with the ROC in 1979.

The model that comes closest to full diplomatic relations not upgraded to full recognition is what is termed 'reciprocal recognition' (*xianghu chengren*). This was first used by Taipei when relations with Vanuatu were put on firmer ground with the signing of a joint communiqué on 24 September 1992. On 26 May 1995 the same model was used to develop relations with Papua New Guinea. Taipei claims that what is distinct about 'reciprocal recognition' is that the two governments concerned will treat each other in conformity with the principles of international law, particularly regarding economic, trade, technical and international co-operation (FCJ, 2 June 1995). It falls short of establishing full diplomatic relations, however, because there is no exchange of ambassadors (UDN, 27 April 1995). Although this is a fine distinction, the fact that Beijing has not broken off relations with Vanuatu or Papua New Guinea indicates that this model is within the limits of acceptability, at least for very small states. For Taipei, size is not as important as the symbolic confirmation that the ROC exists as an international entity that is conferred by such ties.

How far other states within the substantive category can be persuaded to stretch the one-China policy depends on the efficacy of Taipei's diplomacy and how its results are perceived by Beijing. Because Beijing will not accept recognition of the ROC by other states, Taipei's diplomacy has to accept working through non-state organisations. It is thus that Taipei's diplomacy has been christened 'pragmatic diplomacy' (*wushi waijiao*). As described above, this has been developed since the days of Chiang Ching-kuo and can even be traced back to his premiership, when in February 1973 he outlined a strategy of 'total diplomacy' (Fu 1992: 79). This was envisioned as mobilising every kind of resource – political, economic, scientific, technological, cultural and sporting – to develop 'substantial' links with states that had terminated diplomatic relations, in the hope of gaining political concessions.

There would be little reason for other states to reciprocate in this process, however, unless it was complemented by what is colloquially called 'dollar diplomacy'. This amounts to offering substantial financial and technical assistance and other forms of economic co-operation to those who are willing to reciprocate politically. What has made this possible is, above all, the economic muscle that comes from the important role Taiwan plays in world trade. Not only has Taiwan built up foreign exchange reserves that compete with Japan's for the highest level in the world, but it has diversified its markets to become an important trade partner in most regions.

The mobilisation of Taiwan's economic resources has been aimed at a variety of states, ranging from the less developed to the industrialised. It is directed both at maintaining the loyalty of the ROC's formal allies and at pushing those in the 'substantive' category further towards recognition. Concerning the less developed states, it has been systematised somewhat through the creation of an International Economic Co-operation and Development Fund to help friendly states upgrade their economies, and hopefully their diplomatic relations. Some US$420 million was put aside for this purpose as of fiscal 1993 (*ROC Yearbook* 1994: 171), and by the end of May 1994 the government had approved eighteen applications totalling US$266.84 million in loans from the fund. Seven other cases, totalling US$94 million, were being processed. Countries allocated soft loans from the fund in 1994 included Poland (US$20 million), the Philippines, Paraguay and Latvia (US$10 million each), and Vietnam (US$5 million) (FCJ, 17 June 1994). Technical aid has also been an important arm of diplomacy, with the ROC stationing some 317 personnel in technical missions throughout the world as of December 1992 (CEPD 1994). As well as maintaining relations with the ROC's remaining allies, this also fits in with the ROC's general strategy to raise its international profile by using financial resources to aid other developing countries as a form of 'feedback' to the international community.

A good example of how dollar diplomacy combines with pragmatic diplomacy in dealing with Taipei's allies could be seen when Lee Teng-hui attended the inauguration of Nelson Mandela as president of South Africa in May 1994. This involved stopping over in Nicaragua and Costa Rica. As the first official presidential visit to diplomatic allies for seventeen years, this was a highly symbolic act for the ROC. That dollars lubricated the process is indicated by the announcement by the ROC embassy in Managua of an agreement to cancel 75 per cent of the debt owed on a US$10 million loan made in the 1980s (with interest this had been pushed up to US$22 million) to help Nicaraguan cotton farmers (FCJ, 13 May 1994). A joint communiqué was also issued which committed the ROC to continue collaborating with international organisations to provide funds for Nicaraguan projects, following a US$30 million syndicated loan from the ROC and the Inter-American Development Bank in 1993 to assist with agricultural reforms (FCJ, 13 May 1994).

When Lee Teng-hui finally arrived in South Africa, there had been much speculation that the change of regime in Pretoria would mean the loss of Taipei's one remaining ally of any real weight in world politics. However, the fact that some 300 Taiwanese-owned companies are located in South Africa, employing 40,000 workers, proved to be a strong bargaining chip when dealing with the new government. The degree to which the ROC was prepared to bend the one-China principle to maintain relations with South Africa had already been made evident when, on 5 May, ROC Vice Foreign Minister Steven Chen explained that dual recognition would be preferable to breaking relations with Pretoria (FCJ, 13 May 1994). According to the ROC ambassador to South Africa, Nelson Mandela told Lee Teng-hui in a private audience in Pretoria that the new regime would not take the initiative in breaking ties with the ROC (FCJ, 10 June 1994).

When diplomatic relations have been terminated, Taipei has used the mechanism of substantive ties to maintain co-operation with other states.

Links have thus been maintained with Saudi Arabia since it switched recognition in July 1990, in the form of regular conferences and technical and economic co-operation. After the Republic of Korea established relations with Beijing in August 1992, substantive ties were developed just over a year later in the form of a pact to promote economic, trade and cultural exchanges. Representative offices have been established under the names 'Taipei Mission in Korea' and 'Korean Mission in Taipei'.

Dollar diplomacy has also been used as part of a more sophisticated strategic policy in Taiwan's immediate environment, aimed in part at creating conditions to draw Taiwanese investment away from the PRC. This has been developed under a 'southwards policy' directed towards South-east Asia. The diplomatic wing of this initiative began over the Christmas–New Year period of 1993–4. It took the form of breakthrough visits by Lee Teng-hui and Lien Chan to Singapore, the Philippines, Indonesia and Thailand. Although Lee and Lien were officially on holiday during their tours of South-east Asia, they were treated in a fashion appropriate for state guests and they met state leaders in all these countries. A precedent was thus made for what has come to be called 'vacation diplomacy'.

The economic dimension of the 'southwards policy' was given legal form in January 1994, when the ROC Ministry of Economic Affairs drew up a draft bill to strengthen trade links with South-east Asia. This includes measures such as signing bilateral agreements on transport, removing taxes on freight, and seeking agreement from the Labour Department for Taiwanese businesses with investments in South-east Asia to train employees in Taiwan. That this has a solid trading foundation to build upon can be seen by the increasing volume of trade with the ASEAN states. The ROC is an important trading and investment partner for most of the countries in the region. Total two-way trade of the ROC with the region in 1992 was in excess of US$14 billion. Taiwan is the primary source of investment in Vietnam and the second largest source for Thailand. Taipei was also quick to take advantage of the US withdrawal from Subic Bay in the Philippines, joining with the Subic Bay Metropolitan Authority to back investment by Taiwanese companies. These numbered forty-five in 1994 and promises were made to invest US$423.7 million to develop a 30-hectare industrial park in the centre of the zone (FT, 15 March 1995).

The political gains won by Taipei from the 'southwards policy' are significant. They can be seen in the shape of support from Thailand and the Philippines for Taiwan's application to join GATT, seen largely as an exchange for an agreement on the legal import of workers from those countries (FEER, 12 March 1992). It has also been suggested that the development of Subic Bay is part of a long-term strategy to provide an alternative to Hong Kong as an entrepot for mainland trade, or at least to use this possibility to exert leverage in negotiations with Hong Kong over renewal of aviation agreements spanning 1997 (UDN, 6 January 1994). The diplomatic pay-off can also be seen in gestures such as allowing the word 'Taipei' to be included in the ROC's office in Thailand, the reciprocal opening of economic and cultural offices in Taipei, Ho Chi Minh City and Hanoi in July 1993, and the commencement of flights between Vietnam and Taiwan by China Airlines and Taiwan's private carrier, EVA Air.

Ministerial-level delegations from Indonesia have also visited Taiwan to solicit investment, and invitations have been extended for Lee Teng-hui to visit President Suharto for his 'vacations'. With Taiwan playing such an important economic role in the development of South-east Asia, it is understandable that when the PRC complained to Malaysia about Taipei's vacation diplomacy, the Malaysian foreign minister replied that his country could not overlook Taiwan's economic position and maintained its right to engage in discussions and exchanges with Taiwan. In the context of what is perceived by many states in the region to be an increasingly threatening PRC, it has also been claimed in Taiwan that ASEAN and Vietnam might see Taiwan as a useful balance to the influence of the PRC (UDN, January 1994).

In some respects the strong economic presence of the overseas Chinese in South-east Asia means that the 'southwards policy' has also involved areas of overlap with the developing concept of a Greater China. The special 'Chinese' relationship with Singapore remains significant on this count, with Lee Kuan-yew often playing the role of honest broker between the different communities of Greater China. As mentioned in Chapter 5, that ROC Premier Lien Chan discussed joint development of Hainan Island during his 'vacations' in Singapore is particularly interesting in light of Lee Kuan-yew's views on networking among the Chinese business communities of the world.

As well as maintaining substantive links with states in South-east Asia, pragmatic, dollar and vacation diplomacy have also begun to be successful in cultivating relations with states in other regions. When Lee Teng-hui took his 'vacations' in the United Arab Emirates and Jordan in April 1995, this was presented in the Taiwan press as a breakthrough in Middle East policy. The dissolution of the Soviet Union and the demise of Russian Communism have also given Taipei a host of opportunities. Poland established a representative office in Taipei in mid-November 1992, which is fully authorised to grant visas. The bans on direct trade and investment with the Soviet Union were in fact lifted before disintegration, in March and April 1990, and non-governmental exchanges were relaxed. In the following years visits by low-ranking officials, parliamentary members, academics, performing artists and business delegations from the former Soviet states have all increased. Particular emphasis has been placed on developing relations with Russia, Belarus, Ukraine and Kazakhstan, with large offers of food and medical aid being made. Trade with Russia expanded from US$74 million in 1989 to nearly US$600 million in 1992, and in June 1992 the ROC and Russia signed an agreement to establish economic and cultural co-ordination offices in their capitals (*China Yearbook* 1994: 176).

As for the world's three main markets of North America, the European Union and Japan, the launching of a Six-Year National Development Plan by Hau Pei-tsun in 1991 can be seen in many respects as a central plank in ROC diplomacy. The honey pot certainly attracted a swarm of ministerial-level 'friends from afar' who paid 'unofficial' visits to the island. Hau claims that the plan even led directly to the crucial breakthrough in arms procurements that occurred in 1992, when the United States agreed to sell 150 F-16 fighter planes to Taipei. Threats of retaliation from the PRC seem to have proved lacking when weighed against the survival of General Dynamics Corporation in a US election year. This also overcame French hesitation to sell Taiwan sixty Mirage 2000-5 multi-role jets and 1,500 missiles. The closure of the French consulate in the mainland's Guangdong province and the exclusion of French companies from bidding for a subway contract there also proved ineffective when weighed against the survival of key defence contractors such as Dassault, which had not had a single military export for four years.

The general raising of the ROC's profile that was achieved in this period was symbolised by significant political developments, such as a resolution by the European Parliament on 28 May 1992 acknowledging the importance of Taiwan. It was heralded as a 'political breakthrough' when the European Community agreed to hold bilateral trade talks for the first time in Taipei in October (SCMP, 8 September 1992). Australia also broke a twenty-year ban on ministerial visits when its tourism and resources minister 'unofficially' led a trade delegation to Taiwan. As an Australian government spokesman succinctly put it, 'The visit does not mean that Australia has detoured from its one-China policy. The visit, rather, further demonstrates the fast-growing economic ties between Australia and Taiwan' (FCJ, 6 October 1992).

Even the United Kingdom, which had to be especially wary about provoking the PRC in the period leading up to the transition of Hong Kong to PRC sovereignty, began to take a more positive view of Taiwan in the 1990s. An Anglo-Taiwan Trade Committee and British Council representation were established in Taipei to pursue the objectives of the Foreign and Commonwealth Office in developing exports and commercial involvement with Taiwan, and cultivating educational and cultural links. Taiwanese representation in London was also expanded and given higher status. Beginning in February 1992 a number of visits were made to the island by British ministers at the invitation of private organisations. Appearances by celebrities such as former Prime Minister Thatcher also went down well.

Visits to Taiwan by UK parliamentary committees also appear to have had the desired impact. In March 1994 the Foreign Affairs Select Committee made a report on relations between the United Kingdom and China in the period up to and beyond 1997. It reflected a clear willingness to recommend developing ties with Taiwan, including strengthening economic and cultural links, establishing relations with the Legislative Yuan, and relaxing some restrictions on Taiwan's representative office in London (HC 1994: xxiii–iv). Noting Taiwan's economic and political achievements and its important role in the world economy, as well as the prospects for increasing two-way investment, the committee also reiterated support for Taiwan's entry into GATT (HC 1994: xxxiii). Again, this took place against the background of important economic developments, such as the announcement by the Taiwan textiles group Hualon of the breaking of ground for a textile factory in Northern Ireland, the biggest inward investment for the province in a decade (FCJ, 17 June 1994).

Concerning relations with Japan, in Beijing's eyes recent history makes Tokyo's links with Taipei as sensitive as those between Taipei and Washington. Despite this, the historical links and close geographical proximity of the two islands means that there is a special relationship, with 1.5 million Japanese visiting Taiwan in 1991 alone. There also remain close personal ties between elderly Taiwanese and their former Japanese teachers and friends, and close relations between the KMT and the LDP. However, the relationship is also dogged somewhat by Taiwan's persistent deficit with Japan, standing at US$14.2 billion for 1993, and the dispute over the Senkaku (Diaoyutai) Islands, which remains a running sore on Chinese and Taiwanese nationalist sensitivities. Although the ROC's demands that Japan do something to redress the trade balance are rebuffed by Tokyo, a positive development of substantive relations was claimed when the ROC's four representative offices in Japan were allowed to change their names from 'Association of East Asian Relations' to 'Taipei Economic and Cultural Representative Offices' on 20 May 1992. As the *ROC Yearbook* points out, 'The new name refers to the ROC more specifically and concretely than the former vague "East Asian" designation, marking another step towards stronger relations with Japan' (*ROC Yearbook* 1994: 177).

Most significant, however, has been Washington's development of substantive relations with Taiwan. Following the Japanese model, the United States is represented by a large institution called the American Institute in Taiwan (AIT). Taipei was also allowed to maintain a Co-ordination Council for North American Affairs (CCNAA) with thirteen offices throughout the United States, including one in Washington. Some indication of the scale of 'unofficial' activity overseen by these organisations is given by the observation that between 1982 and 1992 no less than 400 Congressmen and Senators visited Taiwan, along with more than 1,100 Congressional staffers. Some thirty-five states have signed sister state agreements with Taiwan and about twenty states have trade offices in the island (Laux 1992: 19). Much to Beijing's annoyance, the USA continues to sell arms to Taiwan and to upgrade their quality. Meanwhile, the flood of students from Taiwan to the USA and the counter-flow of young Americans seeking job opportunities in Taiwan continues to develop strong cultural and social bonds between the two societies. As with other states, the official status of visitors from the USA has crept higher. On 30 November 1992 the first cabinet-level visit since 1978 was made when Trade Representative Carla Hills took part in the sixteenth joint conference of the ROC–US and US–ROC economic councils.

After Bill Clinton won the presidential election, future relations looked rosy when he announced in a Washington Chinese restaurant that he had visited Taiwan four times and 'loves the country' (CN, 20 November 1992). The Bush administration's policy of supplying advanced weaponry to the ROC was also maintained under the new administration: Clinton endorsed a bill which came into effect on 30 April 1994 by which the stipulation in the Taiwan Relations Act that sufficient armaments should be supplied to enable Taiwan to defend itself was given priority over the commitment to reduce arms sales to Taiwan contained in the 1982 PRC–US joint communiqué. The bill also recommended supporting Taiwan's participation in international organisations, high-level exchanges, and changing the place of origin of Taiwanese in the United States to 'Taiwan' (FCJ, 6 May 1994).

'Dollar diplomacy' and 'pragmatic diplomacy' have also helped Taipei's attempts to gain a higher standing in international non-governmental organisations. Taipei is represented in 794 such bodies, ranging from scientific and technological to sports and cultural. A variety of methods are used to get around the barriers erected by the PRC. To 'represent the country' diplomatic personnel are substituted by professors and business people, with organisations such as the ROC Red Cross Society playing an important role (Lee Teng-hui 1992b: 115). Non-governmental organisations are in fact a specially appropriate setting for

Taipei's style of diplomacy. This is particularly so for organisations with a high East Asian membership, where the style of diplomacy tends to be conducive to a blurring of the distinctions between official and unofficial activities and where states with problematic relations can work towards consensus-building through non-binding dialogue (Woods 1993). It is in such a context that Taipei has made some of its most significant breakthroughs, for example Beijing's 1986 acceptance to attend PECC alongside a delegation from Taiwan on the grounds that this organisation is non-governmental.

The use of the formula 'Chinese Taipei' for the Taipei delegation at PECC, first used by Taiwan's team at the 1984 Olympics, was deemed appropriate by Beijing, despite the less clear-cut distinction between Taipei's personnel and 'officials' when compared to athletes. The best example of this can be found in the figure of Koo Chen-fu. Not only did Koo lead the Chinese Taipei delegation to PECC, he is also international president of the other main non-governmental economic organisation, the PBEC. Koo is ostensibly qualified to hold these posts as a leading Taiwan industrialist and financier. In this persona, Koo is head of the Chinese National Association of Industry and Commerce, and president of Taiwan Cement Company.

Yet such qualifications hide Koo's status as the ROC's most important ambassador-at-large. Koo is in fact a member of the KMT's central committee and chairman of the Straits Exchange Foundation, and receives funds from the Foreign Ministry for his diplomatic efforts, which include meetings with heads of state and political figures whom ROC leaders are unable to meet due to Beijing's objections. As seen above (p. 119), it was also Koo who represented Taipei in the Koo–Wang talks between the unofficial organisations from the two sides of the Strait in Singapore. The division between unofficial and official representation becomes increasingly blurred as one follows the activities of Koo. In the 1990s the Koo family-controlled China Trust Commercial Bank, Taiwan's biggest privately owned bank, has begun to build a global network. In the words of the bank's senior executive in charge of commercial banking, Wu Ching-mai, the bank's mission is 'not just to make profits, but also to play a quasi-diplomatic role'. That unofficial business is not always separable from official business is made clear by Wu when he adds, 'Of course, Taiwan's efforts to gain recognition internationally was one of the important original motivations behind our overseas expansion, but at the same time it makes good business sense' (Tyson 1994).

THE LIMITS OF DIPLOMACY

Having looked at some of the achievements of Taipei's diplomacy, it is necessary to see where its limits lie in order to get a picture of what kind of international status has been achieved for Taiwan. Rather than portraying Taipei's diplomacy as an unmitigated success, it might be better to view it as having led to a stalemate with the PRC, as can be seen by the oscillation of small states which can enjoy considerable benefits by switching recognition between Taipei and Beijing. Thus to welcome in the new year in 1994, the PRC successfully won over Lesotho, reducing the number of states recognising the ROC to twenty-eight, to which the ROC responded by swaying Burkina Faso into its own camp. This stalemate can also be seen in the case of larger states. Following the decision of France to sell jet fighters to Taiwan, for example, protests from Beijing and the closure of the French consulate in Guangzhou led Paris to embark on an intense diplomatic effort to bring about rapprochement. This culminated in the signing of a series of large commercial contracts during an official visit to Paris by Jiang Zemin in September 1994 (FT, 12 September 1994).

The deadlock in Taipei's diplomacy is also evident in its attempts to join international governmental organisations. Here, although Taiwan often gains some kind of raised status, when the PRC joins such bodies, Beijing always insists that the island's representation must fall short of anything that would imply sovereign statehood. The result is often a farcical quibbling over what appear to outsiders to be trivial issues. The PRC's entry into the ADB is one example. So sensitive are Taipei and Beijing to the implications of their membership of such organisations for their claims to sovereignty that at the ADB's twenty-sixth annual conference, the governor of Taiwan's Central Bank of China, Samuel Shieh (Xie Senzhong) launched a campaign to drop the comma from the ROC's membership title, 'Taipei, China'. The comma is objectionable to Taiwan because it can be interpreted as implying that the ROC is a local municipality or provincial government of the PRC. 'Taipei China', it is held, would be more acceptable as reflecting the ROC's status as a Chinese government currently situated in Taipei (FCJ, 7 May 1993). Shieh threatened to stop making donations to the bank's Asian Development Fund unless the comma was expunged.

Taipei's application to join the GATT-WTO has also been plagued by stalemate over objections from the PRC. In line with 'pragmatic diplomacy', the Lee administration has been extremely careful to present its application 'in such a way and under such a name as to solve the purely political objections raised by Mainland China'. The case for accession is thus made on the grounds that the territories of Taiwan, Penghu, Kinmen and Matsu form a 'customs territory', over which the government representing that territory possesses full autonomy in the conduct of its external commercial relations. It is argued that this permits accession under GATT Article XXXIII, and Taipei has stressed that accession is a purely economic affair not supposed to achieve a secondary political purpose (*Accession* 1990: 11). In support of its position that the promotion of trade, growth and world-wide living standards should be 'strictly separated from unrelated questions of diplomatic recognition or national sovereignty', the ROC refers to two principles agreed upon by the UN Security Council in 1950. Under these, the act of voting to support accession of an applicant to an international organisation is separated from diplomatic recognition.[13] Beijing, however, seeing this issue as inevitably concerning sovereignty, demands that 'Chinese Taipei' must be added to the name 'Customs Territory of Taiwan, Penghu and Matsu' and strongly opposes Taiwan's accession ahead of the PRC. Ultimately it was Beijing's view that was supported by the majority of GATT contracting parties when the Council of Representatives met to consider Taiwan's application in September 1992 (GATT 1992: 95–6). As has already been pointed out (p. 78), the indignant reaction in Taiwan to a statement that its status was only equal to that of Hong Kong indicates that it sees the issue as in reality much more than the purely economic one it claims it to be.

By far the most adventurous move to gain improved international status for Taiwan, however, has been the ROC's attempt to re-enter the UN under the two-seat model adopted by East and West Germany. The declassification of the PRC government as a 'rebel' group during the constitutional reforms of 1991, and the recognition that the ROC only has effective control of Taiwan and the off-shore islands, laid the domestic legal foundation for the ROC's application. The political context was provided by Lee Teng-hui's movement away from Chinese nationalism under intense pressure from the opposition to do something to raise Taiwan's international status. It was thus on 6 August 1993 that seven of the states in the UN that recognise the ROC[14] sent a letter to the Secretary-General to request that an ROC application for membership be considered by the General Committee when it convened the following month.

The response from Beijing came in the form of the White Paper *The Taiwan Question and Reunification of China*, which has already been quoted several times above. Here, Taiwan's position as a symbol of the violation of the integrity of the Chinese state and nation remains as strong as it did in the early 1980s. In the context of such opposition, the following December Secretary-General Boutros Boutros-Ghali signalled that Taipei's campaign would be a difficult one when he said, during a visit to Japan, that the UN has resolved that Taiwan is a part of China and that it cannot become a UN member. Although the ROC Foreign Ministry objected that Resolution 2758, which expelled Taiwan from the UN in 1971, only actually expelled 'the Chiang Kai-shek regime', this blurring of distinctions did not impress other states (UDN, 23 December 1993). Despite an escalation in 1994 of Taipei's campaign its case failed to get on to the agenda. The ROC might have increased support for its case, with seven member nations actually speaking out on its behalf compared with three the year before, but the PRC also mobilised seventeen member nations against the ROC, up from eleven the previous year. Moreover, while ROC support was confined to a handful of small Central American, Pacific island and African states, those which spoke in opposition included not only the PRC itself, but also Russia and India (UDN, 23 September 1994).

Concerning relations with other relatively influential states, the limits of Taipei's diplomacy were again indicated by the reaction of the Foreign and Commonwealth Office to the House of Commons Select Committee recommendations for improving UK relations with Taiwan: it drew back from agreeing to any changes which might unilaterally affect the status of Taiwan in international law (HC 1994: xxiii–iv). While the ROC's lobbying and economic activities might have impressed the British Parliament, the Foreign and Commonwealth Office maintained that the clear priority was to develop 'a wide-ranging relationship with China'. In this view, Britain's 'vital interest' is the maintenance of stability in the Asia–Pacific region and the expansion of trade and investment with the PRC, the UK's twelfth largest export market (*The Times*, 1 July 1994). As ROC lobbyists were reminded by MPs at a seminar held in London to promote the ROC's entry into the UN, businessmen in their constituencies would not be happy with anything that might upset their opportunities for doing business not only in that growing market, but also with Hong Kong after 1997.

What Taipei's diplomacy tells us about the relationship between Taiwan's identity and its international status, as far as international society is concerned, then, is that there is a considerable degree of latitude for a state to carve an international niche for itself without the privilege of diplomatic recognition. The development of such a niche is important in a number of respects. Firstly, there is a demand within Taiwan for a higher international profile of some kind. This is important not only in terms of regime legitimisation, but also to prevent Taiwan falling under the shadow of the PRC in the eyes of other states as transactions mount across the Strait. From Taipei's perspective, even if the ROC is not widely recognised as a state, at least its lobbying activities and the internationalisation of the Taiwan problem have led to an increase in awareness of its claims and of its difficult situation among the international community. When the PRC decides to take stronger actions against the ROC, as it did in 1995–6, it is harder to present its case as one of 'China's internal affairs'.

This being said, however, the costly diplomatic stalemate should be attributed not only to the fact that Beijing is often able to match many of Taipei's diplomatic methods but, more significantly, to the fact that Taipei's diplomacy is also hampered by the lack of clarity of the political aims it is supposed to fulfil. It will be shown below that this uncertainty inevitably arises from the difficulty of seeking the best possible dispensation for Taiwan in the context of a fluid situation not only in the domestic politics of Taiwan and the mainland but also in international society.

TOWARDS A NEW INTERNATIONAL DISPENSATION?

Concerning the changing international situation, a fairly clear idea of Lee Teng-hui's vision of international politics after the Cold War can be gained from the principles he advocated in a September 1991 speech on the ROC in the new Asian–Pacific situation. These were enumerated as follows:

1 Respect democracy and human rights, which includes redefining the concept of sovereignty.
2 Replace military force with negotiation, and abandon war as a means of resolving international disputes.
3 Promote a market economy that incorporates a mixed economic system.
4 Strengthen the collective security system that incorporates regional organisations and the UN.
5 Promote the concept of *Gemeinschaft* (common community), and foster the consensus that joys and sorrows are to be shared and problems jointly tackled in the 'global village' that we live in.

(Lee 1991d: 122)

If these points are understood primarily as an attempt to distinguish the ROC's understanding of world order from that of the PRC, it can be seen that the first and the last are a sharp departure from the hard conception of sovereignty and rejection of cosmopolitanism that are characteristic of the Chinese nationalist tradition. In developing this theme, ROC spokespersons cite examples such as European integration and the dual representation enjoyed by the two Germanys and the two Koreas in the UN as evidence that sovereignty need no longer be seen as an 'all or nothing' concept. This was the gist of remarks made by ROC Foreign Minister Frederick Chien in August 1994 (UDN, 17 August 1994) and such views have also been aired in Taiwan by influential foreigners such as James Lilley, a former director of the American Institute in Taiwan and former US ambassador to Beijing. Lilley is reported to have told a seminar in Taipei that the PRC's idea of sovereignty is rooted in a nineteenth-century conception and is archaic when faced by problems such as the status of Taiwan, Hong Kong, Tibet and Xinjiang (CT, 22 August 1991).

Lee Teng-hui himself talks increasingly in terms of regional identities, and even global identities. As he went on to explain in the September 1991 speech:

> We are happy to see the efforts that the Asian-Pacific nations are making in the area of integration and development by positively moving toward the establishment of many different organisations for economic co-operation. We hope that these will transcend political borders and accelerate the interaction and development in regional economy and trade.
>
> (Lee 1991d: 122–3)

In this speech, then, it can be seen how the idea of the *Gemeinschaft*, originally developed as a foundation for state legitimacy in domestic politics, is extended beyond the state to the region and even the 'global village'. The idea has at different times been stretched from meaning the community of people on Taiwan, to the community of Chinese in the world, to an East Asian community, and at times to a world community, depending on the audience being addressed. It is this elasticity of the concept that allows the notion of a *Gemeinschaft* to be tailored into a wider vision of international relations which would seem to offer more room for manoeuvre for the ROC in carving out a new identity and status for itself.

Why this context of regional identities and international co-operation is important as a background to ROC diplomacy is that it enables the edges between national identity and statehood to be significantly blurred. Thus, although the existence of something called one 'China' is acknowledged by the Lee administration, this can be interpreted as an entity that is something other than the conception of the nation-state as traditionally understood in international society. As *There Is No 'Taiwan Question' There Is Only a China Question* says, something called 'China' may well exist, but this does not alter the reality that the government of the ROC and the 'Chinese Communist authorities' have exercised government powers within it for some time (MAC 1993: 11).

What this loosening of the link between Chinese identity and statehood enables is the development of a different claim to state legitimacy, based not on the congruence of nation and state, but on moral criteria. This can be seen in the way that central to the ROC's claims for a higher international status is an argument about legitimacy which amounts to the demand that Taiwan *ought* to be represented internationally because its democratic and economic achievements entitle it to such representation. Democratic constitutional reform lends real credibility to the claim that the liberal democracies have a moral duty to support the island. The Tiananmen massacre certainly provided the perfect backdrop against which Taipei could explain to an international audience why resolving the differences between the political situations on the two sides of the Strait had to come before unification (Lee 1989a).

By the early 1990s the 'silent revolution' had become a central theme in Taipei's campaign to foster foreign support and to portray the ROC as a 'partner nation' of the west in Asia, appearing in international publications such as *Time, Newsweek,* the *International Herald Tribune, The Financial Times* and the *Asian Wall Street Journal,* among others. The message being promoted was that the ROC on Taiwan should be recognised for its political achievements, and this became an important theme in the campaign for ROC representation at the United Nations (GIO 1993, 1994; Hu 1994: 8–9).

As well as parading these political achievements, spokespersons also reel out statistics which draw attention to the island's economic achievements. These include the size of the ROC's foreign exchange reserves, which in the early 1990s were competing with Japan for the honour of being the largest in the world, and the fact that the island's volume of world merchandise trade hovers between thirteenth and fourteenth highest in the world. Taipei can also claim it is committed to implementing free trade practices, low tariff rates and a liberalised financial and services sector.

Underlying this moral vision, however, there are also neo-liberal assumptions about the nature of power in the post-Cold War period. Primary among these is the assertion that 'geo-economics' is taking over from 'geo-politics' (Lee 1994b). The graphic image used by Lee Teng-hui to illustrate where the locus of this economic power lies is that of the 'flying geese' model of economic development. Here Japan takes the lead, followed by the newly industrialising countries, then the ASEAN countries and mainland China. Yet although Japan takes the lead in Asia, this formation ultimately relies on the US market (Lee 1992b: 150).

Accompanying the hegemony of economic power in Lee's vision of the new world order is that of political power in the shape of 'democracy'. With the KMT claiming legitimacy on democratic grounds, the ROC can look forward to being a 'partner nation' of the west in Asia (Lee 1991e: 80) on the side of a tide of democracy said to be sweeping the world. In this view, any territory that is aligned with the global free market and the forces of democracy will be part of a process of development and progress. If any member of the Asia–Pacific community should swim against this tide, however, then all will suffer.

In many respects, then, Lee's vision of world order is one in which the United States and Japan play the beneficial role of hegemonic stabilisers. Opposed to their efforts, and those of Taiwan, to promote regional linkage are those nations which are unable to abandon narrow-minded ideology and self-centred nationalism, or to consider the collective security and development of the region. For Lee, the main hope for overcoming such resistance is that the USA will continue to exert a powerful influence to eliminate barriers created by trade protectionism, while Japan will take responsibility as the 'economic navigator' of the region (Lee 1992c: 143).

In conformity with this view of world order, ROC spokespersons tend to present Taiwan's international role as one which could be described as integrationist and functional, in so far as it questions the assumption that the state is irreducible and that the interests of governments prevail, and actively considers schemes for co-operation, is peace-oriented and seeks to avoid a win–lose stalemate (Groom and Taylor quoted in Dougherty and Pfaltzgraff 1990: 132–3). Rather than resist what Sun Yat-sen and Mao Zedong would have considered to be the imperialist tide of the global economy, Taipei wants to dive in head first. For Lee Teng-hui, therefore, Taiwan's development to become a hub for transportation in the western Pacific and a major Asian financial centre constituted two of the most important aims of the Six-Year National Development Plan (Lee 1991c: 116).

Naturally, the more important Taiwan's role in the global economy becomes, the stronger are its arguments that its exclusion from international organisations is unreasonable. It is unfair to its population, prevents the ROC from making an appropriate contribution to world affairs, and distorts the work of international organisations by depriving them of important information. The ROC not only signals its belief in the benefits of economic liberalisation and integration, but can also claim to have put this into practice. In bilateral relations this is most clear in the response to pressures from Washington to co-operate on intellectual property protection. It has also reduced Taiwan's trade surplus with the United States by the adoption of a 'Trade Action Plan' in May 1989, bringing the level down from a peak of around US$18 billion in 1987, to below US$10 billion in the 1990s.

Multilaterally, the commitment to trade liberalisation and integration can be seen in initiatives such as moves towards becoming a member of NAFTA and ambitious plans for forming strategic alliances with multinational corporations jointly to develop the Asia–Pacific market.

Taipei ultimately envisions Taiwan as the financial and communications centre for the whole Asia–Pacific region, and has gone to some lengths to meet the requirements for GATT membership. Equal treatment with their American counterparts has been given to European and Japanese insurance companies. Foreign banks have been permitted to set up head offices and the heavily protected agricultural sector has been liberalised, despite this being a highly charged issue for the regime's rural power base. The ROC application to GATT has thus won considerable support in an international community which no doubt realises the inconsistency of excluding such an important trading entity from the GATT-WTO, with even the United States and the European Union states supporting accession.

Taipei's appeals for recognition according to its political and economic credentials have had the most significant impact in the United States. There they have attracted a tide of bipartisan support in Congress and the media for a reassessment of ties with Taiwan. This began to build up into an irresistible force when the Clinton administration refused a request for Lee Teng-hui to be allowed to stay overnight in Hawaii while *en route* to Latin America in May 1994. This triggered off a campaign in support of a visit by Lee to the USA itself. The call also went out for support for Taipei's UN application and for the revision of sections of the Taiwan Relations Act which prohibit US officials from visiting Taiwan. A bipartisan petition to the president, started on 16 May, had gathered the signatures of fifty-four Senators by the end of June. A resolution in support of Taiwan's entry into the UN was passed by the Senate on 10 June. On 1 July, the Senate also ratified a proposal to revise the Taiwan Relations Act so as to permit visits by the president of the ROC and high-ranking officials to the USA. On 12 August, thirty-seven Congressmen signed a joint invitation for Lee to visit the USA.

Such developments looked promising for Taiwan as the administration began to change its tune, with Secretary of State Christopher hinting on 1 July that if the administration did not recognise what had been achieved in Taiwan, this would make him 'uncomfortable'. The complexity of the Taiwan problem and of Taipei's arguments, however, makes it difficult for states to respond to the discomfort that they might feel with the status quo over Taiwan. Sam Gejdenson, chairman of the Congressional Subcommittee on Economic Policy, Trade and Environment, for example, argues that given the island's commitment to democracy and its declining trade deficit with the USA, Washington should stop treating Taiwan 'like a second class country' (HR 1993). Yet how does the implication that Taiwan should be treated like a 'country' fit in with the demands on US policy-makers that arise from cultivating links with the economies of the

'Chinese Economic Area' (see p. 148)? And how does it fit in with Taipei's attempts not to provoke Beijing more than is necessary by going so far as to declare independence?

Taipei's success in gathering domestic support in the USA left the Clinton administration on the horns of just such a dilemma. With the PRC's importance as an economic partner growing, the choice seemed to be one of pursuing American economic interests or supporting an old ally that was actively promoting American values of democracy and free trade. Although Clinton had come to power on a platform of taking a hard line on human rights in the PRC, he was also elected to revive a flagging economy. It was this latter theme that had tended to prevail in relations with Beijing. As Donald Anderson, president of the US–China Business Council told Congress in the hearings on how to deal with Beijing's human rights abuses, withdrawing or putting conditions on China's MFN status would lead to the loss of over 150,000 jobs, US$8 billion in lost exports, and at least US$14 billion in higher import prices for American consumers (HR 1993). In May 1994, Clinton finally delinked the PRC's MFN status from its human rights record, and a US trade mission to the PRC led by Commerce Secretary Ron Brown at the end of August was celebrated as opening a new era of 'commercial diplomacy' (IHT, 30 August 1994). The signing of US$5 billion worth of agreements between leading US firms and Chinese counterparts followed, while Brown announced the determination of the USA to get its 'fair share' of the US$250 billion worth of infrastructure projects before the end of the century. For Brown, China's strategic and economic importance demanded the construction of a more comprehensive relationship. The thinking behind this was made clear when Brown told a meeting of the US China Business Council that US exports to the PRC were growing at four times the rate of exports to the rest of the world (FT, 31 August 1994).

Although the figures of the business lobby are persuasive, Figures 6.1, 6.2 and 6.3 show that they reveal not so much a predominance of PRC trade links with the USA but rather a situation in which disruption of business with either Taiwan or the mainland would have serious repercussions for the USA.

That the Clinton administration's review of its Taiwan policy, unveiled on 7 September 1994, satisfied neither Beijing nor Taipei reflects Washington's desire to keep good relations with both. Granting permission for high-level bilateral meetings to take place in government offices, changing the name of the CCNAA to the Taipei Economic and Cultural Representative Office, and permitting private visits by officials to the island, were seen by critical observers in Taiwan as merely keeping up with changes made in European states, Japan and Australia in their

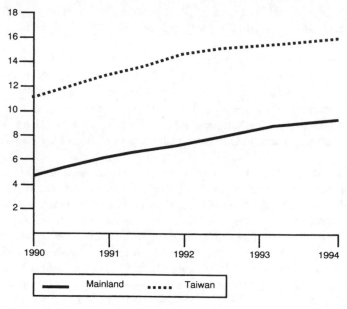

Figure 6.1 US exports to the mainland and Taiwan, 1990–4 (US$ billion)

Source: US Bureau of Economic Analysis, 'Survey of Current Business, August 1994', *Statistical Abstract of the United States 1995*, Washington, DC.

relations with Taiwan. These had failed to address the fundamental issue of Taiwan's status (Cai 1994). Yet most disappointing for the Lee administration was the failure of the Clinton administration to back its bid for representation at the UN. But despite assurances from the State Department that the changes did not represent any departure from the one-China policy, even these limited concessions by Washington sparked off an angry reaction from Beijing. Reports in the Hong Kong press claimed that the PRC had drafted a 'war plan' to suppress Taiwan's diplomatic gains (FT, 9 September 1994). Perhaps such reactions were inevitable when what Washington was trying to do was to keep both sides happy.

What is interesting about the Clinton administration's policy of keeping working relations with both Taipei and Beijing is that in many respects it seeks to formulate policy so as foster, rather than damage, the special relationship that has grown up between the two sides of the Strait. Underlying the resulting policy there has developed a US strategy based on a particular view of world economic formations, in which priority is given to doing business in 'Big Emerging Markets' (Brown 1994: 56–69), one of which is the 'Chinese Economic Area', consisting of Taiwan,

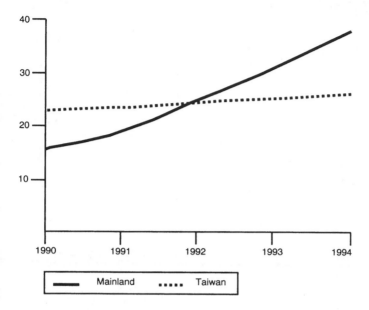

Figure 6.2 US imports from the mainland and Taiwan, 1990–4 (US$ billion)
Source: US Bureau of Economic Analysis, 'Survey of Current Business, August 1994',
Statistical Abstract of the United States 1995, Washington, DC.

mainland China and Hong Kong (Brown 1994: 144). Underlying this view
is an awareness in Washington that policies now have to be developed in
the context of the deep economic and cultural links that have grown
between these three territories. Initiatives towards any one of them will
have profound consequences for the others, particularly because the PRC's
trade surplus with the USA is largely a result of Hong Kong and Taiwan
manufacturers using the Chinese mainland as a production platform (AEI
1992: 9; Lampton 1992: 21–2).

With Washington committed to pursuing American interests by
maintaining working relationships with both Beijing and Taipei, then,
there seems to be little incentive for breaking the status quo that maintains
Taiwan's intermediate status. As was seen when President Clinton granted
Lee Teng-hui a visa to visit the United States, Beijing can raise the stakes
involved in any departure from its version of the one-China principle to
unacceptably high levels. Although during the round of high-level
diplomacy that followed the mobilisation of the PLA in 1995[15]
Washington did not rule out a visa for Lee Teng-hui in future, enough
was said to allow the PRC to accept that the Americans remained

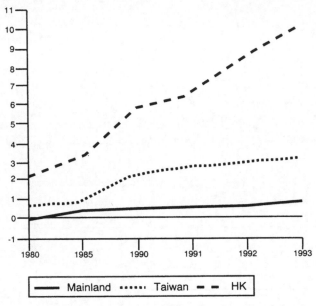

Figure 6.3 US direct investment in the mainland, Taiwan and Hong Kong, 1980–93 (US$ billion)

Source: US Bureau of Economic Analysis, 'Survey of Current Business, August 1994', *Statistical Abstract of the United States 1995*, Washington, DC.

committed to the principle that Beijing is the only legitimate government of China and that Taiwan is a part of China (IHT, 2 August, 27 October 1995). When Lee Teng-hui was asked by *Newsweek* after the election whether he would visit the USA again, his answer that 'America won't let me go' (*Newsweek*, 20 May 1996: 19), and his remarks to the Taiwan press that he feared another visit might further damage Washington–Beijing relations (UDN, 30 July 1995), indicate that the pursuit of national interests in the Washington–Beijing relationship continues to be a powerful constraint on responses to Taipei's appeals for greater recognition.

In terms of the longer historical development of the Taiwan issue as a problem for Chinese nationalism, then, the events surrounding Taiwan's presidential election might best be seen as a testing of the balance of forces that maintain the island's intermediate status. From this perspective the limitations for manoeuvre by all sides may be have been confirmed. First of all, the intervention of the US Navy in the Taiwan Strait between December 1995 and March 1996 signalled that Washington would continue to maintain the security that has enabled Taiwan to carve out its unique status since the 1970s. On the other hand, by the end of July 1995 Lee had decided not to accept an invitation to the joint conference of the US–ROC and ROC–US economic councils to be held in Alaska in September. Lee put this down to the attitude of the USA and to fears of further damaging Washington–Beijing relations. The international constraints imposed by Beijing thus appear to have continued to balance the appeals for greater recognition made by a democratic Taiwan.

TAIWAN'S INTERMEDIATE STATE

These American responses to the dilemma posed by Taipei's foreign policy are informative, then, of how the major international actor involved in the Taiwan problem continues to find ways to accommodate the emerging relationships between Taiwan and mainland China. Just what kind of political relations Taipei can enjoy with other states in this situation takes diplomats into a grey area of compromise and innovation. For Taipei's diplomats, articulating a cogent policy that can both be intelligible to other states and circumvent the obstacles put in place by Beijing requires a kind of semantic balancing act. This often proves too demanding for even the best-trained diplomats and politicians as they have had to talk the language of states. In September 1993, for example, shortly after the ROC's application for UN membership was rejected, Foreign Minister Frederick Chien was widely reported as having told the press, 'It would be better for us not to talk about one China. Over-emphasis on one China will constrain us' (UDN, 22 September 1993).

Chien went so far as to claim that he had not even used the four Chinese characters meaning 'one China' since the termination of the Period of Mobilisation on 1 May 1991. He claimed that Lee Teng-hui and Lien Chan were in full agreement with him on this matter, and that 'sovereignty' had become the most damaging issue for Taiwan, because in international law it was an indivisible concept. To say that 'there is only one China' must imply that Taiwan is under the sovereignty of the PRC and does not have its own sovereignty. Called to account by the KMT, Chien explained two days later that his remarks should only be understood to mean that it is no longer beneficial in relation to international affairs to talk of one China. He did not mean that the government's policy had actually changed from that of pursuing one China (UDN, 24 September 1993). When he addressed the Legislative Yuan he urged that the idea of the 'political entity' should be used when talking about cross-Strait relations, but when pursuing entry to international organisations, the term 'sovereign state' had to be used (UDN, 4 November 1993).

Yet the most blatant statement by a government spokesman of the unspoken implications of the ROC's mainland and foreign policies for Taiwan's identity came, probably inadvertently, from ROC Minister of Economic Affairs Chiang Pin-kung (Jiang Bingkun) at the APEC meeting in Seattle in November 1993. Following a repetition by PRC Foreign Minister Qian Qichen of his government's position that Taiwan is a province of the PRC, Chiang attempted to convey the ROC position to the world press. Trying to give a faithful representation of the official line, Chiang told his audience that the ROC had adopted a policy which he called a 'transitional two Chinas policy' (*jieduan xing liang ge Zhongguo*). As the press back in Taiwan commented, while the 'China' of Qian Qichen is political, concrete and exclusive, that of Chiang Pin-kung actually consists of three Chinas: the ROC, the PRC and a future united China. Yet it also came across that central to Chiang's message was the admission that there are now two sovereign Chinese states (UDN, 22 November 1993), while the mainland press condemned it as yet another departure from the one-China principle (*Liaowang* 1993: 46). Perhaps what Chiang had really achieved was to demonstrate just how difficult it had become for his government to describe Taiwan's intermediate state between independence and unification when addressing the different audiences of his domestic constituency, Beijing and international society.

7　Conclusion

This work has attempted to understand the development of the Taiwan problem in terms of people thinking and acting to resolve a variety of problems in a changing historical situation. From this perspective, the Taiwan problem can be understood as part of an ongoing political debate which takes place on a variety of levels of analysis, from the individual search for identity, to the search for political stability, and ultimately to the quest for international order. In such a situation the main actors must work to manipulate a fluctuating balance of political power and to develop the vocabulary of political discourse that they inherit. The result is a process of historical change in which established patterns of power and old concepts tend to take on new meanings as the context changes.

The overall context within which the Taiwan problem has developed must be seen as intimately tied up with the entry of China into international society. Central to this process has been the development of a theory of state legitimacy founded on the principle that the national unit and the political unit should be congruent. With the legitimacy of the ruling party being linked with the integrity of the national unit, theories of democracy and self-determination have been subsumed under the imperative for national unity, justifying a theory of party dictatorship in times of national division. The national unit concerned has been imagined in terms of fluctuating historical, ethnic and territorial criteria, extending at times to all the territories of the former Qing empire. Taiwan was given a prominent place as a part of this Chinese identity when the Second World War provided Chinese nationalists with the international support to make territorial claims against Japan. On becoming part of the Chinese nation, Taiwan became a criterion of the nationalist credentials of political parties. Following the 1949 retreat of the KMT to Taiwan and the US intervention in the Taiwan Strait in 1950, the situation of national division made Taiwan and the one-China policy a central criterion of state legitimacy in the politics of both sides of the Taiwan Strait.

The further development of the symbolic importance of Taiwan's relationship with the Chinese mainland in the post-war period must be understood in the context of the need to prove the legitimacy of the regimes that ended up facing each other across the Taiwan Strait. Neither of them has been free from serious crisis for any significant period of time. These crises, however, have led to very different outcomes concerning the development of Chinese nationalism. In mainland China the failure of Communism has led to an increasing saliency of the nationalist elements of Chinese political thought. In Taiwan, disillusion with the KMT has taken place in the context of increasing international isolation due to the claims of Chinese nationalism. Under the umbrella of the unique status provided by the Taiwan Relations Act, this isolation has not led to a solution to the problem of Taiwan's international status in terms of statehood, but has provided the context for a deconstruction of Chinese nationalism to take place.

The deconstruction of Chinese nationalism that has taken place in Taiwan has challenged the KMT's legitimacy to govern and made the link between state and society the central theme of political discourse. The response of the regime has been to find a new form of legitimacy by initiating reforms aimed at introducing representative government. Yet any such moves have had to circumvent the international implications of acknowledging that the population of Taiwan exercises sovereignty over the island. The resulting ambiguity in the relationship between Taiwan's identity and status has had to be accommodated by numerous devices, such as maintaining symbolic representation for the Chinese nation in representative bodies.

Yet democratisation has proved to possess its own momentum. This has led the Lee Teng-hui regime to proceed with increasingly radical reforms. Consequently, nationalists in the KMT's ranks have been alienated as the difference between the claims of the one-China policy and the reality that sovereignty now lies with the population of Taiwan has become increasingly apparent. As bureaucratic and legal arrangements have been needed to systematise and oversee transactions with the Chinese mainland, and as the one-China policy has continued to isolate Taiwan internationally, debates on constitutional reform have ultimately been unable to avoid the issue of national identity. This has especially been so concerning issues where the symbolic representation of the Chinese nation is impossible, such as the election of the president.

Under pressure to be seen to be putting Taiwan first, Lee Teng-hui has attempted to increase his democratic credentials. This has meant finally breaking with nationalists in his own party and their ideological legacy, and acknowledging that sovereignty is located in the population of Taiwan.

For this he has received much support from the opposition and moved into a position of being more the president of Taiwan than the leader of the KMT. The reform process has culminated in a concentration of power in his hands along the lines of a French-style presidential system. The social cohesiveness upon which this new political dispensation must rest, moreover, has had to break with the divisive ethnic criteria characteristic of Chinese nationalism. This has been replaced by a definition of the *demos* in subjective terms of shared interests and loyalties, of society as a 'living community' of 'shared destiny'. The result is a 'post-nationalist' identity established on a sense of what Lee Teng-hui calls *Gemeinschaft*.

This development of a post-nationalist identity in Taiwan has meant that a new conception of the island's relationship to Chinese identity has had to be arrived at. This can be seen in attempts to depoliticise links with the overseas Chinese through taking away their rights to representation in Taiwan's political system, while simultaneously building up economic and cultural links. The same process can be seen in the tendency to locate Taiwan within a 'Greater China' consisting of an economic and cultural community including the Chinese mainland, Hong Kong and Macao. The process of integration with this entity has been successfully managed so as to satisfy the demands of business and kinship ties while forestalling demands for political amalgamation. Its political limits are shown by the deadlock over the issue of sovereignty and jurisdiction in the 'unofficial' negotiations held to establish better working relations between the two sides.

While this process has been going on, the centripetal forces of the mainland Chinese economy have been balanced by a parallel process of integrating Taiwan into the global economy. This has also been complemented by a diplomatic drive to secure an international status for the island and to stop Taiwan being thought of as a part of the PRC by other states. As the regime has freed itself from the nationalist form of legitimisation in domestic politics, it has finally reached a stage at which it can present its claims in terms of statehood, culminating in the campaign for representation in the United Nations. Despite winning much approval for its economic and political achievements though, Taipei has been unable to break out of its intermediate state between independence and unification, so long as Beijing insists on upholding the one-China principle in international society.

With Taipei and Beijing moving along different trajectories, at some point there had to be a showdown in which the balance of forces could be clarified. This occurred with the events between Lee Teng-hui's 1995 visit to the United States and the 1996 presidential election in Taiwan. The outcome of the reactions to these events appears to have indicated that the stalemate between the two sides of the Strait continues. While sovereignty is now practised by the population of Taiwan, this has not resulted in the kind of desire to risk secession that appeared when the Baltic states broke away from the Soviet Union. Of course, one of the main reasons for this is the fear of attack from the Chinese mainland. Yet there is also a danger of looking at Taiwan's relationship with China in terms of analogies with Russia and the Soviet successor states. The mainland economy is growing rapidly and thus exerts a centripetal force on the communities around it. Moreover, despite the many destructive policies adopted by nation-building Chinese nationalists over the decades, there remain complex ties between communities in Taiwan, the mainland and throughout the world who identify themselves as Chinese. If Taiwan's position in this web of relationships is under question, on closer examination the process involved appears to be one of metamorphosis rather than collapse. This can be seen by looking at Taiwan's position in the changing nature of Chinese identity and the limitations of international society as the new millennium approaches.

If political change in Taiwan has resulted in a challenge to the nationalist conception of Chinese identity that has been so strong in the twentieth century, the future of the Taiwan problem must be intimately tied up with the future of Chinese nationalism on the mainland. Many commentators outside China have recently raised the possibility that challenges to nationalism are emerging in the PRC. Edward Friedman, for example, holds that by the 1990s Mao-era anti-imperialist nationalism was dead, and points to the development of a new national identity in southern China based on the ancient kingdom of Chu (Friedman 1994). Others have also remarked on the impact of the globalisation of economic and information systems on the evolution of China's national identity and the PRC conception of sovereignty (Kim 1993; Segal 1994a, 1994b). Some writers from Taiwan have gone so far as to claim that the 'deconstruction of China' (*Zhongguo de jieti*) into smaller states is not only inevitable, but will solve Taiwan's problems and most of China's other perennial crises (Huang 1992). One DPP legislator put this in picturesque form when he compared the PRC to a bowl of instant noodles that has been swallowed, while the world waits to see how long it will take for its calories to be burned up (Lin 1992).

Even if such views are right and there is a crisis of national identity in the PRC, this does not necessarily imply a greater degree of freedom for the people of Taiwan to determine what kind of relationship they have with China. If nationalism was born from the ashes of disintegration, the search for stability and security in mainland China may just as well continue to look to the nationalist tradition for inspiration as away from it. The demonstrators who took to the streets throughout mainland China between January 1987 and June 1989 identified themselves most clearly with the May Fourth Movement of 1919, the birth of Chinese nationalism as a mass movement (Calhoun 1994; Schwarcz 1994). The culture of discontent that has taken root in the PRC in the 1990s may represent a rejection of socialism as the key to modernity, but not necessarily a rejection of nationalism. As a slogan from Tiananmen Square put it, 'We love our country, but we hate our government' (Goldman *et al.* 1993: 125).

If CCP rule in mainland China has resulted in an 'authority deficiency', then, this does not necessarily imply that concessions will be made to territories over which the PRC claims sovereignty. The new leaders in Beijing are probably more likely to search for legitimacy by linking economic expansion with Chinese nationalism (Bachman 1994: 47). As nationalist sentiments are stirred up, the symbolic role of claimed territories takes on a heightened significance. Witness, for example, gestures such as the erection of a massive clock in Tiananmen Square in December 1994 to count the seconds before Hong Kong returns to the motherland. This is the context within which a document such as Beijing's 1993 White Paper on *The Taiwan Question and Reunification of China* (Taiwan Affairs Office 1993) and the bellicose reaction to Lee Teng-hui's Cornell visit should be understood. Deng Xiaoping had made it clear when he met Margaret Thatcher in 1982 that any leader who failed on the issue of national unification would have to step down after being condemned by the Chinese people as another Li Hongzhang, the statesman who signed the 'unequal treaties' ceding Qing territory, including Taiwan, to the powers (Deng 1982: 12–13). Shortly before Taiwan's presidential election PRC Defence Minister Chi Haotian told the National People's Congress that if Taiwan could not be liberated, the CCP would be unable to wash away the shame (UDN, 9 March 1996). After the election, in one of the most stridently nationalist statements ever to emerge from mainland China, Jiang was reminded that he, too, has said that any leader who compromises over Taiwan will be condemned as a historic criminal (Zhang 1996: 72).

What this means for Taiwan is that any developments that occur inside the island must inescapably be seen as a part of the much wider debate on the relationship between Chinese national identity and the state. CCP thinking still sees this in terms of the struggle against imperialism, envisioned since the Cold War as taking place between North and South and as a war against socialism through an American strategy of 'peaceful evolution' (Deng 1989). The failure of Beijing's bid for the 2000 Olympics and its hopes to become a founding member of the WTO, pressures from the west over human rights, and what is seen in the mainland as an

American strategy of preventing the PRC from growing too strong, all enabled Lee Teng-hui's visit to the United States to be presented as one link in a grand US strategy of containment which only the CCP is capable of breaking out of (*Liaowang* 1995: 44). The link between unification and legitimacy thus remains as close as ever (Chen 1990; *Liaowang* 1990a: 3) and Taiwan maintains its position as the 'private parts' of China, as one of the authors of the most comprehensive and disturbing statements of Chinese nationalism at the end of the twentieth century puts it (Zhang 1996: 73).

The political function of the Taiwan problem thus remains firmly embedded in the ongoing search for national wealth and power that has lasted throughout the twentieth century. As even dissidents who are arguing for the most radical political reforms in the PRC still locate Taiwan within something called 'China' (Fang 1990: 161–2), albeit along the loosest of federal lines (CDN, 22 February 1991; Yan 1992/3: 14–15), it seems unlikely that this search will result in a departure from Chinese claims to Taiwan. At any rate, so long as nationalism remains the touchstone of legitimacy, any development of a more pluralistic society within the PRC seems likely to occur within a state that places unity when facing the outside world at the top of its priorities.

However, when Deng Xiaoping made unification with Taiwan one of the CCP's three main tasks for the 1980s, it was accompanied not only by opposing hegemonism but also by the task of stepping up economic reconstruction. This draws attention to the developmentalist strategy for achieving national wealth and power that lies at the heart of Deng's nationalism. Although the policy of 'peaceful evolution' and 'one country, two systems' may have its origins in the united front doctrine, it is also a device to bring Taiwan, Hong Kong and Macao under PRC sovereignty without disrupting their economic achievements and without engaging in armed conflict. This is because there is a realisation in Beijing that if the PRC economy is to reach the level of a medium-developed country it will require at least seventy years of peace (Deng 1993: 250, 251–2, 266–7, 372) and it will be helped considerably if there is co-operation from Hong Kong and Taiwan. Such co-operation is only likely to be forthcoming if the Hong Kong transition is successful and the mainland economy is successfully reformed (Deng 1993: 265, 358).

Given this mixture of economic, emotional and political imperatives for unification with Taiwan, how Beijing's policy is implemented will depend largely upon how different factions in the CCP interpret and weigh up the resources that are available. Yet whatever methods are used, the common aim seems likely to remain that of unification with Taiwan. In a political culture where any dissent is categorised as treason, to compromise on the one-China principle is to run the risk of delegitimising one's own activities.

AFTER THE STATE?

If, then, the ongoing development of the Taiwan problem is intimately tied up with the legitimacy of the PRC state, the problem arises of how Taiwan can interact with an international society that has never resolved the conflict between the contradictory principles of state sovereignty and national self-determination. From their responses to this political problem, Beijing and Taipei may be said to have developed visions of global politics that are compatible with 'realist' and 'idealist' conceptions of world politics, respectively, as these terms are used by Martin Wight (Wight 1991).

Beijing's realist vision of international politics must be understood as having its roots in the understanding of world politics that arose as nationalism was generated by the Qing dynasty's entry into international society. Central to this is a hard conception of sovereignty as absolute and indivisible that mainland sources trace back to Bodin and Vattel. European efforts since the nineteenth century to dilute this concept are dismissed as apologies for colonialism (Jia 1993: 112–13; ZDBK 1984: 814–16; Zhou 1981: 167–247). Hand in hand with this understanding of sovereignty goes the belief that its worth must be understood in terms of the configuration of power in international relations at any given moment. The Taiwan problem thus arose from the US policy of using the island to manipulate the balance of power between itself, the PRC and the Soviet Union. In future Japan will replace the Soviet Union in this balance (Jia 1993: 121–2). From this perspective, what Taipei sees as attempts to create a 'win–win' situation by loosening the concept of sovereignty can only be seen by Beijing as part of a zero-sum game. It becomes imperative, therefore, that Taiwan's joining of international organisations is tied as closely as possible to acknowledgement of Beijing's sovereignty. Recognition of Taiwan as a non-state actor, such as a 'customs area' or an Olympic team, must not imply any kind of recognition that the island is a state.

From Taipei's perspective, however, it is in the interests of Taiwan and the whole of China to promote a vision of the world in which conceptions of sovereignty become less significant under the impact of global integration, and as the rights of individuals to determine their own destiny are seen to be on the rise. It is significant to note here that the ROC bid for UN membership is made according to the moral principle of universal representation for individuals in the UN (GIO 1993a, 1994; Hu 1994: 7). Yet if Taipei argues for a move away from nationalist conceptions of the links between state and nation and holds up examples such as the dual representation of the two Germanys and the two Koreas, this must be able to sway other states away from respecting Beijing's narrow interpretation of the one-China principle. What appears to be the trend in reactions to Taipei's assertive foreign policy, however, is that while Taiwan's political and economic achievements tend to gain a favourable hearing for the island amongst parliamentarians and the media in liberal democracies, such reactions are limited by foreign policy organisations which are set up to deal with state interests rather than issues of morality.

The decision to grant Lee Teng-hui a visa to the USA, for example, was strongly opposed by the foreign policy establishment, who tend to see PRC co-operation on a whole range of wider issues, such as North Korea, arms proliferation and trade, as outweighing the ROC's desire for recognition (IHT, 24 May 1995). How far the mobilisation of public opinion and legislatures against executive administrations can promote Taipei's case remains to be seen. Such initiatives, however, run the risk of damaging Taipei's foreign relations in the long run through forcing the hand of foreign governments which do not see why they should jeopardise their relations with Beijing when a reasonably good working relationship with Taipei under the one-China principle appears to have been developed.

Unfortunately, international society cannot boast a good record when it comes to dealing with conflicts between the sanctity of statehood and the principle of self-determination. The stability offered by adherence to the one-China principle is understandably attractive to those who have to formulate and implement foreign policy in times of increasing uncertainty in world politics and of possible instability in the PRC. Rather than forcing states to face this problem head on, the nature of Taiwan's foreign policy has thus had to be to work towards collaboration in the search for mechanisms and concepts that can circumvent and defuse the tensions that arise between the two conflicting principles at the foundations of the international system. In this task, Taipei is at a disadvantage in so far as it is Beijing which is operating within the established vocabulary of international society.

The overall result of this tug-of-war over the relationship between national identity and international status, however, has been a certain creative tension and elasticity from which new concepts emerge. For the CCP, this is most evident in the words and means of 'one country, two systems'. For policy-makers in Taiwan, on the other hand, there is the terminology of the 'political entity', the redefinition of what 'China' signifies, and the development of imaginative diplomatic practices. Much of the time confusion and obfuscation are the result. But it is also interesting to note that Chinese terminology has been taken up by various actors in international society. When, for example, Speaker of the US House of Representatives Newt Gingrich raised the possibility, in February 1995, that the USA could reinterpret the one-China policy as meaning that there is 'currently one China with two sovereign governments who currently represent two different political entities' (FT, 13 February 1995), he was restating Taipei's thinking in a foreign environment. Similarly, the United Kingdom has accepted Beijing's formula of 'one country, two systems' as the basic policy framework for the future of Hong Kong.

What the process of innovation has led to, then, is the development of an identity for Taiwan that is part of the changing Chinese dispensation which needs to be properly accommodated by other states. While the regime in Taiwan has maintained all the characteristics of a state and has embedded itself in international economic structures, it has simultaneously been located as part of a supra-state, post-nationalist Chinese entity embracing communities of Chinese people living overseas and the rapidly expanding economy of the Chinese mainland. This is reflected not only by the actions and words of Taipei's own policy-makers, but also by those of business people and even foreign governments, as in the role of the idea of a Chinese 'Big Emerging Market' in the Clinton administration's China policy. If it is correct to point out that Beijing can enjoy the benefits of a certain cultural identity to support its pragmatic policies towards other Chinas (Scalapino 1993: 228) the same is also evidently true for Taipei.

Of particular interest here is a speech made by Lee Teng-hui in January 1995, in which he coined the new slogan of 'manage great Taiwan, establish a new central plains' (*jingying da Taiwan, jianli xin zhongyuan*) for the coming millennium (UDN, 15 January 1995). This idea was also given a prominent position in his presidential inauguration speech on 20 May 1996 and it is significant for a number of reasons. First of all, when Lee talks about the 'central plains' he is alluding to the mythology that Chinese culture emerged from central China 5,000 years ago (Tu 1991a: 2–3). Lee's 'new central plains' is, of course, Taiwan, which he sees as having successfully resolved the enigmatic problem of combining Chinese tradition with western modernity, and thus providing a model for the rest of China. Rather than pass any judgement on the feasibility of such an ambition, it is more important to note the way that it again draws attention to Lee's continuing balance of the building of a strong state and society in Taiwan against the development of some kind of greater Chinese cultural and economic identity. In this sense, Lee's 'new central plains' might best be translated as a 'new Sinocentrism', with Taiwan as the centre.

It may be something of an exaggeration to suggest that Taiwan can serve as a model for mainland China's development, due to disparity in size alone. However, what can be said about Taiwan's role in Chinese nationalism is that it has become one of the richest sources of new thinking about the relationship between Chinese national identity and the state. From this perspective, the long-term significance of Taiwan's democratisation for Chinese nationalism may lie not so much in Beijing's reaction to the 1996 presidential election as in the flood of books and articles discussing Chinese nationalism and national identity that was triggered by the crisis in all parts of the Chinese-reading world (*Ming bao* 1996; Song 1996; Weng 1996; Wu 1996; Yu 1996; Zhu 1996). Although some of this literature is unsettling, even the most extreme views do at least provoke debate on issues that have remained largely unexplored under CCP rule and under the KMT regime in Taiwan until recently.

From a longer historical perspective, this argument may be seen as the continuation of attempts to adapt Chinese vocabulary to the discourse of a world of nation-states. This has been seen throughout this work in the case of a term such as *minzu*, used as the equivalent of 'nation', or the adaptation of *Zhongguo* (Central Kingdom(s))[16] to 'China'. The term *guo* is a similar case. For thousands of years this pictogram has consisted of symbols representing a population and a sword within a wall, as it still is in Taiwan. It has come to be rendered into English in a variety of ways, including 'state', 'country' and sometimes 'nation'. What should be clear from this work, however, is that the matching of Chinese vocabulary to English terms is a political activity in itself. As part and parcel of the attempt to adapt Chinese thinking to the categories of the European-American tradition of thought, this allows for a degree of creativity in interpretation. It has been shown above that, when looked at in terms of the different demands it is trying to satisfy in dealing with the Taiwan problem, the idea of the *guo* has been stretched to contain a cluster of meanings which it is difficult to catch in English translations. Perhaps the notion of a 'post-nationalist identity in an intermediate state' is the closest it is possible to get to catching Taiwan's identity and status as they have come to exist within the context of the Chinese *guo* at the end of the twentieth century.

Appendix
Glossary of names

Chang Mao-kuei	Zhang Maogui
Chen Che-nan	Chen Zhenan
Chen Li-an	Chen Lu'an
Chen Shui-bian	Chen Shuibian
Chiang Ching-kuo	Jiang Jingguo
Chiang Pin-kung	Jiang Binkong
Chiang Wei-kuo	Jiang Weiguo
Chien, Frederick	Qian Fu
Fei Hsi-ping	Fei Xiping
Hau Pei-tsun	Hao Bocun
Hsieh, Frank	Xie Changting
Hsu Li-nung	Xu Linong
Hsui Sheng-fa	Xu Shengfa
Huang Huang-hsiung	Huang Huangxiong
Huang Hsin-chieh	Huang Xinjie
Huang Kun-huei	Huang Kunhui
Huang Shih-hui	Huang Shihui
Huang Ta-chou	Huang Dazhou
Jaw Shau-kong	Zhao Shaokang
Kao Koong-lian	Gao Konglian
Kaohsiung	Gaoxiong
Kinmen	Jinmen
Koo Chen-fu	Gu Zhenfu
Kuo, Shirley	Guo Wanrong
Lee Teng-hui	Li Denghui
Lei Chen	Lei Zhen
Lien Chan	Lian Zhan
Lin Cheng-chieh	Lin Zhengjie
Lin Cho-shui	Lin Zhuoshui
Lin Yang-kang	Lin Yanggang
Lin Yih-shyong	Lin Yixiong

Matsu	Mazu
Peng Ming-min	Peng Mingmin
Shaw Yu-ming	Shau Yuming
Shieh, Samuel	Xie Senzhong
Shih Chi-yang	Shi Jiyang
Shih Ming-teh	Shi Mingde
Sun Yat-sen	Sun Zhongshan
Tai Kuo-hui	Dai Guohui
Taipei	Taibei
Tao Pai-chuan	Tao Baichuan
Wang Chien-shien	Wang Jianxuan
Wang Yung-ch'ing	Wang Yongqing
Wang Yung-tsai	Wang Yongzai
Wu Che-liang	Wu Zheliang
Yao Chia-wen	Yao Jiawen
Yeh Shih-tao	Ye Shitao

Notes

1 P. 7

This is the import of Sun's key statement, 'minzu zhuyi jiu shi guozu zhuyi'. This phrase is rendered into English in the official translation as the rather meaningless 'nationalism is the doctrine of the state', which overlooks the function of the character *zu*, often translated as 'clan', in the compound *guozu*.

2 P. 24

The background factors leading to the 228 Incident listed here are condensed from the research report into newly released documents carried out by Chen Zhongguang *et al.* (1994). For a version that is highly critical of the KMT, based on first-hand experience, see Kerr (1966). For an alternative interpretation see Lai Tse-han *et al.* (1991).

3 P. 27

The figures for this period are naturally unreliable. Some idea can be gained from the official version in the *China Yearbook* 1980: 143. According to this, the 1940 census taken by the Japanese recorded a population of 5,870,000. In 1946, the population was 6,090,000. Following the fall of the Chinese mainland, the influx of mainlanders left Taiwan's population at 8,128,000 in 1952.

4 P. 47

For a summary of the main documents on 'peaceful unification' and 'one country, two systems' in these years, see Zhan 1993: 31–4.

5 P. 55

GATT Article XXXIII allows for application for accession by a government acting on behalf of a separate customs territory possessing full autonomy in the conduct of its external commercial relations.

6 P. 71

The KMT had in fact originally found through opinion polls that the three ideals most people wanted the ruling party to pursue were summed up by the Chinese characters for 'national security, social stability, economic prosperity'. It is an indication of how the KMT wanted to keep a safe distance from the issue of national identity, however, that by the beginning of October the 'national' had been dropped from this equation and the official campaign slogan had become 'reform, security, prosperity' (UDN, 8 August 1991).

7 P. 74

Existing powers of the National Assembly over appointment and recall of the president and vice-president were reaffirmed, as was the assembly's right to confirm appointment of personnel nominated by the president. An obligation was also introduced for the president to deliver annual reports on the state of the nation. The Third National Assembly, to be elected in 1996, would be given extra democratic credentials by reducing its term from six years to four. Meanwhile, from the next presidential election, the terms of office for the president and vice-president would be reduced from six years to four years, and limited to two consecutive terms.

8 P. 83

They included former premier Yu Kuo-hwa (Yu Guohua), and presidential advisers Nieh Wen-ya (Nie Wenya), Li Kwoh-ting (Li Guoding) and Irwine Ho, and former vice-president and provincial governor Hsieh Tung-min (Xie Dongmin).

9 P. 97

The term *shengming gongtong ti* will be rendered as *Gemeinschaft* hereafter, as it is in official ROC texts and because Lee Teng-hui attributes it to Kant and Goethe. He does not mention Tonnies, with whom it is usually associated.

10 P. 98

A 1992 survey found that the rate of mixed marriages amongst those who had enjoyed higher education stood at 16.1 per cent, just short of the 16.7 per cent it would be if provincial background were not a factor in choosing a spouse (Wang 1993).

11 P. 100

The division made here is based loosely on Townsend (1992). Some adjustments have been made for consistency with the definitions adopted in this work. In particular, Townsend does not include Taiwan, Hong Kong and Macao in what he terms the 'official' and 'unofficial' nations. This gives rise to some confusion that can be avoided by thinking not in terms of 'official' and 'unofficial' when describing relations between Taiwan and the mainland, but in terms of who controls what.

12 P. 105

An indication of the varied nature and extent of links between people of Chinese descent living overseas was revealed by the inaugural meeting of a so-called 'United World Chinese Association' in Hong Kong in September 1992, supposed to be a pan-Chinese organisation aimed at uniting the Chinese mainland, Taiwan and the Chinese overseas, and claiming support from the governments of both the PRC and the ROC. Police investigations revealed, however, that the majority of delegates were in fact international triad leaders. These included representatives of Taiwan's Bamboo Gang, known in the past for its close links with the ROC security services (SCMP, 6 September 1992).

13 P. 140

Namely that 'A member could properly vote to accept a representative of a government which it did not recognise, or with which it had no diplomatic relations', and 'Such a vote did not imply recognition or a readiness to assume diplomatic relations' (*Security Council Official Records*, Fifth Year, Supplement for 1 January through 31 May 1950; reproduced in *Accession* 1990: 16).

14 P. 140

El Salvador, Guatemala, Nicaragua, Costa Rica, Honduras, Panama and Belize.

15 P. 149

Secretary of State Warren Christopher held talks with his PRC counterpart, Qian Qichen, in Brunei on 1 August, Jiang Zemin with Bill Clinton at the fiftieth anniversary of the UN in New York on 24 October, and Jiang Zemin and Al Gore at the APEC summit in Osaka on 19 November (Clinton could not attend, as he originally meant to, due to a dispute with Congress over the US budget).

16 P. 162

Because Chinese nouns cannot take a plural form, the term *Zhongguo*, which has come to be rendered as 'China' in English, can actually be more literally translated as either 'Central Kingdom' or 'Central Kingdoms'. As the philosopher Mencius (372–289 BC) of the Warring States period told King Huan of the Kingdom of Qi, 'You wish to extend your territory, to enjoy the homage of Qin and Chu, to rule over the Central Kingdoms [*Zhongguo*] and to bring peace to the barbarian tribes of the four borders' (Mencius 1984: 219).

Bibliography

ABBREVIATIONS USED FOR NEWSPAPERS

CDN	*Central Daily News* (*Zhongyang ri bao*)
CN	*China News*
CP	*China Post* (*Taipei*)
CT	*China Times* (*Zhongguo shi bao*)
FCJ	*Free China Journal*
FEER	*Far Eastern Economic Review*
FT	*Financial Times*
GSB	*Commercial Times* (*Gonshang shibao*)
IEP	*Independence Evening Post* (*Zili wan bao*)
IHT	*International Herald Tribune*
IMP	*Independence Morning Post* (*Zili zao bao*)
IWP	*Independence Weekly Post* (*Zili zhou bao*)
RRB	*People's Daily* (*Renmin ri bao*)
SCMP	*South China Morning Post*
UDN	*United Daily News* (*Lian he bao*)

WORKS CITED

Accession of the Customs Territory of Taiwan, Penghu, Kinmen and Matsu – GATT (1990) Taipei. (Cited as *Accession*.)

AEI (1992) *American Economic Relations with Greater China: Challenges for the 1990s*, Joint Conference of The American Enterprise Institute and China Business Forum, 5 February, Washington, DC: American Enterprise Institute.

Anderson, B. (1991) *Imagined Communities*, London: Verso.

Armstrong, D. (1993) *Revolution and World Order*, Oxford: Clarendon Press.

Ash, R. and Kueh, Y. (1993) 'Economic Integration Within Greater China: Trade and Investment Flows Between China, Hong Kong and Taiwan', *China Quarterly*, 136: 711–45.

Bachman, D. (1994) 'Domestic Sources of Chinese Foreign Policy', in Kim, S. (ed.) *China and the World: Chinese Foreign Policy in the Post-Cold War Era*, Boulder, Colo., and Oxford: Westview Press.

Bai, Xianyong (Pai Hsien-yung) (1978) *Taibei Ren* (Taipei People), Taibei: Chen zhong.

Beijing Review (1979) 'Message to Compatriots in Taiwan from the Standing Committee of the Fifth National People's Congress', 5 January: 16–17.

Bendix, R. (1978) *Kings or People: Power and the Mandate to Rule*, Berkeley: University of California Press.

Bloom, W. (1990) *Personal Identity, National Identity and International Relations*, Cambridge: Cambridge University Press.

Bosco, J. (1992) 'Taiwan Factions: Guanxi, Patronage and the State in Local Politics', *Ethnology*, 31, 2: 157–83.

—— (1994) 'Faction versus Ideology: Mobilization Strategies in Taiwan's Elections', *China Quarterly*, 137: 28–62.

Breuilly, J. (1993) *Nationalism and the State*, Manchester: Manchester University Press.

Brown, R. (1994) 'The National Export Strategy: Annual Report to the United States Congress', *Business America*, 115, 9.

Bull, H. (1993) *The Anarchical Society: A Study of Order in World Politics*, Basingstoke and London: Macmillan.

Cai, Tongrong (1994) 'Meiguo dui Tai xin zhengce zouxiang' (The Direction of America's New Taiwan Policy), CT, 8 July 1994.

Calhoun, C. (1994) 'Science, Democracy and the Politics of Identity', in Wasserstrom, J. and Perry, E. (eds) *Popular Protest and Political Culture in Modern China*, Boulder, Colo., and Oxford: Westview Press.

Central Committee of the CCP (1981) 'Resolution on Certain Questions in the History of our Party Since the Founding of the PRC', in *Resolution on CPC History 1949–81*, Beijing: Foreign Languages Press.

CEPD (1994) *Taiwan Statistical Data Book 1994*, Taipei: Council for Economic Planning and Development.

Chan, H. (1985) *Legitimation in Imperial China: Discussions under the Jurchen-Chin Dynasty (1115–1234)*, Seattle and London: University of Washington Press.

Chang, G. (1990) *Friends and Enemies: The United States, China and the Soviet Union, 1948–1972*, Stanford, Calif.: Stanford University Press.

Chen, J. (1996) 'Voices of the Past: Oral History Sweeps Deep', *Sinorama*, 27, 21: 78–87.

Chen, Liling (ed.) (1995) *Taiwan ren riben bing de Zhanzheng jingyan* (War Experiences of Taiwanese Soldiers for Japan), Taibei: Taibei xian li wenhua zhongxin.

Chen, Shuibian (Chen Shui-bian) (1989) *Taiwan yao duli* (Taiwan Wants Independence), Taibei: Chen Shui-bian guohui wen zheng bangongshi.

Chen, Zhi (1990) 'Zuguo tongyi shi lishi de da shi' (Unification of the Motherland is a Great Historical Matter), *Liaowang*, 2 April: 6.

Chen, Zhongguang, Ye, Mingqing and Lai Zehan (Lai Tse-han) (1994) *Er er ba shijian yanjiu baogao* (Research Report on the 228 Incident), Taibei: Shibao chubanshe.

Cheng, T. and Haggard, S. (eds) (1992) *Political Change in Taiwan*, Boulder, Colo.: Lynne Rienner.

Chiang, Kai-shek (1947) *China's Destiny and Chinese Economic Theory*, London: Roy.

China Year Book (1929–30) (1931–2) (ed. H. Woodhead), Shanghai.

China Yearbook (1980) Taipei: GIO.
China Yearbook (1994) Taipei: GIO.
Chiu, H. (ed.) (1973) *China and the Question of Taiwan – Documents and Analysis*, New York and London: Praeger.
—— (1992) *The International Legal Status of the Republic of China* (revised edition), School of Law, University of Maryland, Occasional Papers/Reprints Series in Contemporary Asian Studies, No. 5.
Clough, R. (1993) 'Chiang Ching-kuo's Policies Toward Mainland China and the Outside World', in Leng, S. (ed.) *Chiang Ching-kuo's Leadership in the Development of the Republic of China on Taiwan*, Lanham, NY, and London: University Press of America.
Coble, P. (1991) *Facing Japan: Chinese Politics and Japanese Imperialism*, Cambridge, Mass.: Harvard University Press.
Connor, W. (1984) *The National Question in Marxist-Leninist Theory and Strategy*, Princeton, NJ: Princeton University Press.
Copper, J. (1980) 'China's View of Taiwan's Status: Continuity and Change', *Asia Pacific Community*, Spring: 119–29.
Crawford, J. (1979) *The Creation of States in International Law*, Oxford: Clarendon Press.
Cullather, N. (1996) "Fuel for the Good Dragon": The United States and Industrial Policy in Taiwan, 1950–1965', *Diplomatic History*, 20, 1: 23.
Dai, Guohui and Ye, Yunyun (1992) *Ai zeng 228* (Love-Hate 228), Taibei: Yuanliu.
Deng, Xiaoping (1980) 'The Present Situation and the Tasks Before Us', *Selected Works 1975–82*, Beijing: Foreign Languages Press.
—— (1982) 'Women dui Xianggang wenti de jiben lichang' (Our Basic Position on the Hong Kong Problem), reprinted in *Wen xuan*, Vol. 3, Beijing: Renmin.
—— (1983) 'A Concept for the Peaceful Reunification of the Chinese Mainland and Taiwan', in *Build Socialism With Chinese Characteristics* (Zhongguo dalu he Taiwan heping tongyi de she xiang), reprinted in *Wen xuan*, Vol. 3, Beijing: Renmin.
—— (1984) 'Zai zhongyang guwen weiyuan hui di san ci quanti huiyi shang de jiang hua' (Talk to the Third Plenum of the Central Advisory Committee), reprinted in *Wen xuan*, Vol. 3, Beijing: Renmin.
—— (1985) *Build Socialism with Chinese Characteristics*, Beijing: Foreign Languages Press.
—— (1985a) 'The Principles of Peaceful Coexistence are Full of Vitality', in *Build Socialism with Chinese Characteristics*, Beijing: Renmin.
—— (1989) 'Jianchi shehui zhuyi, fangzhi heping yanbian' (Uphold Socialism, Prevent Peaceful Evolution), reprinted in *Wen xuan*, Vol. 3, Beijing: Renmin.
—— (1993) *Wen xuan*, Vol. 3, Beijing: Renmin.
Deutsch, K. (1988) *The Analysis of International Relations*, New Jersey: Prentice Hall.
Dittmer, L. and Kim, S. (eds) (1993) *China's Quest for National Identity*, Ithaca, NY: Cornell University Press.
Dong, Yuhong (1990) 'Taiwan guomindang de jiaose tiaozheng ji qi yingxiang' (The Adjustment of the KMT's Role and Its Impact), *Taiwan yanjiu*, 1: 25–31.
Dougherty, J. and Pfaltzgraff, R. (1990) *Contending Theories of International Relations: A Comprehensive Survey*, New York: Harper & Row.
DPP (1993) *Minzhu jinbu dang dang ling* (DPP Party Charter), Taibei: DPP Secretariat.

Eastman, L. (1986) 'Nationalist China During the Nanking Decade 1927–1937', in Fairbank, John K. and Twitchett, Denis (eds) *Cambridge History of China*, Vol. 13, Part 2, Cambridge: Cambridge University Press.

EY (Executive Yuan, ROC) (1991) *Guidelines for National Unification*, Taipei: Executive Yuan.

—— (1994) *Background Explanation on Taiwan–Mainland Consultations on Travel Safety Guarantees*, Taipei: Executive Yuan.

—— (1995) *Er er ba jinian pai luocheng jinian ce* (228 Memorial Opening Commemorative Brochure), Taibei: Executive Yuan.

Fairbank, J. (1968) 'A Preliminary Framework', in Fairbank, J. (ed.) *The Chinese World Order – Traditional China's Foreign Relations*, Cambridge, Mass.: Harvard University Press.

Fang, Lizhi (1990) 'Dui tongyi de kanfa' (View on Unification), in Yang, W. (ed.) *Haixia liang an guanxi wenji* (Studies of Taiwan–Mainland China Relations), Hong Kong: New Asia Cultural Foundation.

Feldman, M. (1989) 'A New Kind of Relationship: Ten Years of the Taiwan Relations Act', in Myers, R. (ed.) *A Unique Relationship: The United States and the Republic of China Under the Taiwan Relations Act*, Stanford, Calif.: Hoover Institution.

Formosa (1979a) 'Meiyou gaige jiu meiyou qiantu' (No Reform, Then No Future), October: 2.

—— (1979b) 2: 7.

Friedman, E. (1994) 'Reconstructing China's National Identity: A Southern Alternative to Mao-Era Anti-Imperialist Nationalism', *Journal of Asian Studies*, 35: 67–91.

Fu, Dawei (1993) 'The Words Hunter in the Jungle of Bai Lang When Taiwan's Aboriginals Write in Chinese'. Unpublished paper presented to the London–China Seminar, School of Oriental and African Studies, London.

Fu, J. (1992) *Taiwan and the Geopolitics of the Asian–American Dilemma*, New York: Praeger.

GATT (1992) *GATT Activities 1992*, Geneva: GATT.

—— (1994) *1994 Trends and Statistics: International Trade*, Geneva: GATT.

Gellner, E. (1990) *Nations and Nationalism*, Oxford: Basil Blackwell.

Gilpin, R. (1987) *The Political Economy of International Relations*, Princeton, NJ: Princeton University Press.

GIO (1993) *The Republic of China on Taiwan: A Worthy Nation Deserves a U.N. Seat*, Taipei: Government Information Office.

—— (1993a) *Divided China in the United Nations: Time for Parallel Representation*, Taipei: Government Information Office.

—— (1994) *The Republic of China on Taiwan and the U.N.: Questions and Answers*, Taipei: Government Information Office.

Gladney, D. (1990) *Muslim Chinese: Ethnic Nationalism in the People's Republic*, Cambridge, Mass.: Harvard University Press.

Gold, T. (1986) *State and Society in the Taiwan Miracle*, Armonk, NY, and London: M. E. Sharpe.

—— (1993) 'Taiwan's Quest for Identity in the Shadow of China,' in Tsang, S. (ed.) *In the Shadow of China*, London: C. Hurst.

—— (1994) 'Civil Society and Taiwan's Quest for Identity', in Harrell, S. and Huang, C. (eds) *Cultural Change in Postwar Taiwan*, Boulder, Colo.: Westview Press.

Goldman, M., Link, P. and Wei, S. (1993) 'China's Intellectuals in the Deng Era: Loss of Identity with the State', in Dittmer, L. and Kim, S. (eds) *China's Quest for National Identity*, Ithaca, NY: Cornell University Press.

Goncharov, S., Lewis, J. and Xue, L. (1993) *Uncertain Partners: Stalin, Mao and the Korean War*, Stanford, Calif.: Stanford University Press.

Guo, Xiangzhi (1990) '"Yi guo liang zhi" de lilun yu shijian' (The Concept of 'One Country – Two Systems': Theory and Practice), *Taiwan yanjiu*, 1: 5–17.

Haas, E. (1967) 'The "Uniting of Europe" and the Uniting of Latin America', *Journal of Common Market Studies*, 5: 324.

Halbeisen, H. (1993) 'In Search of a New Political Order?', in Tsang, S. (ed.) *In the Shadow of China*, London: C. Hurst.

Han, N. (ed.) (1990) *Diplomacy of Contemporary China*, Hong Kong: New Horizon.

Harding, H. (1992) *A Fragile Relationship: The United States and China Since 1972*, Washington, DC: Brookings Institution.

—— (1993) 'The Concept of "Greater China": Themes, Variations and Reservations', *China Quarterly*, 136: 660–86.

Harrell, S. and Huang, C. (1994) *Cultural Change in Postwar Taiwan*, Boulder Colo.: Westview Press.

Hartland-Thurnberg, P. (1990) *China, Hong Kong, Taiwan and the World Trading System*, London: Macmillan.

HC (1994) *House of Commons Foreign Affairs Committee First Report on Relations between the United Kingdom and China in the Period up to and Beyond 1997*, Vol. 1, London: HMSO.

He, Biao (1993) 'Luntan Taiwan "mingyun gongtong ti"', *Taisheng*, 107: 6–7.

Hobsbawm, E. (1991) *Nations and Nationalism Since 1780*, Cambridge: Canto.

Hong, Ximei (1995) 'Guangfu qian hou zhongguo guomindang Taiwan dang wu de fazhan (1940–1947)' (Taiwan Activities of the China Kuomintang at the time of the Retrocession (1940–1947)), Paper presented to Third Conference on Special Topics in ROC History, Taibei, 19–21 October 1995.

Hoston, G. (1994) *The State, Identity, and the National Question in China and Japan*, Princeton, NJ: Princeton University Press.

HR (1993) *Joint Hearings Before the Subcommittees on Economic Policy, Trade and Environment, International Security, International Organizations and Human Rights; and Asia and the Pacific*, Committee on Foreign Affairs, House of Representatives, 103rd Congress, 1st Session, 20 May, 1993 (Y4 F 76/1:C 44/27).

Hsiao, F. and Sullivan, L. (1979) 'The Chinese Communist Party and the Status of Taiwan, 1928–1943', *Pacific Affairs*, 52, 3: 446–67.

Hu, J. (1994) *The Case for Taipei's U.N. Representation: 'The Virtuous Will Not Be Alone'* (Address to the Atlantic Council of the United States, 17 September 1993), Taipei: GIO.

Huang, Huangxiong (1979) 'Dangqian zhengzhi de liang da keti' (The Two Main Topics of Politics Now), *Formosa*, 2: 15.

Huang, Kun-huei (Huang Kunhui) (1991) *The Key Points and Content of the Guidelines for National Unification*, Taipei: Executive Yuan.

Huang, Wenxiong (1992) *Zhongguo jieti lun* (On China's Deconstruction), Taibei: Zili wanbao.

Important Documents Concerning the Question of Taiwan (1955), Beijing: Foreign Languages Press.

Jang, J. (1967) 'A History of Newspapers in Taiwan', Unpublished Ph.D. thesis, Claremont.

Jia,Yibin (1993) *Lun taidu* (On Taiwan Independence), Beijing: Tuanjie.

Jiang Jingguo (Chiang Ching-kuo) (1986) 'Zai zhongguo guomindang di shier qie san zhong quanhui kai hui dianli zhici-zhongguo zhi tongyi yu shijie heping' (Speech at the Opening Ceremony of the Third Plenum of the KMT Twelfth Central Committee – China's Unification and World Peace), in Jiang Jingguo, *Jiang zongtong Jingguo xiansheng qishiwu nian yanlun ji*, Taibei: GIO.

—— (1987) *Jiang zongtong Jingguo xiansheng qishiwu nian yanlun ji*, Taibei: GIO.

—— (1991) *Jiang Jingguo quan ji*, Vol. 14, Taipei: GIO.

Jiang, Yongjing (1985) 'Sun Zhongshan xiansheng de geming sixiang' (The Revolutionary Thought of Sun Yat-sen), in *Zhonghua minguo jian guo shi* (The History of the Founding of the ROC), Taibei.

Jiang, Zemin (1990) Speech to Central United Front Work Conference, RRB, 12 June.

—— (1995) 'Wei cujin zuguo tongyi da ye de wancheng er jishu fendou' (Continue to Struggle to Facilitate Completion of the Great Task of Uniting the Motherland [Jiang's 'Eight Points']), RRB, 31 January.

Jin, Hongfan (1989) 'Shehui zhuyi chuji duan yu "yi guo liang zhi" gouxiang', (The Initial Stage of Socialism and the Concept of 'One Country – Two Systems'), *Taiwan yanjiu*, 2: 1–11.

Jiushi niandai (1996) 'Jiu liang an wenti – zhankai guangkuo taolun', 319: 50–99.

Johnson, C. (1962) *Peasant Nationalism and Communist Power: The Emergence of Revolutionary China 1937–1945*, Stanford, Calif.: Stanford University Press.

'Joint Communiqué Between the People's Republic of China and the United States of America' (1972) in Han, N. (ed.) *Diplomacy of Contemporary China*, Hong Kong: New Horizon.

'Joint Communiqué on the Establishment of Diplomatic Relations Between the People's Republic of China and the United States of America' (1978) in Han, N. (ed.) *Diplomacy of Contemporary China*, Hong Kong: New Horizon.

'Joint Communiqué of the United States of America and the People's Republic of China' (1982) in Han, N. (ed.) *Diplomacy of Contemporary China*, Hong Kong: New Horizon.

Kamenka, E. (1976) 'Political Nationalism – the Evolution of an Idea', in Kamenka (ed.) *Nationalism: the Nature and Evolution of an Idea*, London: Edward Arnold.

Kao, K. (1993) *Trade and Investment Across the Taiwan Straits: Maintaining Competitive Advantage, Pursuing Complementarity*, Taipei: MAC.

Kerr, G. (1974) *Formosa: Licensed Revolution and the Home Rule Movement 1895–1945*, Honolulu: University Press of Honolulu.

—— (1966) *Formosa Betrayed*, London: Eyre & Spottiswoode.

Kim, Key-hiuk (1980) *The Last Phase of the East Asian World Order: Korea, Japan and the Chinese Empire 1860–1882*, Berkeley: University of California Press.

Kim, S. (1993) 'Mainland China and a New World Order', in Lin, B. and Myers, J. (eds) *Forces for Change in Contemporary China*, Columbia, SC: University of South Carolina Press.

'Kuaizi wenhua' (Chopstick Culture) (1992) CDN, 7 April.

Kuhn, Thomas S. (1970) *The Structure of Scientific Revolutions*, Chicago: University of Chicago Press.

Lai, Tse-han, Myers, R. and Wei, Wou (1991) *A Tragic Beginning: The Taiwan Uprising of February 28, 1947*, Stanford, Calif.: Stanford University Press.

Laitinen, K. (1990) *Chinese Nationalism in the Late Qing Dynasty – Zhang Binglin as an Anti-Manchu Propagandist*, London: Curzon.

Lamley, H. (1964) 'The Taiwan Literati and Early Japanese Rule, 1895–1915: A Study of their Reactions to the Japanese Occupation and Subsequent Responses to Colonial Rule and Modernisation'. Unpublished Ph.D. thesis, University of Washington.

Lampton, D. (1992) *The Emergence of 'Greater China': Implications for the United States*, Report on a project of the National Committee on US–China Relations, Inc., National Committee China Policy Series, No. 5.

Lan, Bozhou (1994) *Ri ju shichi Taiwan xuesheng yundong* (The Taiwan Student Movement During the Japanese Occupation), Taibei: Shibao.

Lasater, M. (1989) *Policy in Evolution: The US Role in China's Unification*, Boulder, Colo., and London: Westview.

Lau, J. (1983) 'Echoes of the May Fourth Movement in Hsiang t'u [xiang tu] Fiction', in Tien, H. (ed.) *Mainland China, Taiwan and US Policy*, Cambridge, Mass.: Oelgeschlager, Gunn & Hain.

Laux, D. (1992) 'Taiwan's Economic and Trade Relations with the United States, Hong Kong and China', in AEI, *American Economic Relations with Greater China: Challenges for the 1990s*, Washington, DC: American Enterprise Institute and China Business Forum, 1992.

Lee Teng-hui (1988a) 'Message to the Nation on Assumption of Office', in Lee Teng-hui (1989) *President Lee Teng-hui's Selected Addresses and Messages 1988*, Taipei: GIO.

—— (1988b) 'First International Press Conference', in Lee Teng-hui (1989) *President Lee Teng-hui's Selected Addresses and Messages 1988*, Taipei: GIO.

—— (1989) *President Lee Teng-hui's Selected Addresses and Messages 1988*, Taipei: GIO.

—— (1989a) Interview, *Asian Wall Street Journal*, 21 October: 9.

—— (1990a) Speech to Central Standing Committee, in CDN, 8 March.

—— (1990b) 'Opening a New Era for the Chinese People Inaugural Address', in Lee Teng-hui (1992a) *Creating the Future*, Taipei: GIO.

—— (1990c) Speech to closing session of National Affairs Conference, CDN, 6 July.

—— (1991a) 'Constitutional Reform, National Unification and the Future', in Lee Teng-hui (1992a) *Creating the Future*, Taipei: GIO.

—— (1991b) 'Love and Faith', in Lee Teng-hui (1992a) *Creating the Future*, Taipei: GIO.

—— (1991c) 'From Uncertainty to Pragmatism – The Shape of the Age to Come', in Lee Teng-hui (1992a) *Creating the Future*, Taipei: GIO.

—— (1991d) 'Towards the 21st Century Arm in Arm – The Republic of China and the New Asian-Pacific Situation', in Lee Teng-hui (1992a) *Creating the Future*, Taipei: GIO.

—— (1991e) 'Constitutional Reform, National Unification, and the Future', in Lee Teng-hui (1992a) *Creating the Future*, Taipei: GIO.

—— (1992a) *Creating the Future*, Taipei: GIO.

—— (1992b) 'Regional Security and Economic Cooperation: The Case for the Asian-Pacific Region', in Lee Teng-hui (1992a) *Creating the Future*, Taipei: GIO.

—— (1992c) 'Growing Linkages and Global Implications for the Asian Regional Economy', in Lee Teng-hui (1992a) *Creating the Future*, Taipei: GIO.

—— (1994) Speech to KMT Annual Retrospective, CT, 31 December.

—— (1994a) Speech on the State of the Nation 19 April, CT, 20 April.

—— (1994b) '83 nian, zui chongman xiwang, zui xuyao douzheng de yi nian' (1994 a Year Most Full of Hope and Requiring Most Struggle), UDN, 1 January.

—— (1995) 'Zhong gong fangqi dui tai yong wu – liang an heping tanpan qianti' (The CCP Renouncing Use of Force is the Precondition for Peace Negotiations [Lee's 'six points']), UDN, 9 April 1995.

—— (1995a) Speech Commemorating 228 Incident, UDN, 1 March. (Extracts and summary in English, FCJ, 3 March.)

—— (1995b) New Year speech, UDN, 1 January.

—— (1996a), Inauguration Speech, Chinese and English versions in *Sinorama*, June 1996, 16–19.

Leng, S. (1993) (ed.) *Chiang Ching-kuo's Leadership in the Development of the Republic of China on Taiwan*, Lanham, NY, and London: University Press of America.

Leng, S. and Palmer, N. (1961) *Sun Yat-sen and Communism*, London: Thames & Hudson.

Li, Ao (1987) *Taidu fenzi kan dalu* (A Taiwanese Independence Activist Looks at Mainland China), Taibei: Quan neng.

—— (1991) 'Gonghe shenme?' (Republic of What?), IEP, 12 December.

Li, Dahong (1994) 'Taiwan zhengtan chongman jiaoju de yi nian' (A Year Full of Political Competition in Taiwan), *Liaowang*, 24 January: 36–7.

Li, Jiaquan (1988) 'Jiang Jingguo zhi hou Taiwan zhengju de sikao' (Considerations on the Political Situation in Taiwan After Chiang Ching-kuo), *Taiwan Yanjiu*, 2: 13–16.

Li, L. (1993) 'The Search for Local Self-Government', *Sinorama*, November: 76–85.

Li Qing (1987) '"Yi guo liang zhi" yu ai guo tongyi zhanxian de xin xingshi' ('"One Country, Two Systems" and the New Form of the Patriotic United Front'), in Zhongyang shehui zhuyi xueyuan tongyi zhanxian lilun jiaoyan shi (Central Socialist Academy United Front Theory Teaching and Research Office) (ed.) *'Yi ge guojia, liang zhong zhidu' li lun yu shijian wenxian ziliao xuanbian* (Selected Documentary Sources on 'One Country, Two Systems'), Shumu wenxian chubanshe.

Li Shenzhi and Zi Zhongyun (1988) 'Jin hou shi nian de Taiwan' (Taiwan in the Next Ten Years), *Taiwan yanjiu*, 1: 3–11.

Liaowang (1990) 'Guo gong liang dang ying duideng tanpan tuijin guojia tongyi' (The KMT and CCP Should Hold Equal Talks on Furthering Unification of the Country), 2: 7–8.

—— (1990a) 'Aiguo zhuyi he renmin minzhu' (Patriotism and People's Democracy), 11 June: 3.

—— (1993) 'Chi "jieduan xing liang ge zhongguo" miu lun' (Denounce the Fallacy of 'Transitional Two Chinas'), 49: 46.

—— (1995) 'US Urged to Abandon "Cold War" Syndrome', 24 July: 44.

Lin, Manhong (1996), 'Liang an wenti xiangguan ji ge lishi guan', *Lishi yuekan* (Historical Monthly), July 1996.

Lin, Zhongsheng (ed.) (1994a) *Chen Yisong hui yi lu*, Taibei: Qianwei.

—— (1994b) *Zhu Zhaoyang hui yi lu*, Taibei: Qianwei.

Lin, Zhuoliu (1987) *Taiwan lianqiao*, Taibei: Nanfang congshu.

—— (1993) *Wu hua guo*, Taibei: Qianwei.

Lin, Zhuoshui (Lin Cho-shui) (1992) 'Wenhua, zhongzu, shijie yu guojia' (Culture, Race, World and Nation), Paper presented to Conference on Provincial, Ethnic and National Identity, April 1992, published in IEP, 30 May.

Liu, F. (1992) 'The Electoral System and Voting Behaviour in Taiwan', in Cheng, T. and Haggard, S. (eds) *Political Change in Taiwan*, Boulder, Colo.: Lynne Rienner.

Liu, Fengsong (1979) *Formosa*, 3: 76.

Liu Shao-chi (Liu Shaoqi) (undated), *Internationalism and Nationalism*, Beijing: Foreign Languages Press.

Liu, Wenzong (1993) RRB, 30 November.

Long, S. (1991) *Taiwan: China's Last Frontier*, London: Macmillan.

Lu, A. (1992) 'Political Opposition in Taiwan: The Development of the Democratic Progressive Party', in Cheng, T. and Haggard, S. (eds) *Political Change in Taiwan*, Boulder, Colo.: Lynne Rienner.

Luo, Q. and Howe, C. (1993) 'Direct Investment and Economic Integration in the Asia Pacific: The Case of Taiwanese Investment in Xiamen', *China Quarterly*, 136: 746–69.

MAC (Mainland Affairs Council) (1992) *Direct Transportation Links Across the Taiwan Straits: Problems and Prospects*, Taipei.

—— (1993) *There is no 'Taiwan Question' There is Only a 'China Question'*, Taipei.

—— (1993a) *Questions and Answers Related to Government Policy on Hong Kong and Macao* (Mainland Policy Backgrounder), Taipei.

—— (1993b) *The Repatriation of Illegal Migrants from Mainland China*, Taipei.

—— (1993c) *Fishing Disputes*, Taipei.

—— (1993d) *The Third Round of Follow-up Negotiations on Practical Issues Held Between the SEF and the ARATS*, Taipei.

MacFarquhar, R. (1972) *Sino-American Relations 1949–1971*, Newton Abbot: David and Charles.

Mao, Zedong (1934) 'Report of the President of the Central Executive Committee of the Chinese Soviet Republic', reprinted in V. Yakhontoff (1974) *The Chinese Soviets*, Westport, Conn.: Greenwood.

—— (1939) 'On New Democracy', in *Selected Works*, Vol. 2, Beijing: Foreign Languages Press.

Mayall, J. (1993) *Nationalism and International Society*, Cambridge: Cambridge University Press.

Meisner, M. (1967) *Li Ta-Chao and the Origins of Chinese Marxism*, Cambridge, Mass.: Harvard University Press.

Mencius (1984) *The Mencius* (translated by D. C. Lau) (1984) Hong Kong.

Ming bao yue kan (1996) Special issue on 'Zhongguo xin minzu zhuyi de diaogui' (The Paradox of Chinese Nationalism), March.

Minzu cidian (Dictionary of Nationalities) (1987) Shanghai: Cishu.

MOFA (Ministry of Foreign Affairs, ROC) (1992) *Dui wai guanxi yu waijiao xingzheng* (External Relations and Diplomatic Administration), Taipei: MOFA.

Moody, P. (1992) *Political Change on Taiwan: A Study of Ruling Party Adaptability*, New York: Praeger.

Nathan, A. and Ho, H. (1993) 'Chiang Ching-kuo's Decision for Political Reform', in Leng, S. (ed.) *Chiang Ching-kuo's Leadership in the Development of the Republic of China on Taiwan*, Lanham, NY, and London: University Press of America.

NPC (National People's Congress) (1954) 'Constitution of the People's Republic of China', in Wang, J. (ed.) (1976) *Selected Legal Documents of the People's Republic of China*, University Publications of America Inc. Vol. 1.

—— (1978) 'Constitution of the People's Republic of China', in Wang, J. (ed.) *Selected Legal Documents*, Vol. 2.

NUC (National Unification Council) (1992) *The Meaning of 'One China'*, Taipei.

Pan, W. (1945) *The Chinese Constitution: A Study of Forty Years of Constitution-making in China*, Washington, DC: Catholic University of America.

Peng Mingmin (Peng Ming-min) (1972) *A Taste of Freedom: Memoirs of a Formosan Independence Leader*, New York: Holt, Rinehart & Winston.

Peng Mingmin Educational Foundation (ed.) (1994) *Peng Ming-min kan Taiwan* (Peng Ming-min Views Taiwan), Taipei: Yuanliu.

Provisional Central Government of the Soviet Republic of China (1934) 'Circular Telegram of the Provisional Central Government of the Soviet Republic of China Declaring War Against Japan', reprinted in V. Yakhontoff, *The Chinese Soviets*, Westport, Conn.: Greenwood.

Pye, L. (1986) 'Taiwan's Political Development and Its Implications for Beijing and Washington', *Asian Survey*, June 1986: 618–19.

Qian, Qichen (1995), New York press conference, 30 September, in UDN, 2 October.

Qiushi (1995) 'Shixian zuguo tongyi shi zhonghua minzu de zui gao liyi' (Realising Unification of the Motherland is in the Greatest Interests of the Chinese Nation), Interview with Wan Guoquan, deputy chairman of the Chinese People's Political Consultative Congress (CPPCC) and head of the China Association for Promoting Peaceful Unification, 16 May: 9.

ROC Yearbook (1991–2) Taipei: GIO.

ROC Yearbook (1993) Taipei: GIO.

ROC Yearbook (1994) Taipei: GIO.

Rousseau, J.-J. (1979) *The Social Contract and Discourses*, translated by G. Cole, New York: Everyman.

Scalapino, R. (1993) 'China's Multiple Identities in East Asia', in Dittmer, L. and Kim, S. (eds) *China's Quest for National Identity*, Ithaca, NY: Cornell University Press.

Schram, S. (1989) *The Thought of Mao Tse-tung*, Cambridge: Cambridge University Press.

Schwarcz, V. (1994) 'Memory and Commemoration: The Chinese Search for a Livable Past', in Wasserstrom, J. and Perry, E. (eds) *Popular Protest and Political Culture in Modern China*, Boulder, Colo., and Oxford: Westview Press.

SEF (Straits Exchange Foundation) (1993) *A Resume of the Koo–Wang Talks*, Taipei: SEF.

Segal, G. (1994a) *China Changes Shape: Regionalism and Foreign Policy*, Adelphi Paper 287, London: IISS.

—— (1994b) 'Deconstructing Foreign Relations', in Goodman, D. and Segal, G. (eds) *China Deconstructs*, London: Routledge.

Shen, Guofang (1996) Press conference in Beijing, in UDN, 8 March.

Shi, Weiquan (Shih Wei-ch'uan) (1992) 'Minzu guojia de shenhua jiegou yu er er ba' (The Mythical Structure of the Nation State and the 228 Incident), IEP, 10 November.

Smith, A. (1986) *The Ethnic Origins of Nations*, Oxford: Basil Blackwell.

Snow, E. (1978) *Red Star Over China*, Harmondsworth and New York: Penguin.

Song Qiang, Zhang Zangzang and Qiao Bian (1996) *Zhongguo keyi shuo bu* (China Cay Say No), Beijing: Zhonghua gongshang lianhe.

Spence, J. (1982) *The Gate of Heavenly Peace: The Chinese and Their Revolution, 1895–1980*, London and Boston: Faber & Faber.

Sun, Qingyu (1992) *Min jin dang de xian xiang* (The DPP Phenomenon), Taipei: Ri zhi tang.

Sun, Yat-sen (1927) *Memoirs of a Chinese Revolutionary: A Programme of National Reconstruction for China*, London: Hutchinson.

—— (1969) *San min zhuyi* (Three Principles of the People), Taipei: Da zhonghua tushu.

Taida Qingnian (1971) 'Wei baowei diaoyutai yundong shuo ji ju hua' (A Few Words in Defence of the Diaoyutai Movement), *Daxue Zazhi* (The Intellectual), 43: 28–31.

Taiwan Affairs Office (1993) *The Taiwan Question and Reunification of China*, Beijing: Taiwan Affairs Office and Information Office, State Council of the PRC.

'Taiwan renmin shi "xinxing minzu"?' (Are the Taiwan People a 'New Nation'?) (1995) IEP, 15 February.

Tao, Baichuan (1993) 'Jianli zhonghua mingyun gongtong ti de jiji huhao' (Urgent Appeal to Establish a Chinese Community of Shared Destiny), UDN, 3 November 1993.

Tien, H. (1989) *The Great Transition*, Stanford, Calif.: Hoover Institution.

Townsend, J. (1992) 'Chinese Nationalism', *Australian Journal of Chinese Affairs*, 27: 97–132.

Truman, H. (1950) 'Statement on the Mission of the Seventh Fleet in the Formosa Area', reprinted in MacFarquhar, R. (1972) *Sino-American Relations 1949–1971*, Newton Abbot: David and Charles.

Tsang, S. (ed.) (1993a) *In the Shadow of China*, London: C. Hurst.

Tsang, S. (1993b) 'Chiang Kai-shek and the Kuomintang's Policy to Recapture the Chinese Mainland, 1949–1958', in Tsang, S. (ed.) *In the Shadow of China*, London: C. Hurst.

Tu, W. (ed.) (1991) *The Living Tree: The Changing Meaning of Being Chinese Today*, Stanford, Calif.: Stanford University Press.

Tu, W. (1991a) 'Cultural China: The Periphery As Center', in Tu, W. (ed.) *The Living Tree: The Changing Meaning of Being Chinese Today*, Stanford, Calif.: Stanford University Press.

Tuchman, B. (1970) *Sand Against the Wind*, London and Basingstoke: Macmillan.

Tudor, H. (1972) *Political Myth*, London: Pall Mall.

Tyson, L. (1994) 'Bank Goes to Bat for Taiwan', FT, 11 November: 14.

US–ROC (1958) Joint Communiqué, reprinted in Chiu, H. (ed.) (1973) *China and the Question of Taiwan*, New York and London: Praeger.

Wang, Chuozhong (1996) 'Tai ci qiye xiehui kai chuang yi pian tian kong' (Taiwan Business Associations Open New Space), CT, 12 August.

Wang, Feng (1958) 'Report to the Fifth Meeting of the Nationalities Committee of the First National People's Congress, February 9, 1958', in Leng, S. and Palmer, N. (1961) *Sun Yat-sen and Communism*, London: Thames & Hudson.

Wang, Fuchang (1993) 'Shengji ronghe benzhi' (The Nature of Provincial Integration), Paper presented to Conference on Provincial and Ethnic Identity, October 1992, published IEP, 10 May.

Wang, G. (1981) *Community and Nation: Essays on Southeast Asia and the Chinese*, Singapore: Heinemann.

Wang, J. (ed.) (1976) *Selected Legal Documents of the People's Republic of China*, University Publications of America Inc. Vols 1–2.

Wang, Lixing (Wang Li-hsing) (1994) *Wu kui* (No Regrets), Taipei: Tianxia.

Wang, Renjie (1971) 'Dui waijiao shang de yixie xiao yijian' (A Few Minor Opinions on Foreign Policy), *Daxue zazhi* (The Intellectual), 44: 4.

Wang, Zaixi (1993) 'Taiwan xian shi zhang xuanju qingkuang toushi', (Perspective on the Situation of Taiwan's Elections for County Magistrates and City Mayors), *Liaowang*, 13 December: 31–2.

—— (1994) 'Zongguan Taiwan sheng shi zhang xuanju jieguo' (An Overview of the Results of Taiwan's Elections for Provincial and City Heads), *Liaowang*, 26 January 1994: 55.

Weber, M. (1978) *Economy and Society*, Roth, G. and Wittich, C. (eds and trans) Berkeley, Los Angeles and London: Routledge.

Weng, Songran (1996) 'Zhongguo weixie lun zhuyi' (Ruminations on the 'China Threat'), *Ershi shiji*, April: 18–24.

Wight, M. (1991) *International Theory: The Three Traditions*, London: Leicester University Press.

Wilson, R. (1983) 'Political Socialization of the Children', in Hsiung, J. (ed.) *The Taiwan Experience 1950–1980*, New York: American Association of Chinese Studies.

Winckler, E. (1988a) 'Mass Political Incorporation, 1500–2000', in Winckler, E. and Greenhalgh, S. (eds) *Contending Approaches to the Political Economy of Taiwan*, Armonk, NY, and London: M. E. Sharpe.

—— (1988b) 'Elite Political Struggle 1945–1985', in Winckler, E. and Greenhalgh, S. (eds) *Contending Approaches to the Political Economy of Taiwan*, Armonk, NY, and London: M. E. Sharpe.

Winckler, E. and Greenhalgh, S. (1988) *Contending Approaches to the Political Economy of Taiwan*, Armonk, NY, and London: M. E. Sharpe.

Woods, L. (1993) *Asia-Pacific Diplomacy: Nongovernmental Organizations and International Relations*, Vancouver: UBC.

Wu, Guoguang (1996) 'Yi lixing minzu zhuyi kangheng "wei du zhongguo"' (Use Rational Nationalism to Counterbalance 'Containing China'), *Ershi shiji*, April: 25–33.

Wu, Micha (1991) Comments to IMP Seminar on the Formation of the Modern Chinese Nation, in IMP, 1 December.

Wu, Sanlian and Cai, Peihuo (1990) *Taiwan minzu yundong shi* (History of the Taiwan National Movement), Taipei: Zili wanbao.

Xie, Zongmin (1990) *Zhu wai ren kan Taiwan zhengzhi* (Looking at Taiwan Politics from Abroad), Taipei.

Xin Chaoliu (1984a) Translation of Harry Beran, 'A Liberal Theory of Secession' (taken from *Political Studies*, 32) *Xin Chaoliu*, 1.

—— (1984b) Coverage of FAPA statement of 18 November 1984, rejecting the Hong Kong model for Taiwan and insisting on the right of self-determination for Taiwan's population, *Xin Chaoliu*, 25: 47.

Yahuda, M. (1993) 'The Foreign Relations of Greater China', *China Quarterly*, 136: 687–710.

Yakhontoff, V. (1974) *The Chinese Soviets*, Westport, Conn.: Greenwood.

Yan, Chuanrong and Yang, Huasheng (1990) 'Taiwan zhengzhi zhuanxing de tedian ji zhuyao maodun' (Special Points and Contradictions of Taiwan's Political Transformation), *Taiwan Yanjiu*, 1: 18–24.

Yan Jiaqi (1991) 'Zhongguo tongyi: cong shenfen guo zouxiang lianbang' (China's Unification: From Personal Country to Federation), CDN, 22 February.

—— (1992/3) 'Towards the Federal Republic of China', *China Now*, 143: 14–15.

Yan, Jing (1995) 'Taiwan dangju weibei "yi ge zhongguo" yuanze juzheng', *Liaowang*, 19 June: 22–3.

Yang, W. (ed.) (1990) *Haixia liang an guanxi wenji* (Studies of Mainland China Relations), Hong Kong: New Asia Cultural Foundation.

Yao, Jiawen (1979) 'Aiguo lun: you sheng min zhi guo, ze you aiguo zhi min' (On Patriotism: With a Country that Supports the Livelihood of the People, There is a Patriotic People), *Formosa*, 3: 93–7.

Yao, Yiping and Liu, Guofen (1989) 'Taiwan "tanxing waijiao" pingxi' (Analysis of Taiwan's 'Flexible Diplomacy'), reprinted in Yang, W. (ed.) (1990) *Haixia liang an guanxi wenji* (Studies of Mainland-China Relations) Hong Kong: New Asia Cultural Foundation.

Ye, Shitao (1990) *Zou xiang Taiwan wenxue* (Towards Taiwanese Literature), Taipei: Zili wanbao.

Ye, Yang (1985) 'Xin shiqi tongyi zhanxian de fazhan' (Development of the United Front in the New Period), in Zhongyang shehui zhuyi xueyuan tongyi zhanxian lilun jiaoyan shi (Central Socialist Academy United Front Theory Teaching and Research Office) (ed.) *'Yi ge guojia, liang zhong zhidu' li lun yu shijian wenxian ziliao xuanbian* (Selected Documentary Sources on 'One Country, Two Systems'), Shumu wenxian chubanshe.

Yen, S. (1965) *Taiwan in China's Foreign Relations 1836–1874*, Hamden, Conn.: Shoe String.

'Yi ren kan xuanju' (Artists Look at the Elections) (1994) UDN, 4 December.

Yu, Ying-shih (1996) 'Feidan xia de xuanju – minzhu yu minzu zhuyi zhi jian' (Elections under Missiles – Between Democracy and Nationalism), CT, 29 March 1996.

ZDBK (1984) *Zhongguo da bai ke quan shu* (fa xue) (Great China Encyclopedia (Law)), Beijing.

Zhan, J. (1993) *Ending the Chinese Civil War*, New York: St Martin's Press.

Zhang, Maogui (1992) 'Shengji wenti yu minzu zhuyi' (The Provincial Problem and Nationalism), Paper delivered to Conference on Provincial and Ethnic Identity, Taipei, 12 April 1992, published in IMP, 13 April.

Zhang, Zanzang (1996) 'Zhongguo ren: leng zhan houdai de qinggan ji zhengzhi xuanze' (The Chinese: Post-Cold War Sentiments and Political Choices), in Song Qiang, Zhang Zangzang and Qiao Bian, *Zhongguo keyi shuo bu* (China Can Say No), Beijing.

'Zhenghe hua nan jingji chuan – Xianggang jiushi qi shi guanjian' (Complete a South China Economic Sphere – Hong Kong 1997 is the Crux) (1991) UDN, 7 December.

Zhou, Gengsheng (1981) *Guoji fa* (International Law) Vol. 1, Beijing: Shangwu yinshu guan.

Zhu, Aili (1990) 'Taiwan "zongtong" xuanju de zhengce zouxiang' (The Direction of Policy after Taiwan's 'Presidential' Elections), *Taiwan Yanjiu*, 1: 1–4.

Zhu Gaozheng (1996) 'Minzhu yu minzu zhuyi' (Democracy and Nationalism), *Lishi Yuekan* (Historical Monthly), August: 84–93.

ZMZS (1981) *Zhonghua Mingguo zhongyao shiliao chu bian* (ROC Important Historical Materials), Sec. 3, Vol. 3, Taipei: Academia Sinica.

Index